OPERATION THUNDERHEAD

THE TRUE STORY OF VIETNAM'S FINAL POW RESCUE MISSION—
AND THE LAST NAVY SEAL KILLED IN COUNTRY

Kevin Dockery

BERKLEY CALIBER, NEW YORK

THE BERKLEY PUBLISHING GROUP
Published by the Penguin Group
Penguin Group (USA) Inc.
375 Hudson Street, New York, New York 10014, USA
Penguin Group (Canada), 90 Eglinton Avenue East, Suite 700, Toronto, Ontario M4P 2Y3, Canada
(a division of Pearson Penguin Canada Inc.)
Penguin Books Ltd., 80 Strand, London WC2R 0RL, England
Penguin Group Ireland, 25 St. Stephen's Green, Dublin 2, Ireland (a division of Penguin Books Ltd.)
Penguin Group (Australia), 250 Camberwell Road, Camberwell, Victoria 3124, Australia
(a division of Pearson Australia Group Pty. Ltd.)
Penguin Books India Pvt. Ltd., 11 Community Centre, Panchsheel Park, New Delhi—110 017, India
Penguin Group (NZ), 67 Apollo Drive, Rosedale, North Shore 0632, New Zealand
(a division of Pearson New Zealand Ltd.)
Penguin Books (South Africa) (Pty.) Ltd., 24 Sturdee Avenue, Rosebank, Johannesburg 2196,
South Africa

Penguin Books Ltd., Registered Offices: 80 Strand, London WC2R 0RL, England

The publisher does not have any control over and does not assume any responsibility for author or
third-party websites or their content.

Copyright © 2008 Bill Fawcett & Associates
Cover design by Richard Hasselberger
Front cover photograph courtesy of U.S. Navy
Book design by Kristin del Rosario

PRINTING HISTORY
Berkley Caliber hardcover edition / November 2008
Berkley Caliber trade paperback edition / November 2009

Berkley Caliber trade paperback ISBN: 978-0-425-23000-8

The Library of Congress has catalogued the Berkley Caliber hardcover edition as follows:

Dockery, Kevin.
    Operation Thunderhead : the true story of Vietnam's final POW rescue mission—and the last Navy
SEAL killed in country / Kevin Dockery. —1st ed.
        p. cm.
    Includes index.
        ISBN 978-0-425-22373-4
    1. Vietnam War, 1961–1975—Prisoners and prisons, North Vietnamese. 2. Prisoners of war—
United States. 3. Prisoner-of-war escapes—Vietnam. 4. Dramesi, John A. 5. Vietnam War,
1961–1975—Search and rescue operations. I. Title.

    DS559.4.D63 2008
    959.704'37—dc22

                                                                                    2008019857

PRINTED IN THE UNITED STATES OF AMERICA

10   9   8   7   6   5   4   3   2   1

*This book is respectfully dedicated to the memories of
United States Air Force Captain Edwin Lee Atterberry
and
United States Navy Lieutenant (SEAL) Melvin Spence Dry.
They knew the true cost of freedom and paid it.
We are diminished by their loss.*

[CONTENTS]

[CHAPTER 1]

VIETNAM

While at Seymore Johnson Air Force Base in North Carolina, John Dramesi was flying F-105D jet fighter bombers when he received a call from his old squadron commander. The commander was going to Fort Lewis, Washington, a major Army base, to be the air liaison officer. As such, his job would be to coordinate the integration of the Air Force and the Army at the base. The conversation with his old commander was an interesting one, as Dramesi learned that he had just volunteered to be a forward air controller with the 4th Infantry Division at Fort Lewis.

A forward air controller or FAC was about as far from being a fighter pilot as one could be and still have something to do with aircraft. The FAC controls close air support missions to integrate the local Air Force assets with the infantry fighting on the ground. Since the enemy and the infantry can be very close to each other in combat, it takes a knowledge of just what an aircraft can do, and what the effects of the ordnance it has on board are, to safely engage the enemy at what are known as "danger close" distances. The FAC can also tell ground commanders just what kind of air support is immediately available to them, what it can do, and what the best ways to employ it are.

In Vietnam, many forward air controllers operated from small, relatively slow-moving aircraft such as the prop-driven Bronco OV-10. They directed incoming air support via radio and marked targets on the ground with white-phosphorus smoke rockets. There is also the FAC who operates on the ground, working very closely with the infantry as they're right there in the mud together. That kind of FAC is a ground-pounder with a radio and very big "friends" up in the sky.

That job was going to be John Dramesi's next assignment as his old commander literally yanked him from the squadron he was in and ordered him to Washington State. At that time there was an attempt in the military to get some of the best fighter pilots in the Air Force into FAC positions. That would allow the Air Force officers to help educate the Army about the ability of the Air Force to deliver close-air support to the fighters on the ground. There was a turf war going on between the Air Force and the Army as to just who would command the close-air-support units when they were working with the Army units. The Army felt that their commanders on the ground knew best just what they needed in the way of close-air support and how they wanted enemy units attacked. The Air Force knew best just how the aircraft and their bombs, rockets, and guns could be applied.

Although Dramesi had an opportunity to do some flying during his FAC assignment, he was a grounded bird: a pilot wearing boots and in the mud. After extensive training at Fort Lewis, John Dramesi deployed to South Vietnam with the 4th Infantry Division in 1966. This was the first time that forward air controllers had trained directly with an Army division prior to it being deployed to combat.

As a pilot, Dramesi was now getting direct experience in ground combat. He had worked with the men he would be fighting beside. FACs were armed with the normal weapons of an infantry soldier. For Dramesi, his primary weapon was hanging under the wings and in the ammunition boxes of the aircraft flying overhead.

Not a lot of pilots experience direct combat during their careers. That time gave him a direct knowledge of operating and living in the jungles of Southeast Asia that was very different from his Air Force survival training. And it would give him information that he would strive to keep from his captors later in North Vietnam.

As far as Dramesi knew, he was the only one at the time who had in-country and out-country experience as a forward air controller. That included his time in the 4th Infantry Division and his time later as an F-105 pilot bombing North Vietnam.

As a pilot, John Dramesi had already received experience on the ground during his survival training at Stead Air Force Base in Nevada. During that training, Dramesi and his fellows were not only taught how to live off the land, they were given experience as to just what they might expect if they were captured after a shoot-down over enemy territory. No pilot ever fully believes that such a thing would happen to him, but the training makes sure that each man has a least a small idea what could be waiting for him on the ground if he did ever have to punch out.

In the prison camp during training, Dramesi and the other pilots were thrown together to suffer various privations and an enthusiastic instructor cadre. When the instructors, acting as the part of the enemy, would interrogate the students, they knew they were giving the pilots but a taste of what to expect at the hands of the enemy. Many of the instructors had either directly known or studied the reports from POWs who had been held by the North Koreans. In some survival schools, some of the instructors themselves had been POWs. For John Dramesi, being a POW held no appeal whatsoever and he sought to escape at his earliest opportunity.

Not something a student usually did, John Dramesi successfully escaped from the POW camp at Stead Air Force Base during his survival training. He was the only one to do so that he knew of.

When Dramesi arrived at the camp, the students were supposed to organize for an escape. The students planned to crawl through a hole they'd noticed in the wire fence, one that seemed to have been overlooked by the instructor/guards. Dramesi could see the plan wasn't going to work, and he was proved right. When the remainder of the group "escaped" though the wire, they immediately ran into the instructors, who were there waiting for them. The instructors had known the hole was there, and the students could now experience what kind of repercussions they might receive for such a failed attempt.

The instructors had promised the students a free breakfast if they successfully escaped the camp. The idea of some food appealed to everyone as the rations at the camp were meager at best—another attempt to give the students some idea of what they could expect. No matter how unpalatable the food, the students were to eat all of it to keep up their strength to take advantage of an opportunity to escape, as well as to aid their resistance to interrogation.

Dramesi earned his free meal. During the debriefing afterward, he was told by the instructors that he should try not to shoot anyone during an escape. Shooting at the enemy made it more likely that Dramesi himself would be shot.

Durng the debriefing, Dramesi also had to explain to the instructors how he had managed his escape. Watching the guards go in and out of the camp gave Dramesi the first clue as to what his avenue of escape might be. It was dark around the camp; when the students walked out on a work detail—particularly when the group was going out with the camp commander—the guard at the gate came to attention. That meant the guard's attention was on something other than his immediate job.

When Dramesi went out on a detail with the camp commander, the guard came to attention as expected. Seeing his opportunity, Dramesi grabbed the guard's weapon and wrestled it from his grasp. With a rifle in his hands, Dramesi shot the guard and the camp commander. As a couple of additional guards gave chase, Dramesi shot them as well as he retreated from the camp, walking backward and firing as he moved.

The escape resembled a child's war game: Dramesi was firing on the move, the flames from his blank cartridges jetting out into the darkness, the sound reverberating through the desert. The only real problem was that an approaching guard wasn't stopping as Dramesi fired.

Shouting, "You're dead! You're dead!" Dramesi ran from the camp. His head start was enough that the guard couldn't catch the escapee, no matter how much he ignored being dead.

The instructors poured from the camp to locate the escapee. Searching through the dark desert, the instructors could not find where Dramesi had run to, or where he might be hiding. The reason for this was simple enough to Dramesi: He wasn't where they were looking. When he ran from the camp and finally slipped into the darkness, Dramesi then turned about and went to the opposite side of the camp, skirting around the area in the darkness. As the instructors were searching for him, the escapee was on the far side of the camp watching everything that was going on.

A short time later, Dramesi decided to try for his free breakfast and turned himself in. It was daylight and there really wasn't anyplace else for him to go except deeper into the desert. It was a training program and not a real escape. Risking the very real possibility of becoming lost in the desert was not a very good option.

So Dramesi turned himself in and got his free breakfast. The instructors debriefed him immediately and that was when they told him that he shouldn't shoot anybody during an escape. As far as Dramesi was concerned, it was a good debriefing. And he didn't forget the lessons he learned during the exercise.

But the experience of what it would be like to be a POW wasn't over. He received his reward of a meal, then Dramesi was put right back in with the rest of the POWs. Only now, he was thrust into a little box for isolation and punishment. The box was around five feet long and maybe 1½ feet wide. It was anything but comfortable, and for anyone with a trace of claustrophobia, the box would bring it out for everyone to see.

The dirty rats, as Dramesi considered the instructors, slipped him into the box. They had said they would give him breakfast, which they did, and that was all. The exercise had not ended.

Dramesi escaped again.

Using his metal belt buckle, Dramesi attacked the area of the door at the end of the box. Instead of a lock, the instructors had wrapped a wire around some protrusions to secure the door. Pushing the door open as far as it would go, Dramesi was able to just reach the wire in the opening between the door and the frame of the box around it. With his belt buckle, Dramesi scraped at the wire, finally breaking it and releasing the door.

When the door was open, Dramesi slipped out of the box, paused, and rewired the end closed. Anyone looking in to the area would just see the same thing that had been there before: a long box with the door at one end wired shut. There was no way to tell the box was empty without either opening it or getting the "occupant" to say something.

The instructors didn't know that Dramesi had once again escaped. And he wasn't making the same mistake in turning himself in again. He went missing from the box all day long and into the next day, when the exercise was declared over. Then he once again turned himself in.

It seemed that John Dramesi was just going to be a troublemaker for anyone who took him prisoner.

After his tour with the 4th Infantry was completed, Dramesi once more returned to the air, again as the pilot of an F-105D. In August 1964, the first F-105 aircraft moved from Japan to Korat Air Base in Thailand. The planes were to have provided supporting cover for air rescue operations throughout Southeast Asia. Far more often, they were used as strike support for CIA operations in Laos.

By 1966, the U.S. government admitted that Thunderchief aircraft were operating out of Thailand. The number of planes had increased considerably and the Air Force was operating two tactical fighter wings out of two air bases in Thailand. Assigned to the tactical fighter wing operating out of Korat Air Base, John Dramesi piloted his craft on bombing operations deep into North Vietnam.

Flying into what had become one of the most heavily defended air spaces in the world, Dramesi would have to steer his craft into target zones known as Route Packages (RPs). The most defended of these packages was RP-6A, the zone in and around the North Vietnamese capital of Hanoi. Heading into Hanoi was called going "downtown," in part from the lyrics of a popular song of the time. Everything that a pilot wouldn't want to meet was waiting in and around downtown in the form of SA-2 surface-to-air missiles supplied to the North Vietnamese by the Soviets; 100, 85, 57, 37, and 23mm antiaircraft cannons in mounts holding from one gun to four; and 14.5 and 12.7mm machine guns, also in single, double, and quadruple mounts. All of that artillery was reinforced by the population, most of whom had weapons they'd use to fire at aircraft. It is not known how many North Vietnamese MiGs may have been brought down by this incredible umbrella of steel and fire, but hundreds of American aircraft were taken out of the sky by it.

The F-105D Thunderchief was the workhorse aircraft in bombing many of the targets in North Vietnam. Nicknamed "Thud" by many of the pilots and ground crew who flew and supported the F-105D, the planes did the dangerous missions in part because of the very fast flight the craft could do at low altitude. That also meant Thuds were exposed to the brunt of the antiaircraft fire available to the North Vietnamese.

At the peak of the air war over North Vietnam, the chances of a Thud pilot completing 100 missions was considered to be only about 75 percent. Loss of the craft was high; in part there were so many of them in the air at one time, that a hilly area in the approach pathway to the Hanoi target area was known as "Thud Ridge." Attacking Hanoi, going downtown, cost the United States Air Force 124 F-105 Thuds during 1966. Nearly four hundred of the aircraft were lost during the air war over Vietnam, almost half of the F-105s ever made.

On April 2, 1967, Captain John Dramesi, flying under the call sign "Lover Lead," climbed into the cockpit of his F-105D for his fifty-ninth Thud mission over Vietnam. The target was a truck park near Package One, the area around Ba Don in the North Vietnamese province of Quang Binh. The bombing mission was to be conducted in two flights of four aircraft each and a single flight of two aircraft. Dramesi would be leading the single flight of two aircraft, with Ken Gurry as his wingman.

The ordnance load for the attack would have ordinarily been a half-dozen M117 750-pound bombs carried on a single multiple ejector rack (MER) along the bottom of the fuselage. That bomb load added up to 2¼ tons of "smash." That was enough ordnance to do considerable damage to a carpark or any jungle target, especially when multiplied by the ten aircraft making up the three flights.

Locating the target area, Dramesi and his wingman turned in on their bomb run. The rest of the flights had made their attacks and the target area had been pretty well saturated. Pulling away from the area, Dramesi called for permission to conduct an attack on a secondary target.

Each of the Thuds was armed with an M61 Vulcan cannon and more than 1,000 rounds of 20mm ammunition to feed it. The six rotating barrels of the cannon could put out that high-explosive ammunition at a rate of one hundred rounds per second. That load of ammunition and the M61 Vulcan cannon would be more than enough to conduct an armed reconnaissance of a road northwest of Dong Hoi. The location where the road ran was known to be a staging area for enemy strikes into the border area between North and South Vietnam.

Having received permission for their secondary target, the two Thuds in the flight were heading up the valley where the road was located, moving at a speed of over 575 miles an hour. The speed wasn't defense enough from the enemy in the jungle below.

The North Vietnamese were quite adequately using what was available for air defense. It wasn't sophisticated; it wasn't high-tech. It was simple and brutal. Barrage fire from 37- and 57-millimeter cannons pumped as much high-explosive ammunition as they could into the air ahead of the moving jets. Often enough, the speeding aircraft simply passed through the rain of steel coming up at them.

Dramesi heard two or three loud distinct booms, and suddenly his plane was shuddering as it tried to stay in the sky. Gurry's words came in over Dramesi's radio. "Lover Lead, your wing tanks are gone, and you have fire in your tail."

Dramesi's F-105D had been hit by some of the dense cannon fire coming up from the jungle below. He was at 2,500 feet and moving fast as his canopy filled with smoke and the plane started coming apart. Grabbing at the handles that controlled his ejection seat, he pulled them up and squeezed the triggers. The canopy blew away from the plane as the ejection seat rocketed into the air, up and away from the stricken plane.

[CHAPTER 2]

FEAR

A soldier—anyone serving in the military—has a lot to fear from time to time. Just the nature of their jobs means that soldiers work with materials and objects intended to kill people and destroy things. In combat, a soldier has a fear of being killed or wounded. This is a normal, healthy thing; it is the fight-or-flight reaction built well within all of us, deep in the basic survival centers of our brains.

In spite of that fear, members of the military have to train long and hard to be able to function in a combat situation. Soldiers have to be able to use their weapons, move, and communicate. Sailors have to operate machinery that makes their ships such great fighting machines. And pilots have to work in an environment where technical actions have to take place smoothly and effectively, and decisions have to be made with split-second speed.

One fear that never goes away with training centers on the enemy and their actions. If a soldier is killed, then their concerns are pretty much over. If wounded, there will be a period, possibly a long one, of pain and suffering. There's the possibility of going home—perhaps not as physically whole as when the individual left for the service—but home is a reward of its own. But one thing will keep a military man from going home, wounded or dead: being taken prisoner, captured by the enemy. As a prisoner of war, a POW, no member of the military knows when he will ever see freedom again, or what treatment he will receive at the hands of an enemy who holds him helpless.

It is that feeling of utter helplessness, knowing that everything concerning your life, including life itself, is dependent on the whims of your captors, that brings on despair in the minds of men taken prisoner. History has shown that that the fear of being held prisoner can be well founded indeed.

Conflict, war in a simpler term, has been a part of mankind's past since before recorded history. For millennia, the idea of a prisoner of war did not exist. When an enemy was defeated, he was killed, wounded or not. Resources were too limited, food too hard to come by, for any of it to be wasted on a vanquished enemy. Usually his home was put to the fire; his village or town was sacked, with anything portable of value being taken; and any family, women, children, or elderly killed—though the women at least stood a chance of being taken as slaves.

It was into the time of recorded history that the idea of taking prisoners started to become more of a common thing, at least for larger, more organized nations. The defeated survivors surrendering on the battlefield were not simply taken prisoner; they were enslaved by the victor. When the defeated laid down their arms, they became chattel, property of the victors, to be used or disposed of at whim. They were even made the stuff of entertainment in some societies, paraded before a joyous populace celebrating the victory of their military, and the lessening of their chances of becoming slaves. In very limited numbers, some of those slaves could be made to fight for their lives, if not their freedom, in shows for the multitudes. Those captured in war were now property, part of the spoils taken by the victors.

Captured prisoners, enslaved or otherwise, had to be fed and cared for at least to a minimum extent. Warriors would be lost on both sides of an extended conflict. Valuable skills would be lost to each side as the men were taken and held by the opposition. And their care was a burden. Killing unarmed prisoners out of hand became less popular because the opposite side would consider that a reason to treat the prisoners they held in the same brutal fashion.

Prisoner exchange and the ransom of high-ranking nobility taken on the battlefield became more common as the millennia progressed, and the victors realized that such actions could work to their benefit if their turn came up in the prison pens. By the Middle Ages, the enslavement of captives happened less often, though the ransoming of ranking officers (knights) as well as nobility was fairly common throughout what was considered the "civilized" world. It was only in the religious wars such as the Crusades where the captured fighters of the opposing faith were still commonly put to death as unbelievers, heretics, or whatever label fit.

Eventually, the exchange of prisoners captured during war became the normal practice. The release of prisoners after a conflict was over wasn't officially recognized until the practice was finally put in print in the mid-1600s in the treaty that ended the Thirty Years War.

For hundreds of years, the threat of retaliation in kind kept most prisoners in some kind of security after their capture. But excesses still happened on a regular basis. During the American Civil War, the brutality of prisoner-of-war camps was well-known. Nearly a quarter-million prisoners were taken on both sides of the conflict. Thousands died from malnutrition, disease, and a form of organized neglect, particularly at some of the larger camps. At the hellhole known as Andersonville, Georgia, more than 10,000 prisoners died while incarcerated. The commander of that camp, Captain Henry Wirz, was later hanged after being tried and convicted on charges of murder and conspiracy. He was the only Confederate soldier convicted of war crimes after the Civil War.

While the Civil War was still raging in the United States, in Europe, representatives from twenty-six governments of the world gathered in Geneva, Switzerland, to try and limit some of the suffering of war. For the warrior, the conference resulted in a convention that at least respected the rights of wounded soldiers on both sides of a conflict.

The first Geneva Convention also had close ties with the founding and recognition of the International Committee of the Red Cross. One of the successes of the meeting was the international agreement to respect the neutrality of hospitals and other buildings bearing the symbol of the Red Cross.

With the beginnings of a new century, the world tried again to control at least the worst excesses of war. At The Hague Peace Conference of 1899, the leader of the Russian Empire, Tsar Nicholas II, called representatives of the world together to try and establish a "real and lasting peace." Additionally, the tsar wanted to limit the development of the weapons of war and restrict the world to the armaments that existed at that time. It was a worthwhile effort that is remembered today for outlawing the use of expanding bullets (soft-nosed or "dumdum" ammunition) for military use. The intent was to try and limit the pain and suffering that had been so prevalent just a few decades earlier when soft lead bullets had smashed into soldiers, shattering bones and causing numberless amputations to save a soldier's life.

Most of the other declarations of that first Hague Peace Conference didn't last the lifetime of the tsar. The prohibition on the use of poison gases was ignored inside of fifteen years. The other prohibition, outlawing the firing of projectiles from balloons, wasn't ignored as much as rendered obsolete. Balloons as military aircraft were soon overshadowed by the invention of the powered airplane. The dropping of bombs from the air, from aircraft or balloons (zeppelins), hadn't been really considered at the conference.

A second Hague Peace Conference, held in 1907, also tried to limit the destructive capability of military weapons. Again, it to failed to reach that goal. There was a greater range of rules of war established at The Hague, but any form of peace conference was doomed as the world hurtled toward the biggest war mankind had conducted to date.

The assassination of Archduke Franz Ferdinand of Austria on June 28, 1914, at the hands of Bosnian Gavrilo Princip was the spark that ignited the Europe powderkeg. The resulting explosion of combat was known to the combatants at the Great War. To history, it was World War I, to those who lived through it; it was the War to End All Wars.

Nearly every country in Europe clashed during World War I, the bulk of the fighting happening across France. There were more than 40 millions casualties from the fighting and bombardments of the war that lasted from 1914 to 1918. Those casualties included the nearly 20 million dead among both the military and civilian populations. As the lines of the war ebbed and flowed, prisoners were captured on all sides of the conflict.

The nearly 500,000 prisoners of war on both sides of the American Civil War paled in comparison to the almost 8 million men held in prison camps during World War I. The United States only joined in the fighting during the last two years of the war. Of all the soldiers and Marines that the United States sent off to that war, only 4,120 men were captured and interned as prisoners of war. Of the U.S. prisoners held, more than 3,900 of them were repatriated at the end of hostilities in November 1918. In spite of relatively good treatment of the Americans at the hands of their captors, 147 men died while POWs. Most of these men passed away as a result of wounds received in combat.

Among the prisoners of other combatants, the mortality rate was much higher. Nearly 8 million soldiers became prisoners and hundreds of thousands died as a result of their captivity. Many of the POW deaths were in areas such as Russia, where food was short and famine became rampant, starving prisoner and civilian alike. In other countries, even with food shortages, there were relatively few prisoner deaths. As compared to the nearly 20 percent of all Russian prisoners dying of starvation, less than 5 percent of the prisoners held by Germany died while in captivity.

In the aftermath of World War I, another effort was put forward to make the treatment of wartime prisoners more humane. More than forty countries signed or agreed to the articles of the 1929 Geneva Convention on the treatment of POWs. Several countries limited their acceptance of the new conventions regarding prisoners. Japan and the Soviet Union stood out in their opposition to most of the rules in the agreement and did not consider the agreement binding to their countries' actions during wartime. The new convention was soon tested, as war broke out ten years after its creation.

The opening years of World War II resulted in more U.S. military personnel being taken prisoner than at any other time in our history. In Europe, the USSR, and in Asia, millions of soldiers were taken prisoner as the Axis forces made up primarily of Nazi Germany and Imperial Japan swept across their areas of conflict. From 1939 to 1945, World War II ravaged the landscape. Millions of soldiers died, but not all during combat.

Though Nazi Germany treated captured Soviet forces in a subhuman manner, the regime maintained many of the principles of the Geneva Convention of 1929 in regards to their treatment of British and American prisoners. As the war progressed, many American prisoners held by the Germans came from downed air crews. Being held in European prison camps gave the POWs a real chance at escape, many of whom did so during the war. Escaped POWs had a possibility of blending in with the local population, especially if they managed to learn some of the language. The existence of local resistance groups gave active aid to escaping prisoners, once contact could be established.

In Asia under the Imperial Japanese Empire, the situation was drastically different. In the first full year of the war in the Pacific, thousands of Americans were taken prisoner as the Japanese seized island after island. In the Philippines, American forces held out against the approaching Japanese for months. Cut off from resupply and any reasonable means of escape, the Americans forces finally surrendered after holding out for four months. This was when the Japanese first held large numbers of U.S. soldiers and civilians as prisoners.

The military class of Imperial Japan followed the Bushido code of moral principles to guide their actions. It was the greatest honor to follow the orders of their emperor to the death. Surrender was an almost inconceivable disgrace, one that could only be slightly relieved by the death of the individual. When the Japanese were in possession of thousands of surrendered military prisoners, they felt disgust that such men had not committed suicide rather than face such shame. The arrogance of the Imperial Japanese military allowed them to feel superior to any other race on the planet to begin with. It was very easy for them to consider the POWs they held to be something less than human, and to treat them as such.

The first major example of how the Japanese treated the prisoners under their care came when the captured men were forced to march ninety miles to a camp. Thousands died along the way from bayonets, shootings, and beheadings at the hands of Japanese officers and non-commissioned officers (NCOs). The men who died quickly were considered lucky when compared to the many who died as a result of subsequent beatings, starvation, dehydration, heat, and untreated wounds. Of the 11,796 American POWs who took part in the Bataan Death March, 600 to 650 men died along the way. Some escaped into the jungle to fight alongside the Philippine people, who also suffered greatly at the hands of their captors. Of the approximately 72,000 prisoners, the bulk of whom were Filipino, about 54,000 lived to reach the camp.

More than half of all U.S. prisoners held by the Japanese during World War II died at the hands of their captors, either by neglect or design. The Japanese subjected their prisoners to starvation diets and brutal labor tactics. Just surviving day to day took a terrible toll on the prisoners, knowing that at any moment they could be killed by any

Japanese soldier for any reason—or even no reason at all. Disease was rampant in a population of prisoners weakened by starvation and heavy labor. Escape was considered difficult at best because the Americans, even in their emaciated states, stood out among the local populations. For the POWs held in the camps on the main Japanese islands, escape was barely a dream.

To transport prisoners, the Japanese packed them aboard transport ships, quickly named "Hell Ships" by their suffering human cargo. The unmarked transports were sent through areas known to be hunting grounds for Allied submarines. More than 3,800 American prisoners were killed when their transports were targeted by U.S. Navy submarines. Of the more than 25,000 American POWs taken by the Japanese, nearly 11,000 died at the hands of their captors. After the war ended, it took years to prosecute Japanese camp guards, commanders, and staff for war crimes.

The brutality of prisoners during World War II was addressed soon after the end of the war. It was not just the Japanese who mistreated their prisoners in a criminal fashion. The Germans killed the Russians and the Russians killed the Germans, both sides causing the deaths of more than 1 million men each. In 1949, the Geneva Convention was revised to try and minimize or even eliminate the mistreatment of prisoners. The definition of who would be considered a prisoner of war was expanded, as were the protections and treatment of the prisoners. Prisoners were to be protected from violence or other acts against them by the general public. Nor were they to be exploited by forcing them to work at hard labor, or even simply be on display to the public. The mutilation or torture of POWs, or their being used for medical or other scientific experiments, was expressly forbidden. Medical care was to be given and camps or other holding facilities were required to be open to inspection by neutral parties and the International Red Cross.

As had been specified in the 1929 Convention, a prisoner could not be forced to give information, military or otherwise, to his captors.

By Convention standards, a POW was only required to give his name, rank, service number (if his country used such), and date of birth to his captors.

Over time, more than 150 countries became signatories to the 1949 Geneva Convention. Unfortunately, the ideals of the Convention were not followed by all who had agreed to it. This was proven out within a year of its creation, when war broke out on the Korean peninsula.

Most of the major combatants in the Korean conflict had not formally ratified their agreement to the 1949 Geneva Convention by the time war started. But most involved stated that they would follow the principles of the Convention. The North Korean Communist forces, backed by their allies in Communist China, captured more than 7,100 Americans during the conflict's four years. These prisoners became used for a new form of political warfare fought by the Communists against the rest of the world: the war of propaganda and influencing public opinion to further the aims of the Communists.

Brutal, savage treatment of prisoners at the hands of the North Koreans was comparable to some of the worst excesses of Imperial Japan from only a few years earlier. The Koreans had suffered greatly at the hands of the Japanese, as had much of Asia's overall population. The North Koreans took that barbarism and added some characteristics of their own.

In a kind of nightmare reminder of the Bataan Death March, the North Koreans took American and UN prisoners on forced marches from the frontline areas to the POW camps. POW food was poor at best, though the North Koreans complained that their own soldiers ate the same food. A diet of rice and little else was barely enough to feed the Asian people, who had been living on it for millennia. For American and other UN troops, it was a means of slow starvation. The brutal environment, particularly in the cold Korean winters, helped to cause disease to sweep through the ranks of the POWs, already suffering from malnutrition.

In spite of their protestations that they were treating the POWs humanely, at least 2,701 of the 7,140 Americans held prisoner during the Korean War died while in captivity. Refusing to recognize the International Red Cross as an impartial, neutral organization, the North Koreans did not allow any inspections of the camps where the prisoners were held. If those inspections had taken place, they would have shown a new form of abuse given to the POWs by the Communists.

Physical torture was commonplace as a means of extracting military information from the prisoners. But psychological abuses of prisoners was something new. Beatings, threats, and psychological pressure were all brought to bear to try and force the POWs to admit to knowledge of war crimes—the employment of germ warfare by the UN forces against the people of North Korea was something the Communists wanted to "prove" very much.

Coercion and indoctrination were the methods used by the Communist Chinese who took over the interment of POWs as the war progressed. The intent was to change the political outlook of the prisoners, turn them to the Communist side, and have them confess to war crimes. The confessions were broadcast to the world, particularly the Communist world, as proof that UN forces and particularly the Americans were the aggressors in Korea. The experiences of the POWs in Korea added a new word to the American public and military: *brainwashing*.

At the end of the Korean War, more than 21,000 of the approximately 120,000 Communist troops taken prisoner by the UN forces chose not to be repatriated to North Korea or China. Of the 4,418 American POW survivors who were returned to the United States after the war's end, twenty-one POWs elected to stay in North Korea. The Communist indoctrination had taken hold. For the first time in a major conflict, POWs had become a significant pawn to try and influence the opinion of a population. It was not the last time.

[CHAPTER 3]

CODE OF CONDUCT

The actions of the POWs held by the Communists during the Korean War concerned the staff of all of the services. The new style of interrogations, torture, and brainwashing had soldiers cooperating with the enemy unlike ever before in U.S. military history. Besides revealing military secrets to their captors, soldiers were helping to create propaganda opportunities for the enemy. The Korean War had not only shown the world how warfare with the Communists would be waged, it showed how POWs could be used, manipulated, and exploited in a conflict to influence their populations back home. In spite of only a very few of the total number of POWs being 'brainwashed" and cooperating with the enemy, the problem was considered a different one from those of past U.S. conflicts. It required a new means of training the soldier to resist, and the creation of more practical guidelines for that resistance.

Only a very small percentage of all American POWs captured during the Korean War were U.S. Marines, and out of that number, only one officer cooperated with the enemy. In spite of the relatively few Marine POWs, the Marine Corps was the first U.S. military branch to address captives' behavior while in enemy hands.

During the early summer months of 1955, Marine Colonel F. Brooke Nihart set down on paper a series of principles to guide Marine POWs. The articles were intended to formalize a code of honor that each captive Marine could follow. Colonel Nihart had seen combat during World War II, had taken part in the Battle of Okinawa, and fought hard against the North Koreans during the Korean War. He well knew what the American fighting man was capable of, and what could be expected of him. The final Code of Conduct written by Colonel Nihart consisted of six articles and less than three hundred words. But those words held a particular significance to any member of the American military.

On August 17, 1955, President Dwight D. Eisenhower signed Executive Order 10631, which made the Code of Conduct the official credo for all branches of the U.S. Armed Forces and everyone serving in them.

ARTICLE I

I am an American Fighting Man. I serve in the forces which guard my country and our way of life. I am prepared to give my life in their defense.

ARTICLE II

I will never surrender of my own free will. If in command I will never surrender my men while they still have the means to resist.

ARTICLE III

If I am captured I will continue to resist by all means available. I will make every effort to escape and aid others to escape. I will accept neither parole nor special favors from the enemy.

ARTICLE IV

If I become a prisoner of war, I will keep faith with my fellow prisoners. I will give no information or take part in any action which might be harmful to my comrades. If I am senior, I will take command. If not, I will obey the lawful orders of those appointed over me and will back them up in every way.

ARTICLE V

When questioned, should I become a prisoner of war, I am bound to give only my name, rank, service number, and date of birth. I will evade answering further questions to the utmost of my ability. I will make no oral or written statements disloyal to my country and its allies or harmful to their cause.

ARTICLE VI

I will never forget that I am an American Fighting Man, responsible for my actions, and dedicated to the principles which made my country free. I will trust in my God and in the United States of America.

With the establishment of the order, President Eisenhower had directed that "each member of the Armed Forces liable to capture shall be provided with specific training and instruction designed to better equip him to counter and withstand all enemy efforts against him, and shall be fully instructed as to the behavior and obligations expected of him during combat and captivity."

Now, instead of simply receiving survival training, pilots, air crews, and special operations soldiers who went behind enemy lines would also receive training in how to escape and evade the enemy, as well as what they could expect in terms on interrogation and psychological manipulation. Some of the instructors at military survival schools established following the adoption of the Code of Conduct had been POWs under the Japanese in World War II and the Communists during the Korean War. They well knew what could be done to manipulate a soldier, especially one who would already be experiencing the shock of having been taken prisoner.

The first article of the code was intended in part to fight the shock of being captured. No matter what the soldier's situation, he would be, above all else, a fighting man and remain such. It would be the discipline of the soldier that would help sustain him through the difficulties of his ordeal. It did not mean that he had to die to uphold the ideals of the code, but he had to be prepared to do so from the very beginning in order to fulfill his role as a fighting man. This part of the code was considered so significant that it was repeated in spirit in the last article to remind the soldier of what he was. The soldier was to support the interests of the United States and to oppose its enemies, whether in combat or captivity.

The second article meant that the soldier may never voluntarily surrender while still able to resist the enemy. He did not have to be able to fight, or even defend himself. But he had to exhaust all possible means of escape short of dying without inflicting any damage or losses on the enemy. As long as the leader of a unit had the power to evade the enemy, break out of encirclement, or resist the enemy's approach, he was bound to do so. A leader could not order his men to lay down their arms even if the unit was surrounded, isolated from friendly forces, unless his men no longer had the means to resist—meaning they were out of ammunition, unarmed, or wounded and unable to continue the fight.

It is in article three of the code where a soldier is directed to continue the fight even while a prisoner of war. The fight is not an active one of armed combat but the harder battle of resistance. It is in this arena that the soldier tries hardest to not be exploited by the enemy. Resistance includes fighting against the very real problems of physical and mental stress and manipulation, mistreatment, neglect—particularly when denied medical treatment for wounds received when captured, or political indoctrination and torture.

Part of the means of a soldier's resistance to the trials of being a POW is his duty to try and escape. If he is not able to escape for reasons of illness, wounds, or other physical limitations, he should extend every effort to help his fellow prisoners escape. In the Geneva Convention of 1949, it was stipulated that a prisoner had the right to escape and could not be punished for the attempt outside of disciplinary action and additional surveillance of the individual. Nor could a POW be punished for minor infractions of the law done to support his escape attempt, such as simple theft, forgery (falsifying papers), and being out of uniform (wearing civilian clothing) unless he had committed an act of violence against or caused the loss of life of enemy personnel or the local population.

In the last part of article three, the POW is instructed that he may not accept any special treatment offered by the enemy in return for favors or cooperation. Privileges and better treatment have been offered to POWs in exchange for their promise (parole) not to escape. The promise from a prisoner usually involved his signing a document of some kind that signified an agreement with the enemy. This also meant that the prisoners were not to accept an early release from captivity by the enemy, particularly in exchange for information or statements that could be used against fellow POWs.

Furthering this principle, article four stated that POWs will not work against each other while in captivity or do anything that would bring harm to other prisoners. If there was knowledge of an upcoming escape attempt or that a particular POW may have specific information, a prisoner had to keep that to himself. No matter how great the temptation to give that information over to the enemy, particularly if it would damage the well-being of another prisoner, a POW was not to give it over.

To help reinforce that the POWs were still considered members of the military, their command structure while imprisoned was specified in article four. Leadership would be of great importance in resisting the enemy, or even of simple survival. So would be the discipline necessary to carry out the articles of the code of conduct. Since the population of a POW camp could be comprised of men from various services branches, the senior leader would be the highest-ranking officer no matter what his organization. The mantle of leadership would move to the next highest rank, or precedence, if the commander of a group was incapacitated or unable to act for any reason.

In article five of the code, the basic information that a prisoner is allowed to give the enemy is spelled out. The term *name, rank, and serial number* has been embodied in article five, including the date of birth of the prisoner to complete the identification. This is all that a prisoner can be expected to give and still be considered to have not cooperated with the enemy. According to the Geneva Convention, a prisoner cannot be tortured, physically or mentally, in order to gain more than this basic information.

Oral or written statements, confessions, and appeals to other prisoners or audiences are not allowed. This would mean that a POW cannot take part in propaganda recordings or broadcasts. If they are forced to take part in such actions, they are to resist, limiting their cooperation to the least practical amount.

If a prisoner is tortured, he is to resist to the best of his ability. Such resistance is an individual thing; no two people hold the same tolerance to pain or psychological tortures. Injuries, malnutrition, and lack of sleep lower the ability of someone to hold out against additional tortures. But a soldier is to hold out for as long as he can; if he does break, cooperation should be kept to a minimum.

As in article one, article six reminds the individual that he is part of something greater. He is a soldier and is expected to act like one, whether on the battlefield or in the prison camp. He is responsible for his own actions; each must assist the others in surviving the ordeal of being a prisoner of war.

[CHAPTER 4]

A START

Born in the early 1930s, John Dramesi grew up in a time that saw the United States gear up for war unlike any other period in history. As so many young boys during World War II, the adventures of flying were never far from his mind. Airplanes filled his night sky. Balsa wood models he had built hung from the ceiling in his room. There were so many models, his mother said that you needed a traffic cop just to go into the room.

As the model planes moved with the air currents, John could imagine himself piloting the real craft through the sky. But the reality of just what the aircraft he would fly someday would be like was beyond the reach of even a young boy's dreams. He can't say where he developed his interest in flying, only that it was there and the desire to be a pilot was strong. That love of flying stayed with him throughout his life.

A boy of twelve can recognize what is going on while the country around him celebrates the end of World War II—that war was a time when the entire country moved together to defeat an enemy on both sides of the world. Scrap drives, rationing, war bonds, newsreels, and the radio all served to remind everyone just what was going on elsewhere on the planet. Footage of bombers and fighters moving through the skies of Europe and the Pacific showed young Dramesi just what a flier had to do if he wanted to serve his country. No one had to teach the young man what patriotism meant; he could see it in the actions of others.

Patriotism aside, there are other things to learn growing up in a South Philadelphia row house. Toughness and the ability to depend on oneself to get through a situation counted a lot in Dramesi's neighborhood. Early on, he learned that it took skill and determination to win, not just attitude. His father had been a boxer, and part of that pugnacious attitude seemed part of the boy's genes.

Dramesi continued his education at Haddonfield High School in New Jersey, just across the river from Philadelphia. Sports were something that John enjoyed, and he chose some of the hard ones: football and wrestling. A star wrestler in high school, John knew that it also took brains to get through life. All of his friends on the football and wrestling teams were practically scheduled to go to college. So between the friends who were going to college, and a mother who knew the value of doing so, the motivation was there to work hard, do well, and get the grades that it would take to qualify for a higher education. His efforts paid off when John was accepted to go to Rutgers University.

While at Rutgers, the means to fly opened up for Dramesi when he joined the Air Force Reserve Officer Training Corps (ROTC); it was both a way into the sky and a means to help pay for college. Once more, being average wasn't good enough for the young college man; he excelled in his sport as a wrestler, and as a young officer-to-be. The Scarlet Rifles was a close-order drill team that had been a national competitor since its establishment in 1933. Before graduation, John Dramesi was the commander of that drill team and showed that he could work closely and with precision alongside his teammates. That discipline helped John both as an Air Force pilot and in the greater trials that were to come.

Graduating from Rutgers with a degree in education in 1956, John Dramesi immediately went into active duty with the Air Force. Dramesi had received a letter from the service that he was to report to active duty in the fall of the year following his graduation. In his letter back to the Air Force, the impatience of the young man showed as he plainly told his superiors that the fall of the next year was too late. He wanted to go active duty immediately. The wishes of the new lieutenant were granted, as he received orders to report for duty early in 1956. He was anxious to get going and looking forward to becoming a pilot.

One memory that stood out in training was when Lieutenant Dramesi had an opportunity to do his first solo ride in a Lockheed T33 trainer. The T33 was an old aircraft; the design was developed from the first U.S. jet fighter, the F-80 (P-80), which first flew in 1944. It wasn't a high-performance aircraft—not when compared to the fighters that were in service during the late 1950s. The F-80 had been generally phased out of front-line service with the Air Force shortly after the Korean War, a few years before Dramesi entered active duty. But it was a jet, the kind of bird that wasn't even in the imagination of that young boy watching those balsa-wood planes "fly" across the ceiling of his room.

On that first solo ride, Dramesi piloted his plane down along the Texas coastline. With the ocean on one side and the beach below him, the young pilot went "down on the deck," moving his jet closer to the ground. Being at a low altitude gives the pilot a greater feeling of the speed of his plane, and moving a jet along the beach was a real rush. But an even greater feeling took hold as Dramesi approached someone walking toward him on the beach.

Just as he reached the person, Dramesi pulled his jet up and headed for the sky. Looking back, John could see everything start to get smaller as he gained altitude at a higher speed than anything he had flown in before. This was power at his fingertips and where his joy of flying came from. As he turned around to see the man, beach, and earth growing smaller as his altitude increased, he thought of himself as being in a rocket going to the moon or out into space.

As a young boy, Dramesi dreamed of going into space as so many of his generation did, listening to the radio shows and watching Flash Gordon serials at the movies. Piloting a jet as it screamed up and away from the ground was as close as any human could come at the time to launching up toward orbit. It was years before the first man orbited the earth in a space capsule, but for that moment, the new pilot at the controls of his craft could feel a kinship with those men who would become astronauts.

John Dramesi wasn't an astronaut; he was a pilot in training and had the bug for speed and altitude. The path to high-performance aircraft was by becoming a fighter pilot. The students in Dramesi's class had an opportunity to choose what would be made available to them by the Air Force. But the options were limited by a student's ranking in the class. Choices were more limited as your ranking in the class went down. Other students often became helicopter pilots, cargo pilots, or went on to other assignments. To be a fighter pilot was supposed to be the ultimate peak of high-performance flying. It was where all of the "good" Air Force pilots went first. Standing as number three in overall student ranking put Dramesi tantalizingly close to a jet fighter assignment. But there were only two fighter pilot slots available to the class, and there were two students ahead of him.

With a carefully thought-out plan in his mind, Dramesi moved about with his fellow students, talking about all of the things that young men normally talk about. His emphasis in the conversations was on how great it would be to go to Japan or France, two of the other assignments available to the pilots. In those exotic foreign countries, the beautiful young women would be all over handsome American officers. And as pilots, they would be flying F-86 jets and other planes out there at the forefront of the Air Force's fleet.

His plan proved fruitful, as one of the students in front of him chose F-86 jets and the overseas deployments. His new assignment for further training was going to be at Myrtle Beach Air Force Base on the easternmost point of where South Carolina sticks out into the Atlantic. His plane would be the F-100 fighter craft. Dramesi would be flying faster than the speed of sound.

The North American F-100 Super Sabre was the first supersonic fighter to be in the Air Force inventory. This was an aircraft that was the world's first operational jet fighter that could exceed Mach 1—the speed of sound, or about 760 miles per hour at sea level—in level flight.

During fighter training, Dramesi had exceeded the speed of sound in an F-86. That aircraft was able to break Mach 1, but not in level flight. To go past that magic number for the first time, Dramesi was to take his plane up to a certain altitude and put her nosedown in a dive. As the jet engine pushed at the plane, gravity pulled down and the acceleration increased.

Going into his dive, Dramesi watched his speed gauge, the Mach meter. The needle on the gauge crept up, and the plane dove down toward the ground. The airplane wanted to level out as the dive continued and speed increased. Inside the cockpit, Dramesi watched the indicator creep closer and closer to the red dot, which indicated the speed of sound. He piloted the plane down, continuing his dive as the airframe bucked against him. The ground was coming up; he was going to fly past the safe altitude before that needle would pass the red dot that seemed so important. Finally, he pulled the plane up and out of the dive, disappointed that he hadn't broken the sound barrier.

There was no difference in the feel of the plane during the flight. If he had exceeded the speed of sound, the only indicator Dramesi would have would be that on his Mach gauge. There was no particular sound, shaking, or other dramatic indication that the aircraft would actually be going faster than the sound of its own flight. The noise of its passing would actually be behind it, spreading out in a cone of expanding air and sound known as a sonic boom.

It turned out Dramesi was a little bit in error on his reading of his speed during that flight. Going back to the base after the flight, Dramesi reported to his instructor that he had probably not even reached Mach 1, let alone exceeded it. When asked by his instructor why he hadn't done as ordered, the young lieutenant reported truthfully that he had done as instructed. He had accelerated, gone into the dive, and held it as long as he could. The needle on his Mach gauge had reached quivering toward the red dot, touched it, but had never passed it. The answer back from his instructor was a little blunt.

"You dummy," his flight instructor said, "that red dot is the speed limitation for the airframe. Mach 1 is way back there someplace."

Even though the F-100 could break the speed of sound in level flight, Dramesi learned that it was still difficult to do so. He excelled as a pilot of the Super Sabre at and other assignments, enough so that when a new single-seat fighter-bomber came on line in the late 1950s, he was offered his chance to fly it.

The Republic F-105 Thunderchief is a big, sleek jet with swept-back wings and tail and distinctive "reverse-swept-back" air intakes at the leading edge of both wing roots. The powerful turbojet engine in the body of the Thunderchief pushed the airframe well past Mach 1 to a maximum speed of Mach 2.1, or nearly 1,400 miles an hour. Once in the F-105, Dramesi became a test pilot for the new aircraft. One of the things that had to be done to ensure that all of the aircraft's systems were working properly was to take the plane past Mach 2. Working with the Thunderchief soon gave Dramesi the distinction of being a pilot who exceeded the speed of sound more than most of his contemporary fliers.

During normal flights, even in the F-105, most pilots didn't exceed the speed of sound, certainly not reaching Mach 2 or beyond. Although the airplanes were easily capable of it, exceeding that speed, with the accompanying sonic boom, fuel consumption, and all other considerations involved in high-performance flight, just wasn't done much during peacetime, especially over populated areas.

One time while in Spain, a number of pilots from Dramesi's old squadron showed up while he was piloting the F-105D. When his old friends went past his position, he scrambled his plane to chase them. The speed of the F-105D was such that he was quickly able to catch up with and pass the other fliers. They were at about 20,000 feet, climbing to 25,000 when Dramesi pulled up in front of them, intending to do a loop and join up with the others.

When Dramesi pulled his plane up, he was already at 25,000 feet. In the thin air, his aircraft wasn't acting properly. If he pulled the aircraft around hard, there would have been a good chance that Dramesi could have stalled the plane, possibly going into a spin. Instead, he just let the nose drop. When the nose went down, the plane was going well over Mach 1. When he pulled out, he had full control of the airplane, but his friends had never even known he was in trouble. It didn't take long going at Mach 2 to catch up with his old squadron's flight; his friends were none the wiser.

One thing the pilots trained a lot at doing was a unique bombing action required by the possible tactical use of nuclear weapons. Using a nuclear weapon launched from a fighter-bomber could make a quick, strategic attack against a massed enemy formation possible. The Soviets were known to have a huge reserve of armor. The Air Force's single-bombing action could stop or slow a potential Soviet advance on NATO.

One way to have a relatively small, agile craft attack with a nuclear weapon was with a high-arcing lob of a bomb, releasing the weapon while the plane was in a sharp climb. When the plane released the bomb on a calculated trajectory, the bomb followed its ballistic arc, continuing up into the air along the path of release until gravity pulled the weapon back down to earth. While the bomb was traveling up and over, the releasing aircraft could wing over and rush away from the site of the upcoming nuclear detonation. That would put the aircraft out of the blast radius of its own weapon.

It took a lot of practice to become really proficient at that kind of high-arcing bomb launch, and Dramesi and the rest of his squadron worked diligently to obtain and polish those unique bombing skills. During one training operation near a U.S. base in Libya, before the Air Force gave up the desert base, Dramesi and his fellow pilots practiced releasing ordnance on the range targets.

One of the escape maneuvers for when an aircraft released a nuclear weapon would be for the craft to first overfly, go directly over the target, climb sharply, and release the bomb in a high arc. The plane would have a great deal of recovery speed, so it would complete the loop and dart away from the area before the bomb would drop back on the target.

The first time Dramesi did the action at the Libya range, the range officer had never seen that style of bombing attack before. The range officer thought that Dramesi was being a more than flamboyant pilot, if not all-out crazy and dangerous. As a result, Dramesi was kicked off the range.

After the flight, when Dramesi reported to the operations officer for the mission, he was immediately asked why he had been kicked off the bombing range.

"All, I did was a loop," Dramesi said simply.

"Wow, the officer commented, "a loop, off the ground?"

That kind of maneuver was unheard-of in the regular Air Force.

"Yes, sir," was all Dramesi could say.

"Then I can understand why he kicked you off the range."

"Just a minute." Dramesi spoke up in his own defense. "That is one of the described maneuvers for us in our manuals."

After the attack was described in detail to the operations officer, and why such a maneuver had to be done, Dramesi was put back on flying status.

[CHAPTER 5]

PUNCHING OUT

In terms of technical information and investment in time and money, a modern pilot is the most highly trained individual in the military. Before a pilot is put in command of one of the most complex and expensive single war machines in the world, he has to go through weeks, months, and years of costly training. Long before one of these individuals climbs aboard an aircraft for their first combat flight, he represents an investment of millions of dollars just in training on the part of the government. People who can complete the arduous course of instruction are valuable in and of themselves even without taking into account the cost of training.

During the earliest years of air-to-air combat, there were few options for pilots at the controls of a stricken plane. The man could try to ride the plane down to some kind of landing, spin down into a crash, or, if the plane was on fire, turn a weapon on himself rather than burn to death. During World War I another option was being offered to pilots: the parachute. By the end of the war, the parachute was being used on all sides of the conflict.

In the decades following, the method of parachuting from a damaged plane was fairly simple: The pilot climbed out of the cockpit and fell away. If the parachute was a static-line system, the rig opened automatically as the distance from the aircraft increased. Very quickly, the more flexible ripcord system parachute, opened on command by the wearer by pulling on a handle, became the most popular form of self-rescue for a pilot or aircrew while in flight.

During most of World War II, the only chance to escape from an aircraft involved opening the canopy or a hatch in order to exit. As the speed of aircraft increased, eliminating the open cockpits of earlier years, it became much harder to open a hatch or jettison a canopy against the ever-increasing windblast. The windblast or slipstream created by a speeding aircraft could even hold a pilot back in his seat, preventing him from even climbing out of the cockpit. The time to successfully escape a damaged aircraft was limited; the pilot or crew had to get out before the fuel exploded, fire reached the bombs or ammunition on board, or the plane got too low to successfully bail out of.

A new problem developed as the speed of fighter aircraft increased. Even if a pilot could get out of the cockpit, he had to fall away from the plane far and fast enough so that he wouldn't strike the tail surface of the plane as it went past. The Germans were the first to address this problem when they developed the ejector seat, a powered escape mechanism. Once activated, the ejector seat would push whoever was sitting in it far enough away from the plane that he wouldn't be in danger of hitting the wreckage as it went past.

Other countries were developing the same kind of escape mechanism for fliers, but the Germans were the first to field one. The seats were installed in their earliest jet aircraft, and in many cases was the only means of survival for the pilots. The German jets were introduced too late in the war to significantly change the outcome, but they showed the world the future of combat aircraft. And the nearly sixty Germans who had safely ejected during the war were living proof of the new means of survival for the pilots and aircraft crews.

The early ejection systems were nothing more than a seat strapped to a highly modified gun. During experiments in Britain, it was found that the force of ejection from those single-shot gun systems could seriously damage the spine of the user. When the propellant charge fired the seat up and out of the aircraft, the vertebrae of the user's spine would collide with each other from the severe G-force. Using multiple, smaller charges to quickly build up the velocity of ejection was found to help minimize the injury to the pilot from the seat itself.

The force of the slipstream was another problem. The force of the winds at near-supersonic speeds was incredible. A category 5 hurricane has winds of over 155 miles an hour. It can rip buildings apart, flip cars over, knock down brick walls, and leave a trail of devastation in its path. People cannot stand or walk in such a wind. At Mach 1, the wind blast passing a jet is fives times that fast. Face shields, helmets, and protective clothing could help a pilot survive the damage from the slipstream, at least minimizing injuries to his face and eyes.

In time for the Korean War in the 1950s, the ejection seat was in widespread use around the world. "Punching out" became a popular term for ejection. The expression came from a pilot having to literally blast free of his stricken aircraft, punching through the canopy or ejecting after the cover had been blown clear of the aircraft.

The terrific forces of ejection could leave a pilot dazed and confused at best. Some pilots survived ejecting from the craft only to smash into the ground still strapped to the device intended to save them. Automatic ejection systems were developed that ejected a man from his aircraft, then freed him from the seat and opened his parachute.

New systems were developed that utilized a rocket engine to drive the ejection seat up and away from the aircraft. As speeds continued to increase, the danger to the pilots from the damaging slipstream also increased. Limbs had to be held in by harnesses that automatically pulled the individual into place as the ejection system initiated. Bones would snap if limbs flailed in the awesome winds. There was also the danger of striking part of the cockpit rim if the individual's arms and legs weren't held in their proper place.

The F-105D Thunderchief had a rocket-propelled ejection seat that had been designed by Republic, the aircraft's manufacturer. A drogue chute on the seat itself stabilized it in the air after the rocket had burned out and the seat was clear of the aircraft. The pilot wore his parachute rather than having one that was packed as part of the seat. Once the pilot released his seat's harness, he fell free and pulled the ripcord on his own chute.

To initiate the ejection sequence, the pilot pulls up on the large looped yellow-and-black-striped handles on the outside of the ejection seat. The handles are held in the lowered "safe" position and are located just outside of seat body, where the pilot's thighs would be. Pulling up the loop handle cocks the firing system, moving a lever from the bottom of the loop up to the center. The pilot grabs the center handle with his fingers and squeezes his hand shut, "pulling the trigger" on the ejector seat.

The canopy is blasted free of the cockpit as the ejection sequence starts. The catapult rocket ignites, punching the seat up and away from the aircraft. The rocket engine of the catapult pushes the seat up and away violently enough that the tail of the plane can streak by underneath the ejection seat as the drogue chute deploys to stabilize the system and keep it from tumbling violently through the air. When he releases the ejection seat, the pilot falls away and his own parachute opens automatically. Because some pilots are known to have "frozen" in their seats after ejection, a system was installed that pulled the pilot away from the seat by a strap system.

The whole action takes only seconds, but it's an extremely violent experience. The advertised safe top speed for ejection from an F-105 is reported to have been 525 knots (about 605 miles an hour) but many pilots and crews were forced to eject at higher speeds. On April 30, 1967, Leo Thorsness and his rear seater in the two-seat F-105F Wild

Weasel punched out of their aircraft over North Vietnam while moving at 600 knots (over 690 miles an hour).

Aircraft struck by ground fire or missiles had been seen by other pilots and aircrews to explode shortly after being hit. The explosions sent metal shards flying all about the bird, along with an expanding ball of flame and burning fuel. Waiting for a plane to slow down could use up what precious time there might be before an explosion. The dangers of ejecting at over what was considered a "safe" speed were completely acceptable to men facing a grisly death from their aircraft tearing itself, and them, apart.

An old saying by pilots and fliers was that the average person lost a quarter inch of height when he ejected. No matter how straight the seat might hold someone, it still took a hard blow and high G-forces to get an ejection seat out and past a speeding plane. That force still drove the vertebrae of the spine together, compressing disks and causing damage that normally required bed rest and therapy for a complete recovery. Being seated correctly at least minimized the compression damage from the force of ejection. Combat flying rarely allowed for being correct about much of anything at the moment of ejection. The supersonic slipstream ripped and tore at unsecured limbs, flailing them about, breaking bones and damaging joints. But at least the man would be out of the aircraft and alive. Not many POWs who had ejected from an F-105 or any other aircraft stated that they felt as much injury from a compressed back as they did from all of the other suffering they endured during their incarceration.

No matter how an ejection was completed, it has remained a frightening and dangerous maneuver. It is an action of last resort for a pilot who knows his aircraft cannot survive. When done over enemy territory as the result of combat or air defense fire, the pilot then faces the very real possibility of capture once he does reach the ground.

[CHAPTER 6]

CAPTURED

The smoke had been so thick in the cockpit of the F-105D that Dramesi hadn't been able to see his hand in front of his face. Once he had made the decision to eject, training took over and there was little that he needed to see in order to save himself. He knew that he was going fast and was very close to the ground. Options were limited and it was time to get out. Not knowing whether he was upside down, heading toward the ground, or what his orientation was, his view of the instruments blinded by the smoke, Dramesi punched out. The last thing he remembered was squeezing the trigger.

When the ejector seat shot out of the plane, the windblast was so powerful that it knocked Dramesi unconscious. The next lucid thought Dramesi had was when he found himself standing on the ground, unbuckling his parachute harness. His training had taken him through the parachuting process without his having to think about a single aspect of it. Now came the realization that he was deep inside enemy territory. He had punched out over North Vietnam, and the rest of his training would have to be employed for survival as well as to prevail over whatever was going to come next. And it was probably going to involve a bunch of the same people who had just shot him out of the sky.

The parachute landing had put Dramesi on the side of a brush-covered hill overlooking a small valley. He was unsure of his exact location, but he did have a sense about where he had landed. Getting up onto the crest of the hill he was standing on would also give him a better view of the area, where the rescuing forces would be approaching from—and just where the enemy might be. According to the reports filed later, the location of Dramesi's shoot-down was at coordinates 173800N and 1062300E. That put him about 225 miles south-southeast of Hanoi and seventy miles north of the demilitarized zone between North and South Vietnam. He was deep inside enemy territory, and his only sure way home would be a pickup by a search-and-rescue chopper.

As Dramesi moved up the hill, he heard gunfire coming from the area where he had made his parachute landing. There was little cover beside the brush and the occasional tree as he reached the ridge going along the hill's crest. The high ground was where Dramesi figured a rescue helicopter could most easily find him; the trouble was that a small trail ran along the ridge, which meant the enemy traveled there and they would be able to find him, too. He had twisted his left knee either during the ejection or while landing. Adrenaline had kept the injury from slowing Dramesi down much as he evaluated his situation and planned his course of action.

In the briefing prior to his mission, Dramesi had listened to an intelligence officer tell the fliers what they could expect in the way of assistance if they were forced down in enemy territory. Outside of the American search-and-rescue units, there was basically no help they could expect in North Vietnam. The final admonition of the intelligence officer stuck with Dramesi: It was people who caught people. It was a simple enough rule that so many other pilots forgot in their time of stress after ejecting. It took people—the North Vietnamese—to catch the American fliers who were forced down. To evade capture, you had to avoid people. There was no one to turn to for help except for yourself, and the men whose job it was to come in and rescue you. Everyone else had to be avoided. Dramesi looked around and steeled himself to getting out of his present predicament.

To his west side, there was a small cliff that would help prevent ground troops from approaching from that direction. The cliff ran around to the south of his position, covering him from approach from that direction as well. And the top of the ridge did give him a good position to see the surrounding area. Moving along the path as he headed north, Dramesi could see North Vietnamese moving in the valley below. It was time to hide.

A leap took him off the path and into the brush without leaving any sign of an escape route. On his survival radio, Dramesi contacted his wingman, Ken Gurry, who still orbiting overhead in his F-105D. Gurry had to leave the area due to low fuel, but he had already notified the search-and-rescue teams about Dramesi's situation and location. Rescue helicopters and escort aircraft were already on their way. In spite of his reluctance to abandon his fellow pilot, Gurry had to leave the area before his fuel ran out or the rescue people would have two downed pilots to worry about. Dramesi acknowledged his wingman's message and simply said that he would see him later.

Almost immediately after the jet left the sky overhead, Dramesi heard the sound of the Sandys coming in. The Sandy was the call sign of the Douglas A-1 Skyraider aircraft, which were assigned to escort the helicopters of the combat search-and-rescue units. The radial-engined Skyraider was an attack bomber that had first flown during World War II. The prop-driven aircraft could only go about half as fast as the average jet fighter of the Vietnam War, but it carried four 20mm cannon in its wings and up to 8,000 pounds of ordnance on the hard mounting points under its wings. On top of the heavy punch it could carry, the Skyraider had a long loiter time over target. The fat, slow Sandys were looked at with real affection by downed pilots, as they stayed in the air overhead for close to ten hours at a time.

Trouble was, Dramesi didn't know where the Sandys were, and they didn't know where he was. Getting on the radio to call for help had been his first move, and the right one according to his training. Now he had to find that help, and they had to find him.

The engine noise of a prop-driven aircraft is a distinctive one. Dramesi could hear the planes in the distance, but didn't know in which direction they were coming from. Without that information, he couldn't direct the aircraft toward him; and he couldn't use any signaling device but his radio or the enemy would find him as fast as the planes would. There were enemy troops in the valley below, and they were already making their way up the hill. Soon enough they would reach the crest and the ridgeline where he was hiding in the brush. His only option was to stand up and try to locate the Sandys coming in to help him.

Cupping his hand over his ear to concentrate the sound, Dramesi turned his head to try and hear where the Sandys were. The loudest sound of the props was to his south, so he called over the radio to move them north, in his direction.

"Turn north, turn north!" Dramesi said over the radio. Then he saw the aircraft to his east. "Sandy One, this is Lover Lead. Turn west, stand by, and I will direct you over my position."

With his experience as a forward air controller, Dramesi knew how to apply the approaching Sandys against the enemy forces on the ground around him. Hearing the approach of the planes, he directed them overhead and identified his position. Now that the attack bombers knew where he was, they could address the North Vietnamese forces approaching him on the ground.

Telling the pilots of the Sandys to target the side of the hill rained hellfire on the approaching enemy. White phosphorus rockets roared out from under the wings of the Sandys, punching into the hillside and blooming into yellow-burning petals of white smoke flowers as they detonated. Only two hundred yards away from his position, Dramesi watched the 2.75-inch rockets explode in the brush, sending the enemy forces running back down the hill toward whatever cover they could find. He was in his element, the skills he had put to use for the 4th Infantry still fresh in his mind as he directed the air support units to his location. It wasn't a ground operation he was fighting for now, it was his own freedom. The Sandys were holding the enemy back while the slower rescue helicopters were on their way. The ground experience he had received while working as FAC with the 4th Infantry also helped Dramesi as he hid from the enemy while still maintaining a good observation position.

Every weapon in the valley seemed to open up at once. Now it was time to get the aircraft to a higher altitude, where they would be safe from the ground fire but still available for a rocket or gun attack. As he directed the Sandys away, the aircraft moved to a higher altitude so that they could also cover the area to his south more effectively. And that's when Dramesi's luck ran out.

He was barely sticking up from the chest-high brushline along the top of the ridge, but that had been enough. A rifle bullet coming up from behind smashed into Dramesi's right leg. He knew the enemy had to be close but wasn't sure of their exact location. All they could have aimed at was his head and shoulders, but the overhead roar of the prop-driven aircraft must have shaken someone's aim. The last message he was able to send up to the Sandy overhead was: "They got me, they got me." Lover Lead was down.

With millions of dollars' worth of aircraft and weapons at his command, and the training to use them, John Dramesi was captured by two North Vietnamese men armed with rifles, an officer of some kind, and a young boy in shorts armed with a machete. They came on him while he thrashed about in the brush, frantically trying to get to cover. The bullet had knocked him down but not out of the fight. If he could evade his captors, there was still a chance that the search-and-rescue birds could come in and get him. But the North Vietnamese were on him, stripping him of all of his equipment—especially his precious radio. The Sandys overhead could not do much now, as the man they had come to rescue was shoved along the trail by his captors. Their last option was to do a screaming run at low altitude, just over the heads of the men on the ground. The distraction might be enough for Dramesi to make a break for it.

The North Vietnamese jumped into the brush, but Dramesi couldn't run from the injuries to both his legs. His captors got up and rushed him along as the Sandy pulled away. Limping and trying to move as slowly as he could, Dramesi was prodded along by the gun barrels of the men around him. His hands were tied behind his back, the untreated wound in his leg streaming blood, and his left knee starting to stiffen up and ache as he was forced along.

Other pilots who had been shot down were stunned by their experience. Just surviving the act of ejection could be overwhelming to a man used to being in control while at the controls of a multimillion-dollar aircraft. For Dramesi, he had already been in combat on the ground. He knew what it took to move and survive in the jungle. He also wasn't the kind of person to give up, ever. Even as he was trying to slow his captors down, delay them as best he could, he was constantly staying aware of his surroundings, looking for that chance to escape. He was caught, but he was alive. And there would be search-and-rescue aircraft looking for him.

The North Vietnamese had been fighting wars for a long time. Even the local militias, such as the men who had caught Dramesi, knew not to stay in one place very long. That lesson had been driven home hard when the American they were moving had directed the rockets and cannon fire of the enemy down among them. If they had known that it was Dramesi personally who had been directing those air strikes, they may not have worked so hard to capture him alive.

Just because they wanted him alive didn't mean the North Vietnamese who were holding him would treat him with any consideration at all. Dramesi was tethered to one of the guards for the journey. As they moved downhill, the guards, boy, and their American captive crossed a stream and then followed it downhill before turning off in another direction. The boy was apparently a local, as he was directing the way the group went. A village was coming up in the distance, surrounded by rice paddies filled with water for the new growing season. Perhaps this was where the boy had come from, since it was the only real population center they had come up on. As the group got closer to the village, Dramesi slipped in the mud. Unable to hold his balance with his hands tied, he crashed facefirst into the stinking filth and knee-deep water.

Every time Dramesi tried to climb up out of the muddy water, the guard he was tethered to yanked on the rope. Whether from anger, stupidity, or simple hatred, the yank repeatedly toppled the struggling man. Over and over again, the pilot was tripped up and dumped back into the water. Realizing that he would drown if he didn't do something, Dramesi grabbed at the rope with his tied hands and gave it a yank himself.

The unexpected pull from his prisoner surprised the guard, pulling him off the paddy dike and dumping him into the water. As Dramesi finally got back up, the young boy accompanying them laughed at the guard's dilemma. Angrier with the American than he had been before, the guard crawled out of the paddy, ready to do real harm to his defiant prisoner. Before the other guard had to stop any further attack, the ground started to shudder at the sound of violent explosions.

Off in the distance, American planes were attacking ground targets with heavy bombs. It might have been the Sandys, which were trying to provide Dramesi some cover and distraction for an escape attempt. If it was them, the rules of engagement prevented Dramesi's allies from attacking the village directly. The locals would have had no way to know that, though, and were taking cover as best they could.

The thunder of the explosions frightened the guards as well as the occupants of the village. Following the villagers, the guards quickly shoved Dramesi into a tunnel underneath one of the huts. The twists of the tunnel ended as Dramesi crawled into a low-ceiling bomb shelter, where other villagers were also hiding.

The village shelter quickly filled with people waiting out the air raid. Shoved together in tight quarters, Dramesi could do little more than just look about his surroundings. A mother cradled an infant in her arms, suckling the child for comfort. Others simply watched and waited. The thunder of the bombs finally stopped, and the North Vietnamese now took the time to see the damage to their prisoner.

Slitting up the legs to his flight suit, the guards could see the bullet wound in his leg. The left knee was swelling, but nothing could be done about that. The bullet wound in his right leg was something that could be treated, though only slightly. A dirty rag was tied around the wound, the closest thing to a bandage that Dramesi was likely to get.

A North Vietnamese officer came down into the crowded bomb shelter to get Dramesi up and away from the villagers. Indicating his injured legs, Dramesi shook his head at the officer's gesturing. The inability of his prisoner to cooperate angered the officer. As he shouted at the injured pilot, Dramesi just kept shaking his head and refusing to get up.

The North Vietnamese officer had been with the ground force of men who had been trying to capture Dramesi when the Sandys came in. He indicated that he had lost twenty men to the well-directed air strikes that had been Dramesi's doing. Finally, he pulled an automatic pistol from a holster, cocked it, and pointed it at the prisoner.

The rest of the villagers in the still-crowded bomb shelter started to panic. A gunshot fired in the close quarters of the shelter would probably injure a number of them even if Dramesi was hit with the first shot. A miss could likely kill a number of them. They had just survived a bombing attack; they did not want to die at the hands of one of their own countrymen.

The look of Dramesi's blood-stained leg was bad, though his other leg bothered him even more. Finally the officer holstered his weapon and left the shelter. But he returned shortly and again ordered Dramesi to leave the shelter, crawling if he had to.

Once outside, the injured pilot acted as if his wounds were much worse than they seemed, forcing him to collapse, even when enemy soldiers tried to pick him up. More threats from the officer, including him once more waving his gun about, did nothing to change the situation.

Finally leaving to bring in some additional soldiers, the officer had Dramesi slung in a net hammock underneath a pole. Shouldering the pole, two of the North Vietnamese soldiers carried the American between them. A third carried their weapons. Acting as if every move caused him pain, Dramesi groaned and grunted at every jolt and jiggle. His transport crew entertained themselves for a while trying to make their passenger as uncomfortable as possible. Then they finally settled down to simply carry their prisoner on to the next village.

[CHAPTER 7]

MOVING

Back during his survival training, the instructors had said that the best time for a prisoner to escape was as soon as possible after capture. Not only would the prisoner then have the best idea of just where he was, as in Dramesi's case, but the situation would be at its most confusing. Once the POW reached a camp or traditional prisoner facility, escape was that much harder.

The North Vietnamese who were moving Dramesi had a very good idea how to avoid American aircraft; they just traveled at night. There was enough starlight shining down that the trail in front of the party was a light gray line through the jungle. Following that line in the darkness led the way to a small house instead of another village. People were in the house, nervous folk who had been enduring the American bombs for some time.

In the main room of the house, a small candle was burning on a table. Even that dim light was more than the people would risk when they heard an aircraft passing by overhead. The light was extinguished until the danger had passed.

While Dramesi lay on the ground, one of the soldiers pulled the dirty cloth away from the bullet wound in his leg. The wound had stopped bleeding, but the possibility of infection from the rough bandage was a real one. The enemy soldier must have been worried enough about losing his prize catch that he took the time to treat the wound a little better. Or maybe he just wanted the leg to get better enough that Dramesi could walk instead of being carried. Either way, the soldier placed a standard military-style bandage on the wound, strapping it down reasonably well.

While he was receiving this very limited medical care, one of the house's occupants became incensed at seeing the American. It may have been that Dramesi receiving any kind of care at the hands of his captors was more than the old man watching could take. Or perhaps he was near the edge of his endurance from the stress of the possible bombing attacks. Rushing up to where the American lay helpless, the old man started beating Dramesi about the head and shoulders.

After watching the show for a bit, the guards finally pulled the man away and stopped him from continuing the beating. In mild voices, the guards lectured the man. Dramesi couldn't understand the words, but the tone indicated that the guards weren't all that upset, just that he shouldn't beat the man they had already carried so far.

As the guards spoke to the old man who had been beating Dramesi, a second elderly man entered the room. This man radiated a greater aura of command than anyone else in the room and was clearly in charge of the group, if not also the soldiers. He asked Dramesi in French if he understood that language. When communications didn't open up, he handed the prisoner a piece of paper and indicated that he wanted the pilot to write something down. Dramesi knew that the elderly man wanted his identification, probably what aircraft he had been flying as well. But Dramesi wasn't willing to give up that information and pretended he didn't understand the request.

Finally, the old man left the room. From another room came the sound of an antique telephone, the kind that had to be hand-cranked to make a call. Whatever the conversation was over the phone, it took some time. Finally, the elderly man came back into the room, again with a piece of paper in his hand. He handed the paper and a pencil to Dramesi. In the dim light of the candle, Dramesi could make out writing on the paper, writing that was in English.

The instructions on the paper were that Dramesi was to put down his name, rank, serial number, and type of aircraft that he had been piloting. There were spaces under the questions where Dramesi was to write his answers. Hr wrote, "John Dramesi, Captain, FR 60532," and that was all. The old man who had attacked Dramesi was lurking close by, but still the American refused to write anything further on the paper. Finally, the elderly man took the paper and went back into the room where the telephone was. That signaled the end of the prisoner's first interrogation session.

Ringing someone on the old phone, the elderly man read off Dramesi's answers to whoever was on the other end of the line. This conversation was much shorter than the earlier one had been and the elderly man rang off and returned to where his prisoner was secured. Issuing some instructions to Dramesi's guards, the elderly man had a flat pallet of bamboo brought in, and the injured pilot laid down on it. Loops at the corners of the pallet were long enough to allow a pole to be slipped through them and the prisoner lifted up from the ground.

As Dramesi and his carriers moved back out into the darkness, one of the men who had been carrying him earlier disappeared into the black, moving back the way they originally came. He was carrying the netting hammock that Dramesi had been transported in.

As he watched the stars go by above him, Dramesi lay on his pallet wondering just what might be in store for him ahead. The propaganda that had been coming out from the North Vietnamese said that American POWs were treated well. As a possible future guest of the North Vietnamese, Dramesi considered the possibility that the food in the Hanoi prisons might even be as good as the propaganda said it was. It didn't really make any difference, though; Dramesi had no intentions of staying a POW long enough to try any more of the local cuisine than he had to.

As the sun started to come up the next morning, Dramesi and his captors were approaching another village. In the light, the prisoner started to think seriously about escape. Despite his injuries, he was in relatively good shape. While he was being moved about, the available manpower to search for him was limited.

Sleep was something he needed. In spite of being placed in the bottom of a trench rather than under any real cover, Dramesi found he had little trouble nodding off. Waking up to the pressure of needing to relieve himself, Dramesi realized he was alone in the trench. After attending to his immediate needs, he explored his surroundings; there still were no apparent guards about. The lessons of his prison camp experiences back in training remained him not to accept the obvious way out. That was what his classmates had done at that prison camp in Nevada, and they had been "shot down" for their efforts. In his present situation, Dramesi seriously doubted there would be little hesitation on the part of his guards to shoot him, and they would not be using blanks.

After spending the day in the trench, Dramesi's guard and transport detachment once again showed up just as darkness was falling. Back on his bamboo pallet, he was once more carried off but at a slower pace than the day before. The group traveled through the night. Before the sun came up the next morning, they arrived at another village.

Security at the new village was different from the slit trench at the last one. Before being hidden away for the day, Dramesi was stripped down to his shorts. Whether this was for security reasons or an attempt to humiliate him, he never really knew. Instead of being put on display for the villagers the nearly naked prisoner was placed in a hole in the ground. There was only one entrance to the hole, and the roof of the enclosure was made up of large planks. One possible reason for stripping the prisoner was made clear when Dramesi looked about his new prison. Three walls were stacked floor to ceiling with boxes of ammunition and grenades. He was in an ammunition storage bunker. Without having any clothes, he was certainly not going to be able to hide anything to use against his captors later.

Later in the morning, the roof of Dramesi's prison was opened up as the guards removed some of the planks. This gave the prisoner some fresh air, and also gave the locals access to him. The village children circled the hole, taunting the prisoner within. Shouting insults in a language the prisoner didn't understand wasn't as satisfying to the kids as throwing rocks and other items at their target. Poking at the prisoner with sticks was fun until Dramesi grew tired of the situation and yanked the sticks out of the kids' hands. Throwing some rocks back at his tormentors also convinced the children to go and find another game to play.

The children moved on and left the prisoner to his own thoughts, all except one. As Dramesi sat in the hole, one much more aggressive child crept up to the hole with a knife in his hand. Unseen until the last moment, the child stood and threw the knife at the prisoner. Unlike what has been seen in the movies, a thrown knife is not a very good weapon. Ducking to the side, Dramesi avoided the flashing blade as it went past him. Striking the wall, the knife fell to the bottom of the hole and lay there. The simple weapon would not have done the man much good in his present situation and he had no way to hide it on his person. Dramesi left the blade untouched as the child ran away.

Later in the morning the villagers began returning to their huts. Several of the locals stood about the hole leading down to Dramesi's "holding" pit. One young man stood out from the others; he was wearing boots to all of the villagers' sandals, and had Dramesi come up out of the hole and sit where everyone could see him.

As the villagers started to gather in greater numbers, the young man started to play cheerleader, getting the people riled up and excited. The object of all of the attention was obvious: The young man hated Dramesi and he wanted everyone else in the village to do so as well. Now, Dramesi was starting to feel exposed, much more so than he was just by sitting there in his underwear.

As the village women started to cry and the men got angrier and angrier, the young boot-wearing rabble-rouser may have become concerned himself. The villagers waved farming tools about in a threatening manner. If this was the reaction the young man wanted to get, he had succeeded. Before things got out of hand, Dramesi was put back in his hole and the crowd calmed down.

It wasn't long before Dramesi was once more brought up out of the hole. People were still standing around, but no one appeared particularly threatening. The prisoner was once again sat down on a plank, and a small bowl of rice covered with some green vegetable matter was handed to him.

Along with the villagers, a small dog and swarm of flies kept the prisoner company while he ate. One of the rules Dramesi had been taught back in survival school was you had to eat when you and what you could. He knew that he would need the nourishment, and his captors hadn't been very forthcoming when it came to food. The rice and vegetables weren't much, but it was more than he'd had for several days now. The blob of some kind of matter on top of the rice and greens was something else again. What it was, Dramesi didn't know, and he didn't want to know. It moved, or at least distorted, when he picked it up with his chopsticks. It was easy enough to appear too clumsy with the sticks and the glob fell to the ground. Whatever it was, the dog seemed to think it was edible, as had the flies. The villagers simply looked on and smiled at the prisoner's inability to eat with the simple utensils they used every day.

When dusk came, the procedures that had been followed for the last few nights were changed. After Dramesi was given a red T-shirt and pants, his hands were once more tied behind his back. He would be carried once again, but this time not by stretcher bearers. Just outside of the village, Dramesi was unceremoniously dumped into the back of a small truck, where two guards joined him.

To help break up the outline of the vehicle, plants were strapped to all sides of the exterior. The rolling bush joined a small convoy of other vehicles moving quickly along a fairly narrow jungle pathway. The drivers must have known their route well enough; they drove through the night without lights. Though Dramesi was concerned at the speed they moved in the darkness, his guards didn't seem to care at all. In the preferred posture of soldiers all over the world, the guards slept as the truck convoy continued on.

With the guards asleep, Dramesi managed to untie his hands without making any real noise. In spite of being able to make a hole in the camouflage plants surrounding his truck, Dramesi did not try to escape. He thought the truck was moving east, the direction he wanted to travel when he did escape. Moving in the vehicle was taking him where he wanted to go—or at least in the right direction.

Arriving at another village just before dawn, Dramesi could see one of the reasons the United States was going to have problems moving the air war forward. It took some time to get the truck placed where the guards wanted it because the village was crowded with other vehicles. The vehicles were all trying to stay as close to the huts as possible while remaining under the cover of the jungle canopy. The village was off-limits to U.S. air strikes, the civilians acting as a greater defense than the heaviest antiaircraft guns. Taking further advantage of the situation, the North Vietnamese had ammunition stored everywhere: huts, trucks, even paths were stacked with ammunition crates and containers.

Carried once more by his captors, Dramesi was taken to a small house in the middle of the village ammo dump and truck park. Creature comforts were more than limited; a foot-wide plank was his bed, and nothing else was offered to him until the next day.

While consuming a small bowl of rice the next morning, Dramesi took the opportunity to survey his present environment. The house was sparsely furnished with a few pieces of furniture: a bed without a mattress, tables, some chairs. The walls were made of bamboo tied together with rope, which was also made from bamboo. There was a spot in one corner of the room, between the wall and the roof, where there was a hole large enough for Dramesi to crawl through. A small table underneath would make reaching it possible. What was outside the wall was unknown but Dramesi needed to know the layout of the village in order to plan some kind of escape attempt.

As things turned out, getting outside of the building wasn't a problem. Through one door was a roofed-over but otherwise open kitchen area. Nothing was around that looked like a latrine or bathroom, so he pantomimed his needs to the guards in rough sign language. A guard simply pointed to the open doorway leading outside.

Keeping up the pretense of not being able to walk very well at all forced Dramesi to crawl out the doorway on his hands and knees. Crawling to where he could attend to nature's call, Dramesi looked about but saw nothing notable. The villagers noticed him, though, especially when he was crawling back to the bamboo hut. Some old women who were carrying babies approached him; one of them thought it was funny to place her child on the back of the American "horse." The baby didn't think much of the situation and started to cry. All during the day, villagers came up to the bamboo walls of the hut to stare and poke at the American prisoner.

Before dark, Dramesi was given another meal: rice with some dry chopped peanuts scattered on it. There wasn't another move that night, and the guards settled in to sleep. There were three of them—two men and now a woman—all armed and all sleeping on top of the bed. With Dramesi's crippled act making it look like he could hardly move, the guards left him untied. But they did move the table out from under the opening in the wall and secured the doors.

That night, Dramesi took a chance and stood up in full view of his sleeping guard detail. There was no reaction from any of them as they lay sleeping, each person cradling a weapon in his or her arms. The door was locked and there was no way for the prisoner to open it without making a lot of noise.

There wasn't going to be a way out, not from this hut. Three guards made it impossible for Dramesi to overcome all of them quietly, even if he got his hands on a weapon. Waiting and watching for an opportunity was the best plan for the moment, so Dramesi went over to the corner the guards had set him in and went back to sleep.

More rice and peanuts made up a morning meal served by a young woman who was apparently there to watch him while his guards were away. She gave him water when asked, and did not abuse him.

It was a different situation when the guards came back that evening to continue their journey. Picking Dramesi up on his stretcher, they were moving him to a truck when the villagers closed in. The group attacked the seemingly helpless American with fists and sticks, with the most vicious and dangerous attacks coming from the old women and small children. It didn't matter who was swinging a stick or throwing a rock—at least not to the person on the receiving end.

Rolling off the stretcher to try and protect his face and head, Dramesi fell to the ground. Two of the guards rushed forward and picked him up, pulling him along with his arms across their shoulders. Now the guards were also being struck with sticks and stones.

Threatening the crowd with their weapons, the guards made their way to the truck. Dramesi was put in the back along with some of his guards. They quickly left the village behind as they drove off into the darkness once again.

CHAPTER 8

INTERROGATION

With the occupants of the vehicle safely in place, the truck left the village and riled mob behind. As far as Dramesi could tell, the vehicle was still moving in a generally eastward direction, which made it easier to ride along rather than make an escape attempt on the road. The guards were relatively relaxed since they thought that their prisoner was barely able to move around on his own—an opinion that Dramesi was careful to maintain by crawling whenever possible.

The truck stopped well before dawn. In the darkness, Dramesi was pulled from the vehicle and manhandled into a holding cell. The facility appeared to be a prison of some kind. The room he was thrust into was small, the local equivalent of a jail cell, and appeared to have been built fairly hastily from a standard hut.

There was a board in one corner to act as a bed, but there were no other amenities. It was just a place to hold prisoners until they were moved to a more secure facility. The small room was only about five feet wide and seven long. The main walls of the building were of wood, the outside wall of the cell being one of these. About three feet up from the dirt floor was a window opening with four iron bars set into the sill. A wood shutter closed off the window, blocking the view of the outside area.

A weak point of the structure was the inside wall of the cell; it was made of bamboo secured with the common twisted bamboo twine. Tough but flexible, the twine was used as a construction material throughout of the tropics of Southeast Asia. In addition to the twine, metal wire was also used to secure the bamboo wall together and down to the floor. The bamboo was ill-fitting with gaps between the stalks allowing a view of the areas of the house outside the cell. The bamboo wall was what drew Dramesi's attention; he went to sleep that first night considering the possibilities it offered. He had to learn more about the area around him and who was there before any real plans could be made. Wadding up some old burlap cloth he found in the cell, Dramesi did what was most important for any possible escape: he went to sleep and got some rest.

Daylight the next morning allowed Dramesi to see some of his surroundings through the gaps between the bamboo stalks of the walls. A cooking area was visible, identifiable by the usual pots and pans. A double bed without a mattress indicated where some guards could sleep nearby. To the right of the house was a pen area where a large bull was tied by a brass ring in its nose leading to a tether. A yapping dog chased chickens in front of the house. The bull wasn't going to be a problem if Dramesi stayed out of the reach of the animal's tether. The dog might be an issue—not because of any danger from the animal's bite, but the noise it could make as Dramesi slipped out could alert the guards or anyone else nearby.

There were no sanitary facilities of any kind in the cell. Yelling for the guard and gesturing for what he wanted got Dramesi released from his cell. Maintaining the posture that he was far more injured than he really was, Dramesi crawled out and into the yard after the guard opened the cell door. At the corner of the building he was able to relieve himself while also looking around to the rear of the building. What he saw did not aid any thoughts of escape. Behind the house were additional buildings at some distance past a stretch of barbed wire. That was not going to be the way to go when he broke out of his cell some night.

Once back in his cell and alone, Dramesi made the first practical moves toward an escape. The weak point in the entire structure around him was the bamboo wall of the cell; the top did not extend to the ceiling. By grabbing on to the rafters of the building and pulling himself up, Dramesi was able to see over the bamboo wall. An old man on the other side was squatting and shelling peanuts. When he saw Dramesi watching him, the old man came over and handed the prisoner a handful of the nuts. The food was welcome and tasted good. When Dramesi indicated that he would like some more, the old man passed another handful over to the prisoner. It was obvious from this slight kindness that not all North Vietnamese hated Caucasians on sight.

While watching his peanut benefactor through the spaces in the bamboo wall, Dramesi went to work untying the lines that secured the wall. Patience bore fruit as the bamboo twine could eventually be untied, loosened, and then secured back in place. Eventually, with the wall prepared, it could be shoved over away from the wooden wall of the building. That would give Dramesi room to wiggle through the space between the bamboo and the wall of the hut proper. It wasn't much of a plan for the time being, but it was something constructive to do.

A new guard was on duty that afternoon, who allowed Dramesi to crawl from his cell to relieve himself outdoors. This time, Dramesi crawled to the other side of the house, to the left of where the bull had been secured. The animal was still there and only turned to look as Dramesi added to the muck at the bottom of his pen. Big, powerful, and well-cared-for, the animal impressed the Air Force officer who watched him. The only thing keeping the bull in the pen was the tethered ring through its nose, but that was enough to take its freedom away.

Another small act of consideration was supplied to Dramesi later that afternoon, when he was given a small bottle of wintergreen with which to treat his wound. Cleaning the bullet with the aromatic oil would sting badly, but it might help prevent an infection from gaining a foothold. Dramesi put the bottle away, hiding it for later use. With care, he continued to loosen the fastenings of the wall holding him in. The next day, the situation changed considerably.

Guards came for him the next morning, picking him up and carrying him out of the cell house. They carried him over to a three-walled structure next door to where he had been held and set him down on a stool facing a table. Before the guards left, they tied Dramesi's hands behind his back.

Dramesi faced a number of men sitting at the table in front of him. The two eldest men sat at the center on the far side, one in a military uniform of some type that Dramesi did not recognize. The other elder had a scarred face and wore simple civilian clothes. He was clearly the man in charge, as the rest of the people in the room deferred to him. Sitting on either side of the older men was a younger man. At one end of the table, in a high-backed chair, was a fifth man, the eldest of all of them. He acted as the interpreter for the group, translating the questions of the scar-faced man into English and directing them at Dramesi. It was his first real interrogation at the hands of his captors.

The conversation began with an inquiry after Dramesi's health. His answer was that he was well enough, outside of his two injured legs. One knee was swollen—the one Dramesi injured during his landing—and that no one had attended to the bullet wound in his other leg. Through the interpreter, Dramesi was told that his injuries would be treated. Then he was asked what his name was.

"Captain John Dramesi," he answered.

"Your name is John Dramesi. You have no rank here!"

The real interrogation had begun. The men at the table had no illusions of what the Geneva Convention said about the treatment of prisoners; they simply didn't care about international agreements. As far as they were concerned, the man sitting bound in front of them was their enemy, and they could treat him as they wished.

Questions continued to come from the interpreter. What kind of aircraft did you fly? Where are you from? What is your wing commander's name? Dramesi refused to answer any of them. He expected the worst as the interrogators became angrier with his continued refusal to answer their questions. The only one of the men at the table who didn't seem upset at their uncooperative prisoner was the interpreter. Without showing any expression at all, the interpreter simply sat at the table and spoke, doing his job while remaining indifferent to the situation.

Enraged by the prisoner's refusal to answer the questions, the scar-faced elder finally jumped up from his seat. Grabbing a yard-long bamboo cane as he rushed around the table, the scar-faced man ran up to where Dramesi sat helpless and started beating him with the bamboo.

Again and again, the scar-faced man struck at his prisoner, beating him about the head and shoulders. Unable to protect himself, Dramesi was struck repeatedly. The scar-faced man was so enraged that he apparently didn't notice that he was hitting the ceiling of the low structure every time he raised the cane over his head. That took some of the power from his blows, but there was still enough damage being done. Slipping from his stool, Dramesi fell to the floor.

Giving up on using his bamboo for the moment, the scar-faced man started kicking the prostrate prisoner. Smashing his boots into his prisoner's ribs and back, the man caused tremendous pain but stopped short of actually kicking Dramesi to death. From where he lay, Dramesi thought that the abuse might not last very long and that he could ride it out. His pride kept his jaws tight. No groan of pain escaped his lips.

Finally, the old military officer stopped kicking the helpless prisoner where he lay on the floor. As the man returned to his seat at the table, Dramesi was pulled back up by the guards. Once more sitting on his stool, Dramesi faced his interrogators but still refused to answer their questions. The interrogator spoke in English, and translated Dramesi's refusals into Vietnamese. The scar-faced man became enraged once more and grabbed up his cane to beat the prisoner.

Running up to where Dramesi sat helpless on the stool, the old man swung the cane from his shoulders, as if it were a baseball bat. The painful force of the strikes was not lessened by the cane hitting the ceiling. The hard bamboo smashed across Dramesi's back and shoulders.

Out of his own stubbornness, Dramesi forced himself to stay seated. He didn't fall, nor did he cry out. The blows fell and only the smacking sound of the bamboo strikes could be heard in the room. Dramesi refused to talk, cry out, or even groan. Finally the beating stopped and the scar-faced man once more went behind the table and took his seat. The interrogation continued.

As the questions continued, so did Dramesi's adamant refusal to cooperate. The Code of Conduct stated that he could give his name, rank, and serial number. The North Vietnamese were not interested. What they wanted was specific military information, and Dramesi refused to give it to them. The cycle of questions, refusals, and beatings with a bamboo cane continued. After his fourth refusal to answer questions, an order was shouted to the guards. The beatings were over; now John Dramesi would face the ropes.

The North Vietnamese were masters at inflicting pain with the simplest of items. They could force the human body into contortions that few men believed possible until they had either seen or experienced them. Something as simple and innocuous as a piece of rope could bend a man until he would break—if not physically, then in spirit.

The two guards rushed over to Dramesi and immediately started what was going to be his real ordeal. Though he couldn't see who was doing what behind his back, Dramesi could certainly feel the guards' action on his arms.

His hands were twisted so that the backs were facing each other. Then the rope around his wrists was pulled tight—so tight that Dramesi could feel the circulation stop. What he couldn't see was his hands begin to puff up almost immediately as the skin turned red and then darkened from the lack of circulation. But the hands were just the first action in the use of the ropes to break a man.

The other guard looped a rope around both of Dramesi's arms a few inches above the elbow joint. With a knee in his side for leverage, the guard pulled the looped rope tighter and tighter, which drew his arms together. The two rams coming together so unnaturally forced Dramesi's chest out as his shoulders pulled back. The pain grew more and more intense.

Now, the circulation in Dramesi's arms was cut off from the ropes drawn so tightly around his upper arms. He could feel the swelling in his arms, the thudding of his heart loud in his ears as it tried to pump blood into the tissues that were demanding it. Feeling that even showing pain or emotion would be giving in to his torturers, Dramesi set his jaw tight and remained silent. His blood pressure was skyrocketing as the circulation was cut off to his hands and arms and the noise in his ears grew ever louder.

With a final pull, the guard stopped tightening the rope; Dramesi's arms couldn't be pulled any closer together since his elbows were already touching. Like so many North Vietnamese held POWs before him, Dramesi had no idea that the human body could even be contorted the way his was by the ropes. His arms ached and his shoulder joints screamed with pain as the bones felt like they were being forced from their sockets. Fear and pain warred within his body as both demanded that he give in to his captors. Then, without a word, the men around the table got up and left the room. There were no more questions. There was nothing for Dramesi to say or do but sit in the room and suffer. He was alone with his agony.

Time ticked by. There was no way for Dramesi to actually know how much time had passed as he sat there. He felt that the tissue in his swollen arms would die from lack of blood. Gangrene would set in as the dead tissues would rot while still a part of him. And the pain continued. It was agony just to draw a breath with his arms pulled back so far. His chest was distended, his shoulders pulled back and stretching the muscles across his chest and down his neck.

After perhaps fifteen or twenty minutes, the interpreter reentered the room. Shaking his head at the stubborn prisoner, he sat. He considered Dramesi a diehard, and told him as much. Continuing with the suffering was stupid, and would get the bound man nowhere.

"Tell me the name of your wing commander," the interpreter asked.

"No!"

But the pain was growing worse, or Dramesi's knowledge of it and his image of the damage it could be doing to his arms was increasing. He didn't want to lose his arms, which was just what the interpreter told him could happen if he didn't comply with the questioning. All he had to do was reveal who his wing commander was and the pressure on his arms would be removed.

Pleading now, Dramesi tried to bargain for the pain to stop, to save his arms. He would tell the interpreter what he wanted to know as soon as the ropes were removed. But that wasn't what was going to happen, the old man said. Dramesi would speak the name first, then the ropes would come off.

Dramesi screamed his defiance; he would rot before he said anything.

The old interpreter had patience, and experience. He softly told the suffering man in front of him that only when he answered the question would he be taken out of the ropes.

The pain and anguish were too much. Dramesi agreed to tell the man the name.

Fresh pain roared up as the guard removed the ropes from Dramesi's arms. The returning circulation brought waves of agony as the starved tissues responded to the abuse they had been subjected to. The pain washed over the prisoner like a flood. It overpowered his reasoning, clouded his thinking, and stunned him for the moment.

"What is the name of your wing commander?"

Dramesi told him.

With a sudden awareness of what he had done, Dramesi realized that he had made a terrible mistake. He didn't have to tell this quiet man the real name of his wing commander. He was under no obligation to tell the truth to his torturers. He had been momentarily overwhelmed by what he had just been through. He would not make the same error again.

But the ordeal was not over, and neither were the questions. After a short conversation with the interpreter, Dramesi was told that he should answer the additional questions put to him. The interpreter had seen many other prisoners, and he knew the futility of resistance. The ropes and other techniques would break a man, the pain and fear would force people who thought they could resist into realizing how wrong they were. Dramesi was a diehard, and it was unnecessary. All he would do was suffer needlessly. It could go so much more easily for him if he just told his captors what they wanted to hear.

With a strong sense of personal honor, Dramesi refused to cooperate. He was a military man, an officer of the United States. He was not expected to make things easy for himself. He would not answer questions.

During the conversation, Dramesi learned that the old man had been a professor of mathematics, his wife was a doctor, and his son had been killed during an American bombing raid. He left the room only to return a few minutes later with the rest of the interrogators. The questioning continued.

Now, the questions were far more technical: How did his aircraft attack its targets? What were the weapons he carried? How were they used? How did the aircraft evade antiaircraft fire?

Trying to avoid supplying useful information, Dramesi said he either did not know or wasn't permitted to answer. This was not the cooperation the interrogators were expecting. Finally, a command was given: Dramesi was placed in the ropes once again. With the prisoner trussed and in pain, once more the interrogators got up and left the room.

This time Dramesi gave vent to his feelings. He screamed and cried out from the pain and the frustration. The release wasn't very difficult; he was on the verge of crying out from the pain anyway, so it was easy to act as if the pain and fear of losing his arms had taken their toll of him. Dramesi wailed about his arms dying from the way they were tied.

His cries went on for an hour or more, or so it seemed. His whole world centered on that small room in North Vietnam and the torture he was being subjected to.

When the interrogators returned to the room and released him from the ropes, Dramesi tried to put up a convincing babble. He couldn't answer technical questions, he just didn't know. He was a pilot, and all he did was fly the planes, as fast and as straight as he could.

The arguments about what Dramesi did and didn't know went on for the balance of the session. He gave no more useful information to his captors, in hopes they would think him one of the dumbest pilots they had captured. But they didn't torture him any more that afternoon. They had time, they had patience, and they had him prisoner. He was finally sent back to his dirt-floored cell. They knew that one of the worst tortures that a man could endure was what his own imagination built up for him. They had broken others, and they would break him.

[CHAPTER 9]

ESCAPE

Back in his cell, Dramesi recovered from his ordeal with the ropes and considered what had happened. The situation was a bad one, and it would only get worse. The briefings on North Vietnam hadn't included the lengths the enemy would go to in order to extract information from any American servicemen who came into their hands. He knew he had made a serious mistake in telling them the real name of his wing commander back in Thailand. His captors could use even that little bit of information on the next pilot they captured. It would make evading their questions and lying in answer that much harder for the next guy. He silently vowed to himself that he would not break again. There would be people he would have to face in the future who hadn't broken, who had been strong. He would have to go through what was coming and worse so that he wouldn't have to explain his failure to them.

Even if the tortures cost him his arms, Dramesi would not talk again. He wasn't trying to fool himself. It was a lot easier to think such things to himself while in his cell. Following through when he was in the ropes would be much harder. And there would be more questions.

In the darkness, lying on the board in his cell, Dramesi slept.

Resolve did not go away with the rising of the sun the next day. Until the interrogators sent for him, Dramesi continued to work on untying bamboo wall fasteners. Escape was even more important to him now that he had faced the reality of what it meant to be a North Vietnamese prisoner. The old man was once more shelling peanuts on the other side of the wall. He passed some to Dramesi, who ate them while continuing with his work.

The morning passed without incident. The work of trying to loosen the bamboo wall kept Dramesi busy and his mind off what might happen during the next interrogation session. One of the younger men from the previous day's interrogation session showed up that afternoon. But this wasn't going to be another series of questions, at least not like it had been the day before. This was going to be a period of indoctrination in the right and wrong of the war—solely from the North Vietnamese viewpoint.

After setting up a table and chair, the young man ordered Dramesi out of his cell. Crawling to the table, Dramesi sat and looked at the pamphlets and documents that had been spread out in front of him. The North Vietnamese facing him was a political indoctrinator, and it was fairly obvious the man had a set speech memorized. He spoke for about thirty minutes, repeating over and over how the Americans were going to lose the war, that they were already in the process of losing the war, and that the North Vietnamese would win in the end.

This was the point where the actions that were taking place back in the United States were brought out and used against the prisoners in North Vietnam. The protests of young Americans were used as proof that the people of the United States didn't want to fight, that they were against the unjust war, and fighting the peace-loving people of Vietnam was obviously the wrong thing to do.

This line of logic didn't sit very well with a man who had just been tortured the day before. The "peace-loving people" of North Vietnam had attacked him not more than a few days earlier, throwing stones and hitting him with sticks and their bare fists. But while the young man was talking, Dramesi wasn't being beaten, tied up, or otherwise tortured. But when he was asked how much he must be afraid of the mighty anti-aircraft missile defenses of North Vietnam, Dramesi answered plainly that he wasn't afraid.

The young political indoctrinator was shocked at what he believed must be a blatant lie. Many of the pilots were afraid of the missiles that defended his country. Good-luck charms and tigers' teeth were worn by the hated Americans to try and ward off the terrible retribution of the North Vietnamese people for the violation of their air space.

Dramesi simply repeated that he wasn't afraid. He didn't mention that he had probably never even seen a loose tiger tooth in his life and that dog tags weren't good-luck charms. But the young man had his beliefs, and they were strong ones. Even when faced with the logic of Dramesi's explanation—that the antiaircraft missiles were only really found in upper North Vietnam, and the invincible MiG fighters the young man was so proud of couldn't fly as far as the southern part of North Vietnam—the young politico denied the truth of the words. But the young man wasn't stupid; he was shaken by what he had heard. He fought to regain control of the discussion.

The young man only had his own life experiences to use against the prisoner sitting in front of him. He railed against the president of the United States, stated that he was unpopular because of the taxes he forced the American people to pay in order to support the war they all hated. The people of the United States were tired of paying so much and they did not want to send any more of their rice or buffalo to President Johnson.

The "rice and buffalo" line was a bit odd to Dramesi. But it was mostly a prepared speech, an effort by the young man in trying to reassert his authority. The lecture continued and finally ended with Dramesi being given a number of the North Vietnamese and Communist propaganda booklets. He was ordered to read them.

It was then that Dramesi realized that he had made another mistake in his dealings with his captor. It was not as obvious an error as using his real wing commander's name the day before; instead it was a much more subtle and dangerous one. He had simply talked too much. He had engaged one of his captors in conversation, and enjoyed the young man's confusion. He couldn't talk—mustn't talk. It would be too easy to say the wrong thing, and it would come back to bite him. What he had to do was escape, and as soon as possible.

Back in his cell for the night, Dramesi continued his attack on the bamboo wall. Most of the bindings had been removed or loosened from the bamboo shafts. The wall appeared sound from the outside, but was anything but sturdy anymore. There was some fear on Dramesi's part that anyone leaning against the other side of the wall would bring the whole thing down, but that didn't happen.

The next day, the only thing that happened was that the guards came by to let Dramesi out to relieve himself. What he really wanted was a greater view of the area around the house and beyond. The guard gave him just what he wanted when he was led, crawling all the way, down a path away from the house.

As it led off into the distance, the path wound around several other houses in the village. Farther off, Dramesi could see a small road that went between the crop fields. It looked to be the way out, the path to freedom—if Dramesi could reach it.

Crawling along the path, Dramesi noticed a small pond. The guard stopped and directed his prisoner to a brick pedestal with a lid on it. The use of the open commode was an obvious one, and Dramesi did as he was directed. While making an affair of using the primitive sanitary facility, he looked closely at the surrounding area, memorizing all of what he could of the land's features. While approaching the prison house on the crawl back, Dramesi picked up a bamboo pole and used it to help him along. The guard allowed the prisoner to keep his stick, which gave Dramesi one more tool to use for his escape plans.

During the day's outing, Dramesi picked another very valuable piece of information. The dog that had been yapping so much a few days earlier was nowhere to be seen. The alarm the animal's yapping could have raised had been a concern, but with it being missing, that problem had gone away. There was a mild concern on the part of the prisoner as to just what dog meat in peanut soup, the staple of his meals so far, might taste like.

The burlap cloth that Dramesi had used as a pillow had been made into a rough jacket. That, his bamboo stick, and the bottle of wintergreen that he had saved were the sum total of his escape supplies. Though it was a meager amount and his knowledge of the area was slight at best, he had escaped from the prison camp back in Nevada with less. But that had been training; this was now a matter of life and death.

Darkness fell quickly in Southeast Asia. The fear of putting on lights that could attract attacking aircraft kept the village in the dark. Everyone went to sleep soon after the sun went down, including Dramesi's guards. They slept in the big bed he had seen only feet away from the weakened bamboo wall.

Just before sunset, rain had started to fall, which was just what Dramesi wanted in order to cover his escape. He had his bottle of wintergreen in the pocket of his shirt. Putting on his burlap jacket, he crouched down to work on the bamboo wall. The fastenings he had left in place to hold the wall were easy enough to remove. Now the bamboo poles that made up the wall were free to move away from the floor and the wall of the house. By pushing the bamboo only a few inches, he would be able to squeeze past the poles and the wall and get out of his cell.

As he gently pushed against the wall, Dramesi was careful not to make a sound. The bamboo started to move, though, and then the loose material of the wall started to fall in. The bamboo wall was going to collapse right on top of Dramesi. His hand shot up and pressed against the leaning material, stopping the fall and ending his escape attempt for the moment.

The only noise Dramesi could hear was the sound of his heart thudding in his ears. The guards hadn't wakened and there were no other sounds of alarm. For five long minutes, Dramesi sat on the dirt floor of his cell, holding the collapsing wall up with his hand. Stretching out, he managed to get a grip on the bamboo stick he had picked up earlier. Silently, slowly, he kept himself from gasping out loud as he pulled the length of bamboo up and braced it against the wall. With the end dug firmly into the dirt floor of his cell, the bamboo stick was enough to keep the wall from falling over.

There was now a hole between the bamboo and the rest of the building wall. It was large enough for Dramesi to crawl through if he was careful. One thing was certain: He wasn't going to take the chance on trying to make the hole any bigger.

Slipping through the opening on his hands and knees, Dramesi got out of his cell and into the area where the guards slept. The shoes they had taken from him were at the foot of the bed—a lucky break for him. Picking them up, he continued to crawl slowly from the room as the breathing of the guards in the bed remained slow and steady. Then he saw them: opposite of the bed were the guards' weapons, three automatic rifles that would allow him to fight rather than be recaptured. Weapons, arms—the tools of a fighting man—the guns were a temptation. Dramesi hesitated.

He remembered what his instructors had said back during training. He had shot his way out of that prison camp. But the bullets he had been firing then were blanks. The instructors had made a point of telling him that shooting his way out might look good during training and be a rush, but in the real world it was brains, not bullets, that would serve him best. He turned away from where the weapons beckoned him and continued to crawl toward the door.

Still on his hands and knees, Dramesi crawled from the house and into the courtyard outside. Bracing himself against a small tree, he pulled his shoes on and stood. Tropical rain was pouring down, the noise being more than enough to cover any slight sounds he might make walking down the muddy path. No dogs barked, and the bull didn't make a sound. So far, he was outside of his cell on his feet and undiscovered. He walked down the path, out of the village, and along the dikes of the rice paddies beyond. Frogs and crickets sounded out, but they were natural noises and it apparently didn't disturb anyone but the escaping prisoner. He headed east, toward the South China Sea. That was where the U.S. Seventh Fleet held station, and it was a hell of a lot closer than the Demilitarized Zone, which marked the border between North and South Vietnam. If he could get to the sea, he could steal a boat, gather up bamboo, find a log—anything that would float—and head out to sea and freedom.

The rain was slackening as Dramesi continued east. He had covered an unknown distance from the village when there was the clanging sound of a metal gong being beaten from the direction he had come. Looking back through the diminishing rain, he could see lights coming on as torches and lamps were being lit. Apparently, his little walkabout had been discovered and the troops were turning out to search for him. He still felt that he had a good chance to make something of his escape and continued on heading east. Before very long, he could see the headlights of vehicles coming down along the road that paralleled his course. Trucks and cars from the village were speeding out to try and cut off the escape of what they knew was a man on foot. They didn't know what direction he was traveling in, but there was only the one road that Dramesi knew of.

The area that Dramesi was walking through was mostly flooded rice paddies surrounded by raised earthen dikes. There were paths along the top of the dikes, which could make walking faster, as long as the escaping prisoner made sure that he wasn't outlined by anything in the background. If the clouds broke and he was moving across the top of a paddy dike, he would be silhouetted against the night sky.

Moving as long as he could in the darkness, Dramesi had to pull up as he saw lights approaching him. The searchers were shining flashlights around and that had given them away to Dramesi long before they could have spotted him. The lights kept moving in the distance as he searched for a hiding place. The water wasn't very deep in the rice paddies, but it was dark and anything but clear. Slipping farther out into the paddy, Dramesi watched as the weaving and bobbing handheld lights came closer. The searchers were looking along the paddy dikes, but not going much into the water itself.

Finally, they were too close and Dramesi had to make a move. Taking a deep breath, he ducked down into the muddy water between the stalks of rice. All he could do was hold his breath as long as he could while also forcing his body to be as still as possible. The lights skipped along the water but didn't stop. There were no splashes from the searchers coming for him in the dark water. Finally, the demands of his lungs were too much and he had to come up for air.

In spite of needing to breathe, Dramesi was able to control himself, use his self-discipline to force his body to his will and exhale slowly and quietly. The incoming air was sweet no matter how badly the rice paddy smelled. The enemy had passed him by; there were no searchers standing on the paddy dike. It was time to get up and get going.

Slogging through the soft mud, Dramesi came to the higher solid ground of the surrounding paddy dike. Climbing up the sloping sides, Dramesi came to the top and looked back in the direction of the searchers. What he saw made him freeze into place.

The flashlights were once again approaching him. They were coming back and he was out in the open. There wasn't time to crawl back into a rice paddy and hide in the water. They would be on him before he could quietly hide again. There were thickets of brush on the far side of the paddy dike, away from the direction of the approaching lights. He slipped down the dirt of the dike and struggled to move into the densest of the nearby thickets. He held himself still, scarcely daring to breathe as the lights once again probed around him. The lights illuminated the surrounding brush, but couldn't penetrate deeply into the thicket. The lights paused, and then moved on.

Once more he had escaped detection. Luck was still with him, thought it was touch-and-go for a moment. As he slipped into the paddy, Dramesi noticed that the bottom was very soft and mushy. The water on top of the sludge was also much deeper than the other paddy had been. As he crossed the water, he sank deeper and deeper into it. Near the center of his crossing, his nose was barely above the water. That's when Dramesi felt he was certain it wasn't another rice paddy. He was crossing a cesspool, an open source of fertilizer for the surrounding rice paddies.

After having crossed the repulsive pond, Dramesi climbed up another dike to gain some high ground. Looking back, he could see that the dancing lights of the searchers were still moving across the paddies. But they were looking where he had been, not where he was. And they were gradually moving away in the opposite direction. Finally, the lights were out of sight. Complete darkness closed in and Dramesi was once again alone with only the countless frogs and crickets. Slipping occasionally as he stumbled and splashed across the fields, Dramesi continued due east.

CHAPTER 10

RUN

Passing through two villages during the night, Dramesi kept to the shadows and attracted no attention. He was nearly exhausted, his reserves not being very much after days of captivity and torture. He had to find a place to hide before it became light and people started moving around. But the farmland he had been passing through was mostly flat; the only real feature of the ground all around him were the endless rice paddies. There were no buildings, abandoned huts, thickets, or large trees where he might be able to hide during the day. Time was working against him.

As dawn approached, he crossed a small footbridge. Tired, he almost fell into a group of guards patrolling the area. He slipped into another of the constant rice paddies he had been crossing all night. The guards had not been alerted that the escaped prisoner was practically right next to them, and they continued on their way.

Having passed the night almost constantly on the move, Dramesi was more than a little tired. He was also cold, wet, and hungry. The thin clothes he had on were little more than rags, and soaked through, they helped chill him until his body was shaking. The approaching dawn told him that he had been moving in the right direction. And the increasing light also told him that he had picked up passengers during his many trips through the contaminated water of the rice paddies. There were black leeches all over his lower legs. The calves of his legs had the shiny, wet black slugs all over them, digging painlessly into his skin to draw their sustenance from his blood. They would also transmit diseases into him as they sucked out his blood.

The slippery, slimy creatures would be hard to pull off; and if he did, they would leave a bloody hole behind. But he still had the bottle of wintergreen he had been given back in his cell. With just a touch of the aromatic oil on his fingertip, the parasites immediately released their hold on his flesh. Falling to the mud he was standing in, the leeches slithered away as he touched even more of them with the wintergreen. Finally, his legs were clean of the bloodsuckers.

What he needed in addition to a hiding place right then was water. He had been walking through water all night. But it was hideously polluted and would kill him as surely as a rifle bullet if he drank any of it, though the death would be a much slower one than a gunshot could give. Picking dew-covered leaves off the surrounding plants would supply him with clean water, but there was precious little water actually in the tiny droplets of dew. After licking a number of leaves, Dramesi realized that he was just wasting time and not slaking his thirst at all.

As he had been working at the side of a rice paddy dike, the light had been growing and the local population getting up for their morning work. A trio of water buffalo was slowly approaching him, indifferent to his presence. The more than twenty people who were already working the rice plants nearby also didn't seem to care that he was there, if they had noticed him at all. Even a small group of children passed by and Dramesi was certain that they had seen him. But the children had failed to recognize the escaped American for what he was. All they might have seen was a rag-wearing, muddy, dirty stranger who really didn't stand out much at all.

Moving east but also trying to stay away from people as best he could, Dramesi followed the words he had been given by an intelligence officer back in Thailand: "People catch people." You couldn't be caught if you stayed away from people. It was a simple statement, but a true one. And Dramesi was going to follow that advice.

Coming to a stream of relatively clean water, Dramesi stopped to repair himself a bit and see to a slightly better disguise. The bandage around the bullet wound on his right leg was torn and dangling. Taking it off, he cleaned the wound and then packed mud around it to protect it and hide it from casual observation. Tearing the legs off his red "prison" pants, he made a rough pair of shorts for himself. He smeared the ever-present mud liberally over all portions of his exposed skin: his arms, legs, face, and hands. This darkened his complexion a bit and help disguise him a bit more. His boots went around his neck by their laces and his burlap jacket was crushed up and stuffed up on his back underneath his shirt. With a big bundle of rice straw he had picked up, he looked little more than a farmer whom life had handed a bad deal to in the form of a humped back. The thin disguise was better than nothing and helped Dramesi at least feel a little more secure about his chances.

The poor, deformed, and hopeless-looking peasant walking along didn't draw even a second glance as Dramesi passed a number of people over the course of the morning. He crossed a stream rather than move too closely to a group of old women washing clothes, but no alarm was raised about him going by. A group of children working in the fields didn't care about him and the escaping prisoner didn't even draw any real attention from a soldier standing on a small bridge some distance away.

The sun was nearly directly overhead when Dramesi stopped outside a small village. People crossed a bridge over a canal between himself and the village. After the villagers had passed, Dramesi continued on his way, crossing over the bridge himself and moving toward the small community. The approach of several people on bicycles forced him to hurry across the bridge and then move down into a gully next to the road. Appearing to be just someone tending to a bundle of rice straw, Dramesi kept his head down as the cyclists went by.

Not even a boy sitting on a water buffalo only a few dozen yards away paid any attention to him. The bicycles rumbled across the boards of the bridge and went on their way. That was the signal for Dramesi to get moving again himself and not push his luck. Climbing back up to the road, Dramesi looked in toward the center of the small community.

People were bustling about on whatever business they had. As he grew closer to the village, Dramesi could see that there were just too many people for him to just brazen his way through the area. He would have to circle around the village, which meant going back across the bridge.

He retraced his steps, intending to cross the canal by another, smaller, bridge he had seen in the distance. That meant he would have to cross the grounds of a fairly nice building, a stately old home, to get to the other bridge. But even that risk proved to have benefit.

Near the house, Dramesi came across a small banana grove. The fruits on the trees were small, hard, and unripe. But carrying even the green bananas for a while might allow them to ripen enough to eat, giving Dramesi some much-needed food. He pulled a small bunch of the green fruit from a tree and tucked it into his shirt.

Some distance across the fields was a gang of workers maintaining the levees lining the canals. Then Dramesi saw something that really raised his hopes. As a pilot, he had spent long hours studying the target areas he was expecting to fly over. That work was paying off now big time, as he could see a single hill about four miles away. That hill was a landmark he recognized, one that was on the coast of the South China Sea. He was close to the water; the sun shining in his face was also shining down on the ships of the U.S. Seventh Fleet. He had a real chance of making it as new strength surged through him. Forgotten was thirst, hunger, or exhaustion. Freedom was beckoning to him.

Either by his own error, or simply bad luck, an old man appeared among the rice stalks not a dozen yards from where Dramesi stood. It may have been that the old man saw the "poor peasant" stealing a bunch of bananas; perhaps he thought Dramesi was a trespasser. Whatever got the old man's attention, he approached Dramesi, shaking his finger and scolding him in a rain of Vietnamese.

The simple disguise only worked at a distance really. When the old man approached Dramesi closely enough, he stopped and appeared startled, if not very badly frightened. Suddenly, he turned and ran, waving his arms and yelling toward the gang of workers on the banks of the canal.

The elation Dramesi had felt only a moment before drained from his body as he looked out across the wide-open fields in front of him. There was no way he could run across the rice paddies, surging through the water and the mud with his two injured legs. The shouts of the approaching work gang were coming up behind him as he pushed the bunch of bananas into the mud. At least he wasn't going to be charged with stealing food from the locals. With a last glance at the landmark indicating his lost chance at freedom, Dramesi turned and faced the approaching mob.

The people was actually afraid of the almost pathetic figure in front of them. Dramesi wasn't about to cower in front of them, but he also wasn't going to incite the mob into attacking. He stood stock-still as the locals approached him as if he were some kind of dangerous tiger that could turn on them with tooth and claw.

Seeing that he was unarmed, several of the youngest locals jumped on Dramesi, pulling him to the ground. Once they had his arms tied behind his back, they seemed to feel a lot more secure about their prisoner. The noisy mob headed toward the local village as a number of soldiers arrived. Taking over the prisoner, the soldiers tied a rope around Dramesi's neck and led him off, marching back to the village.

As the group approached the community, the noise of irate people grew louder and louder. None of the locals or the soldiers really knew what to do with their captive, but they certainly didn't like him being among them. After stopping and talking over their next move, the mob and the soldiers began moving through the village.

There was a line of people along the path—very angry people. While one guard lead the prisoner along by the rope, two more guards walked along behind him. As they moved along, the mob shouted and cursed. Dramesi couldn't understand what the people were yelling, but he noticed that it was again mostly old women and the children who were making the most noise. The angry mob drew closer to throw rocks and sticks at the bound man in front of them. The bravest among the mob would be striking out with their fists before long.

Ducking and dodging the bulk of what was being thrown at him, Dramesi could see that there was one male villager who appeared to be trying to keep up with his progress along the road. The man looked like he was trying to find a gap in the solid line of shouting villagers lining the road, and suddenly he found one.

Darting through the villagers, the man ran up to Dramesi, bounded into the air, and tried to strike out with a flying chop to the prisoner's neck. By playing turtle, hunching up his shoulders and ducking his head, Dramesi was able to lessen the power of the blow. The man continued to chop at the prisoner until the guards finally forced him away.

But the angry man wasn't done with his demonstration of martial arts abilities. When he found another gap in the line, he once again charged the bound prisoner, this time punching Dramesi in the back and ribs. The guards again shoved the man out of the way. The mob of people thinned out until it wasn't much more than a bunch of children throwing what they could find at the bound and helpless prisoner. The parade of prisoner and guards finally stopped at a small cottage, the best-looking building Dramesi had yet seen in North Vietnam. That was where the group was going to wait.

The family who lived in the pleasant little home was just as unlike the villagers as their home was different from the rest of the local structures. They gave the recaptured prisoner a large bowl of rice, on top of which was the usual greens and handful of crushed peanuts. The food was welcomed by the hungry, tired man who had been dragged into their home at the end of a rope. An additional treat was given to Dramesi by one of the family's younger female children. It was a small bowl of sweet rice, something the prisoner had not yet tasted during his stay in North Vietnam. The hospitality was a big shock having come so close on the heels of the mob attacks Dramesi had fared only a short while earlier. And it didn't sound as if the attacks may have ended yet.

Outside the house, locals were gathering in larger and larger numbers. Dramesi could hear the noise they were making as he ate. It was possible that he wouldn't make it back to prison. If so, at least the condemned was given a hearty meal—by local standards.

After some time had passed, the mob outside grew quieter but it didn't sound as if the people had gone away. For the time being, Dramesi was the local source of entertainment, and the people wanted their show. The local political leadership knew very well how valuable it was to allow them a view of the enemy. It would help them make even further sacrifices to aid the cause of the Communist North.

Later in the afternoon several people whom Dramesi had already made the acquaintance of arrived at the house: It was the young political officer who had been at his interrogation and conducted the Communist indoctrination outside of his cell. Accompanying the political was another soldier, one Dramesi was also familiar with. The soldier had been one of the men who had ridden in the truck with Dramesi when he was transported to that first prison. Both men were obviously angry their prisoner had dared to try and escape from his just imprisonment at the people's hands.

The two men looked like they were discussing the fate of their prisoner right in front of him, but since Dramesi couldn't understand the Vietnamese language, he couldn't follow the conversation. Whatever was being said, the words were heated and there were a number of quick glances in the prisoner's direction. Whatever was being planned, it probably didn't mean anything good for the recaptured escapee.

The young political officer hadn't been very successful when he had tried to indoctrinate Dramesi during their first session together. But English wasn't his native language and he had been having difficulties trying to get his ideas across to Dramesi in a persuasive manner. The young man's command of Vietnamese was excellent and he was very relaxed in using it. Dramesi found out just how skilled the young political officer was when he took the prisoner outside and showed him off to the gathered crowd.

With his hands tied behind his back, Dramesi was not making a very threatening picture to the crowd. A hush had fallen over the people when the prisoner, surrounded by four armed guards and the political officer, left the house and moved out into the yard. Now there was room enough for everyone to get a look at the prisoner captured by the brave people of the Democratic Republic of Vietnam. The four guards stood about watching the crowd and the prisoner as the young political officer started his speech.

In an almost inaudible tone, the young man forced the crowd into silence in order for them to hear him. Then he started to speak louder and faster. As the sun set and a light rain started to fall, the people hung on the young man's every word. Dramesi didn't know what he was saying, but he could tell that the people were getting worked up again, and their anger was directed at him and no one else. The guards didn't seem to be concerned with what might happen. And the young man extolling the evils of the prisoner might not be able to control the people as well as he thought he could. Dramesi was in for a bad time and he knew it. He was seated on the ground and surrounded on all sides, and the light rain was making him cold. He started to shiver.

The young political officer was nearly shouting in a high-pitched voice. He was gesturing violently and popping out words as if they were bullets, projectiles aimed at the hated American trembling in the mud. One woman started to scream something unintelligible. And that was the trigger for the crowd.

The people rushed forward and started striking at Dramesi. The secured prisoner couldn't protect himself very well, but the crowd's own numbers and their shoving in to get a shot at the helpless man in front of them worked against their goal. People couldn't get much power behind their swings as they struck at Dramesi with bamboo sticks or their fists. The only thing he could do to protect himself was to try and duck his head down between his knees and take the blows on his shoulders and back.

The political officer realized that he had lost control of the situation and the people were reacting more violently than he had expected. Instead of being proud of his manipulation of the crowd, he was starting to be worried that the mob may harm the prisoner. He was a valuable commodity and the punishment the young man could expect for allowing severe harm to come to the prisoner could be very bad. While he shouted at the crowd, the young political officer had the guards also try to push the people back with their rifles. When there was room enough to move, the guards picked Dramesi up from the ground and carried him away.

There was a storage silo nearby, a substantial structure that held and protected harvested rice. The guards tossed their burden into the silo and shut the wooden door. As Dramesi impacted on the pile of rice inside the silo, he heard a lock clicking shut to secure the door. His escape had come so close, only to end on a pile of rice in a locked building. The only good thing he had right then was a dry place to sleep. The rice made a reasonably comfortable bed and Dramesi knew to take his rest when he could.

CHAPTER 11

THE GOOSE AND THE BUG

The rain was gone the next morning. The sun beaming in between cracks in the walls of the silo woke Dramesi where he had been lying on his makeshift bed of rice. It looked to be a bright day for everyone but him. His escape attempt had failed, just when the gateway to freedom might have been in sight.

He lay on the rice and considered his situation, what he had done right and what had gone wrong during his escape attempt. He would have to keep in mind one factor: he'd proven that an American could move across the North Vietnamese countryside, even through population centers, and not draw attention. That had been a big question, but even his very rough costume and "makeup" had worked, at least at a reasonable distance. That was one of the lessons he would have to remember for his next escape; a disguise could help a great deal, was a necessity. And he had to remember not to get overconfident when things went well. People catch people—that rule had been proven and he would not forget.

He wasn't going to speculate too much about the future. Chances were good that he was going to be punished in some way for his escape attempt. It would probably include an extended interrogation session at the hands of the scar-faced man and others he may have embarrassed with his escape. Those ropes, or others like them, were waiting for him somewhere. But thinking about that kind of future did no good.

When a truck arrived, Dramesi was pulled from the silo. Walking to the truck was like passing through a gauntlet, one made up of the locals who were crowding around. The crowd shouted and shook their fists and bamboo sticks at the hated American flier just within reach. But the guards protected their prisoner from the angry mob and got him into the back of the truck safely.

He had spent the night with his hands tied behind his back. Now on board the truck, his ankles were also tied together. The faking he had done to make his wounds look worse than they were wasn't going to work anymore. The guards weren't going to carry him, and they were going to make sure that he could only walk when they wanted him to.

The back of the truck was loaded with supplies: cans of gasoline shared space with the men and a number of hundred-pound sacks of rice. The truck hadn't been as well camouflaged as the others Dramesi had earlier seen and ridden in. They were also going to be traveling in broad daylight, something Dramesi was seeing for the first time. The line of defense of the truck against air attack seemed to be the speed the driver could move it in, even across the primitive country roads.

The vehicle was heading roughly north. Dramesi knew what lay in that direction and a guard answered his suspicions.

"Hanoi?" Dramesi asked.

One of the guards nodded his head. Beyond that, the guards paid him little attention.

From his position on the bags of rice, Dramesi could see that there was very little he could do to affect his situation. He tried to make himself as comfortable as possible. He rested, tried to sleep. It was all he could do, since he wanted to save his energy for later.

The truck drove all day and into the night. Having joined up with a convoy of other vehicles, the group continued north, but at a much safer speed. A speeding driver wasn't the only danger along the roads in North Vietnam at that time. Aircraft roared overhead, illuminating the convoy with the bright light from burning magnesium parachute flares.

People in the rest of the convoy started bailing out of their vehicles as the aircraft lit up the night sky. Dramesi and his guards remained in their positions. In Dramesi's opinion, the flares were too far away to show their truck, and the guards seemed to agree.

Dramesi considered what he might face in Hanoi, in light of the interrogation he had already gone through. He would have to resist their tortures as much as he could, not let himself become intimidated, scared, or confused. If he kept his wits about him and suffered through, when he finally felt himself reaching the end of his endurance, he could lie convincingly.

If a man just broke early and said whatever it was his interrogators wanted to hear, they probably wouldn't believe him. He might face even more torture just to confirm what he had already said. But if a man absorbed the pain and humiliation of torture first, took as much as it would appear someone could stand, then his lies might be more readily accepted as the truth.

Whatever happened, Dramesi steeled himself for what might come. He would speak little and not repeat his earlier mistake. And when he did talk, he would lie whenever possible. He would avoid speaking to the press, hide from cameras, and not speak into microphones or tape recorders. He was an officer in the United States Air Force; his honor was his own and would remain such. The fear of failing at his resolve was the only thing that really frightened him, since it was the only aspect of his life right now that he had any real control over.

If Hanoi was indeed where the truck was going, then it arrived before dawn the next morning. It was still less than two weeks since Dramesi had been shot down. He had been captured, tortured, escaped, and captured again. Now he was somewhere new, and the treatment he received at the hands of his new guards was immediately different.

Getting him out of the truck, Dramesi's hands and feet were untied at last. Guards wearing green uniforms stripped him of all his clothes, and his boots were taken. He was given a pair of black shorts and a short-sleeved black shirt to wear. His hands were once more tied behind his back, though his feet were left untied. A blindfold was put across his eyes so he couldn't see where he was, where he was going, or what might be around him.

The guards led their prisoner into a building of some kind. Dramesi could tell that they had passed through a gate or door of some type and were now indoors. This was confirmed when he was led into a small room of some kind. The sound changed as it bounced off close-in walls. Then they were passing down a tunnel, a corridor within the building probably. The footsteps of the soldiers and the slapping sounds of Dramesi's bare feet echoed off the walls. Stopping, turning, and going up a few steps put the group into another room.

Barefoot, bound, and blindfolded, Dramesi stood in the middle of the room and waited. He didn't have to wait long.

The echoes of footsteps came into the room, and not the sounds of the usual sandals, sneakers, or bare feet. This was the solid sound of military boots striking the floor, and there were a number of them. The bootsteps stopped and there was the sound of chairs scraping and people shuffling about. Then all the sound stopped. The guards moved Dramesi from where he had been standing, put him into position, and removed his blindfold.

Blinking at the sudden glare, Dramesi was in front of a table with two lamps on it, one at either end. As if it were a scene from some kind of old movie, the lamps were pointed at him, their brightness blocking his view of whoever was seated behind the table.

Gradually, Dramesi made out what lay beyond the lights. There were five men seated behind a cloth-covered table. In front of each man was a pad of paper. Each man was wearing some kind of uniform, a few being different from the others, but none showing any signs of rank that Dramesi could recognize. It appeared that the man seated at the center of the table was in charge. At least he was the one who signaled the guards who came up and untied Dramesi's arms. The prisoner just stood and waited.

Finally, one of the men behind the table said in English that it was necessary that Dramesi bow to his captors. He was ignorant and would have to show the proper respect. Standing still, Dramesi remained silent.

The defiance of the prisoner seemed to anger the man speaking. He wanted to know if Dramesi understood what he was supposed to do. He was to stand at attention; he would have to bow. Didn't he understand this?

"Yes," Dramesi said, "I understand."

He spoke, but did not move, and certainly didn't bow. The man at the center of the table once again indicated to the guards. A stool was brought up and placed behind the prisoner. Dramesi was to be seated and face the table. Now that the glare was out of his eyes, Dramesi looked about the room. Over in the left corner of the room was his gear; his torn flight suit and boots were there as well as his prison clothes. Even the burlap jacket he had made was in the pile.

That was all he noticed as he sat down on the small stool. Sitting up straight, Dramesi made a point of staring straight ahead and sitting on his hands. He did not want any unintentional trembling of his hands to give away the nervousness he felt. This was like a scene from an old war film, one where the Gestapo was going to question the captured hero. Only this wasn't a movie; the men behind the lamps and the table were very real, and so was the torture Dramesi was about to undergo. He wasn't the hero in a film. But he was damned if he wasn't going to at least try to act like one.

In poor English, the man seated at the center of the table started to speak. What he had to say was chilling at the least.

Dramesi wasn't a soldier; he was a criminal, the blackest of them. He would have to answer all of the questions put to him, and answer them truthfully. Obey anything that he was ordered to do. And if he repented of his criminal acts, he would be treated in a humane manner.

Then the guard waited for a response from the prisoner.

The man was going to be waiting for a long time. Dramesi hadn't actually been asked a question, and he wasn't going to volunteer anything. He would remain as quiet as possible, not speaking at all if he could. Make the situation seem unworkable and try to end the interrogation session as soon as possible.

The man behind the table stood up, obviously angry at his prisoner's lack of cooperation. He repeated that Dramesi was a criminal, and a diehard. He was a diehard criminal. The criminal acts he had committed had to be punished. Dramesi was the blackest of pirates and would be held accountable for his actions. He would pay! Didn't he understand that he was a criminal?

The man's English wasn't all that good, but Dramesi could make out well enough what he was saying.

"I understand what you have said," Dramesi said.

For whatever reason, the little bit that Dramesi said seemed to calm the man down. He sat back in his chair and appeared to relax. It may have been that he knew very well what was in store for the defiant prisoner seated in front of him. Instead of threats, he offered to be "reasonable."

Soldiers would be going home from the war, the man said, many even before the conflict ended. Didn't Dramesi want to be one of those men who went home?

Of course Dramesi wanted to go home, and he said as much.

Now came the bargaining, the carrot instead of the stick. It was possible that Dramesi could get his wish. And he could have good food, even exercise, while he was still in Vietnam. The man struggled to come up with a word, one he wasn't sure he remembered. *Liquor!* That was it, Dramesi could have liquor! And with that, the man sat back and smiled widely, his big teeth shining.

Smiling himself, but for a completely different reason, Dramesi sat and didn't tell the man that he didn't drink. What he was certain of was that the price for his freedom was going to be cooperation, something he wasn't willing to give.

The rest of the men behind the table began peppering Dramesi with their questions. As during his other interrogation sessions, Dramesi was asked what type of aircraft he flew. And as before, he refused to answer that and other questions as well. The level of anger in the room went up again. Finally, one of the old men behind the table asked a question that Dramesi was going to answer.

"Why did you escape?"

"I am a military man," Dramesi said.

There really wasn't anything else he could add to that short answer. The leader seemed to realize that nothing was going to come from this line of questioning. The man stood and said that Dramesi had a bad attitude. The man would think about that, and he would leave Dramesi time to think about it himself.

One of the guards came up to where Dramesi sat and tied his hands behind his back again. With a push, Dramesi was shoved off the stool and onto the floor. The men behind the table left. The closing doors gave Dramesi a glimpse of daylight. He was alone with his thoughts. It was April 13, 1967.

That afternoon, someone new came into the room where Dramesi sat. The jingling of keys at the door off to his right warned him just before the entry to the room opened up. The man was a very thin individual, appearing tall for a North Vietnamese, but that may have been due to Dramesi being on the floor and looking up at him. He had big feet, which stuck out of both the heels and toes of the sandals he wore. But what Dramesi noticed most of all was the man's long, thin neck, it was a goose neck on a person. That became Dramesi's nickname for the man—the Goose.

Goose had no expression on his long face as he indicated that Dramesi should sit on the stool. Getting up off the floor with some difficulty since his hands were still tied behind his back, Dramesi sat on the stool. Goose dragged a long iron bar and a pair of leg-iron shackles over from the corner. The bar was about two inches in diameter and from ten to twelve feet long. By the way Goose was handling it the contraption must have been heavy. Dramesi was soon to become intimately familiar with that bar and its weight of more than one hundred pounds.

As Dramesi sat on the stool, Goose put the leg irons around each of his ankles. The curved part of the shackles went around the back of his ankles with the open eyelets at the front of each arm of the shackles sticking out of either side of Dramesi's feet. The evil purpose of the huge iron bar became obvious as Goose threaded it through each of the eyelets on the shackles. When this was done to the man's satisfaction, the long bar extended out on either side of the prisoner's feet; the shackles held it in place. Most of the massive bar's weight bore down relentlessly on the bones of Dramesi's ankles and his feet, pressing down and flattening the arches of his feet into the floor.

Having completed his job, Goose left the room. There were no questions asked, there was no bargaining. There was just the growing agony of the bar pressing down on his bones and feet to keep Dramesi company.

To try and distract himself from the pain, Dramesi looked around the room as best he could. What he managed to see chilled him. Off to his left, behind him in the corner of the room, was a small table. On top of that table was a pile of materials including handcuffs. There was also a tangled mound of what could be nylon straps and ropes. There were also smaller pairs of iron shackles, much like the ones around Dramesi's ankles. Either they had prisoners of much smaller stature than the average American, or those shackles could be put around other parts of a prisoner's body.

Speculation about what could be done with the materials that he saw wasn't going to do Dramesi's mind any good at all, so he continued his examination of the room. It was a big room, about twenty by thirty feet; the floor was made up of rough-finished red tiles. The plaster walls were of a mostly uniform filthy white, except where there were streaks of dull green on them. The right rear corner was particularly filthy, as if it had been used as a toilet or where a bucket may have been placed, and missed, by prisoners relieving themselves.

There were dark spots on the walls in places around the room. If he had been able to look closely at them, Dramesi would have recognized them for what they were—splotches of dried blood. Stuck in some of the blood patches were long hairs. They were the mute testimony of where prisoners had their heads driven into the walls. One more ominous sight of what the room was intended for hung down from the center of the ceiling: a large steel hook very much like the meat hooks found in slaughterhouses.

He learned later that this was the terrible room 18 of the Hoa Lo Prison. The French had built the prison when they controlled the area, then known as Indochina, in the early 1900s. The Vietnamese name for the place was very fitting; Hoa Lo translated into "Fiery Furnace" in English; it could also mean a kind of small stove. Either way, it was hell for the prisoners who were held there. The Americans would call the place the "Hanoi Hilton" as a kind of macabre joke among themselves and to use that as a code name for their own communications. Whatever the Vietnamese people had experienced in that repulsive place, they made certain that the Americans had a worse time of it. Room 18 had another name used by the prisoner who spent so much time there: It was the Meathook Room, and the main torture chamber of the prison complex.

These facts would all come to Dramesi later on during his imprisonment. As he sat there during his first day, all he could do was gather as much information about the room as he could by simple observations. He didn't know if it was soundproofed, but it was certainly secure. The double doors off to his right were closed and locked at the center. Windows were in one wall of the prison room; they were shuttered with frosted glass but the bars across the openings were still visible by their shadows on the dirty white glass. Dramesi was still facing what he considered the front of the room—it wasn't like the iron bar securing his ankles allowed him to turn his body in any other direction. The table was still there, covered by that blue cloth. One of the lamps had been taken away, but the five high-backed chairs his interrogators had sat in were still in place.

One of the other features Dramesi had noticed earlier was a large drain hole to his right front. He had already seen a large rat enter the room through the hole. The rodent had looked around, sniffed, and left the way it had come. At least the animal hadn't come up to nibble on Dramesi's toes after his feet were secured in place. There may not have been much he could have done about that kind of situation except shout and wiggle.

As he sat with his pain wrapped about him like a thick blanket, there was the sound of keys at the door again. It was the Goose coming back. Just as before, Goose didn't say a word. He walked in shuffling his feet and pushed the double doors wide open. The flow of air helped clean out the dull smell of the room, and gave Dramesi an opportunity to see some of the area that he had missed coming in blindfolded that morning. He could see the hall leading past the doors, and the archway at the end of the hall itself. Through the archway, Dramesi could see outside of the building a bit; a garden of some kind was growing in the sun.

The reason for the room being aired out was shown shortly. As the prisoner had suspected, the airing-out hadn't been done for his comfort. The old man who turned out to be the camp commander came back into the room, accompanied by two of the other interrogators who had been there during the morning session.

Getting painfully to his feet, Dramesi stood and waited. The pain in his ankles and feet had grown more intense when he moved. He must have given some sign of the agony he felt, or the commander was just very experienced in this kind of thing. Coming up to where Dramesi stood, the commander indicated that the prisoner should sit again.

As soon as Dramesi began to sit, the commander swung his arm hard, smashing Dramesi in the face. The blow toppled him backward, off the stool and falling to the floor.

The commander stood over the fallen prisoner, screaming at him to get up. It was at this point that the screaming camp commander reminded Dramesi of some kind of loathsome insect. Something even worse than the leeches he had taken off his legs just a few days earlier. From that moment on, the commander was the Bug.

CHAPTER 12

TORTURE

As Dramesi struggled to regain his balance, Bug kept shouting at him to get up. As Dramesi got situated a little better, Bug started to explain that the prisoner had to greet him properly, be respectful, bow. He was very demanding about that last word, repeating loudly that Dramesi was to bow when he greeted the commander; he had to bow, to bow!

Understanding the demands but still trying to give as little as possible, Dramesi nodded his head and leaned forward slightly. This show of deference to his superior was far from good enough for Bug. He rushed at the prisoner and struck him again. This time Dramesi was expecting the blow and managed to keep on his feet. The pain in his feet and legs was agony, and if he was knocked down again, there was a real chance he could break one or both of his ankles.

With Bug screaming at him to bow again, Dramesi leaned forward. He bowed, but not all the way. Satisfied with the victory over his bound and tortured prisoner, Bug went back to sit behind the long table again. Bug was still angry at Dramesi's refusal to show respect, but he indicated that the prisoner should sit on the stool again. As Dramesi sat, he could feel the irons digging into his ankles and feet. The metal was breaking through the skin, tearing through it and badly bruising the flesh beneath. The pain was becoming unbearable, and he knew that there was going to be more to come.

The questions started coming at him again. This time they were much more personal as the interrogators tried to build up information on Dramesi's past life. They wanted to know about his family, his childhood, and his parents. Did he have a wife? Did he have any children?

To everything he could, Dramesi gave evasive answers or simply outright lies. He hadn't known what his father did for a living; he had been too young to remember. He didn't know where his mother lived; she had moved since he had joined the service. No wife, no children. Yes and no answers whenever possible, and those given reluctantly.

Then the questioning turned to military matters.

"What is the name of your wing commander?" Bug asked

"I do not remember," was Dramesi's answer.

Again, Dramesi was called the blackest of criminals. And he had to tell what the name of his wing commander was.

But Dramesi just said that he didn't remember.

With a wave of the hand from Bug, Goose came up to where Dramesi sat and knocked him over. Falling off the stool, Dramesi smacked into the hard tile floor, his legs twisting from the iron bar. The skin on Dramesi's ankles was torn and bleeding, but that didn't matter to Goose. Going over to the table in the corner, Goose selected some nylon webbing straps. As Dramesi lay where he fell, Goose slipped the strap loop around his prisoner's upper arm. Putting a foot on one of Dramesi's arms as a brace, Goose hauled back on the end of the strap with all the strength in his arms and legs. Pulling hard again and again, Goose drew both of Dramesi's elbows together. Finally he stopped just at the point where the bones in Dramesi's arms would have broken. The circulation in his arms stopped as Dramesi felt Goose secure the webbing around his upper arms.

But the trussing of the prisoner wasn't done yet. Going back to the table, Goose returned with one of the smaller sets of shackles. The odd-looking handcuffs were connected rigidly together, and they tightened down with screws. Turning Dramesi's hands so that the backs were facing each other, Goose slipped on the shackles and screwed them down tight.

The pressure on his hands and wrists was so bad that Dramesi felt that the bones would break. And he knew what was coming next. The pressure would build in his arms, chest, and shoulders. The numbness would return to his arms and hands. The interrogators would probably go soon, leaving the bound prisoner to suffer in the room alone. This time, they would leave and not come back until the circulation in his arms had been cut off so long that they would die. This time, Dramesi would lose both his arms.

The suffering had really only begun. There were refinements to the use of the straps that Dramesi wasn't familiar with yet. Goose would quickly remedy the lack of experience on the part of the prisoner.

Tying one end of a long nylon strap to the wrist shackles, Goose took the length of webbing and pulled it over Dramesi's shoulder. The action surprised the prisoner as Goose continued to pull the webbing forward, looping it around underneath the iron bar and pulling it back across Dramesi's shoulder again. Putting one knee into the prisoner's back, Goose pulled on the webbing strap, lifting Dramesi's arms and pulling them forward. Since the arms were connected at the wrists and above the elbows, they couldn't bend to relieve the pressure. Instead, the pull of the webbing strap yanked his arms forward and up. Dramesi screamed with all his remaining strength as the agonizing pain washed over him.

The screams of his victim excited the sadistic Goose. He pulled harder on the strap and Dramesi started to struggle, to fight back at the torturer who was slowly killing him. Goose couldn't get the leverage he wanted with Dramesi struggling as hard as he was. Frustrated, the sadistic Goose dropped his end of the nylon strap, pushed Dramesi over on his side, and began kicking at the helpless prisoner's head. If he had been wearing boots, Dramesi's agony would have been over since the impact would have killed him. But Goose was still wearing the sandals that appeared too small for his feet. Every time he kicked at Dramesi's head, he hurt his own toes. That just drove the sadist further into his own madness.

Goose was making a kind of hysterical whinnying sound as he kicked at the prisoner over and over again. Bug realized that the situation was getting out of control and there was a real danger to the prisoner. Bug jumped up out of his chair and ran over to Goose. Grabbing the nearly mad Goose by the shoulder, Bug pulled him away. Then Bug turned back to where Dramesi lay on the ground in agony and shrieked at him to get up.

As soon as Dramesi had gotten up from lying on the floor, Goose was back on him. Putting his foot between the prisoner's shoulder blades, Goose pulled up on the rope, drawing Dramesi's bound arms up away from his back. The pain from Dramesi's shoulders was the most intense thing he had yet felt. He was certain that his screams could be heard all over the prison camp, if not throughout Hanoi—if that was indeed where he was being tortured.

"Will you tell me the name of your wing commander?" Bug shouted over the prisoner's screams.

"Yes!" Dramesi wailed. "Yes I will.'

But Goose continued to pull up on the strap, the pressure on Dramesi's shoulder joints continued, and the pain went on unabated.

"Yes, yes," Dramesi said through a throat hoarse with screaming.

Goose stopped pulling up on the strap, allowing the prisoner's arms to go back down to their lowest position. Now at least Dramesi could breathe a bit in spite of the horrible pain that remained in the whole of his body. When asked about his wing commander, he answered. They already knew the name; he didn't have to try and remember a lie. More questions were asked and the cycle of torture went on; Goose pulled on the straps and Dramesi screamed.

Finally, night came and the straps around his arms were removed. The shackles on his wrists came off as well. That kind of torture could cause a prisoner to suffocate if he passed out and fell during the night. Handcuffs were placed on Dramesi's wrists but the ankle shackles and hateful iron bar remained where they were. Still sitting on the stool, Dramesi passed his first night in the Hanoi prison system.

The punishment and torture continued as Dramesi remained in the room. The routine was quickly set and didn't vary much during the ordeal. The shackles and the heavy iron bar remained on his ankles and across his feet. His arms remained handcuffed behind his back. Twice a day, food was brought to him, his only real breathing space between periods of torture, interrogation, and isolation. The food was poor, just a cup of water, some rice, and a dark-green liquid that might have had some nutritional value. It was a starvation diet at best.

The stool became his world since he was forced to remain on it constantly. The guards tried to keep their prisoner awake constantly. The lack of sleep will sap even a strong person's resolve and ability to resist. It was only during the very early morning hours when the guards were absent from the room that Dramesi was able to drift off into a pain-filled sleep.

He was interrogated on a regular basis. On the second day, he was forced to sit and listen to propaganda tapes reportedly made by other American prisoners held by the North Vietnamese. The tapes were shocking, supposedly made by prisoners whom Dramesi knew by reputation at least. As soon as he identified the people who had made the recording, he would tune out what was being said. The idea of the tapes was obvious: If these people could cooperate with the benevolent people of North Vietnam, then why couldn't Dramesi?

That logic didn't matter to John Dramesi. He was going to resist to the best of his ability and refuse that kind of cooperation, no matter what they did to him. Bug and Goose had a completely different opinion on that subject, and they well knew how to break a man through torture, isolation, lack of sleep, and malnutrition. It was what they did, and Goose in particular took an obscene kind of pleasure in his work.

Dramesi was ordered to make the same kind of tape recordings other prisoners had done, tapes denouncing the American war effort and admitting to war crimes against the North Vietnamese people. To back up the tapes, Dramesi was to sign a confession that he freely admitted to being a war criminal. And Bug wanted letters to be written by the prisoner in front of him. The letters were to be sent to other members of Dramesi's squadron back in Thailand, telling them to disobey orders and not fly missions over North Vietnam.

One particularly strange request was that Dramesi was to write a letter to U.S. senator J. William Fulbright, chairman of the Senate Foreign Relations Committee. An early dissenting voice against the war, he held a hearing on U.S. conduct in Southeast Asia. But he probably wouldn't have even bothered to read a letter addressed to him from an Air Force officer, even if Dramesi had been willing to write it.

Besides the demands for letters and tape recordings, Dramesi had military questions put to him. What were the names of the other squadron pilots he flew with? What were the number and types of missions he had gone on? His answers were limited, when he said anything more than he didn't know or didn't remember. When the cooperation that Bug wanted didn't come, Goose would step up with his shackles, straps, and ropes.

The soundproofing in Room 18 prevented much of the tortured prisoner's agonized cries from making it past the bloodstained walls. Goose didn't lose control of himself again, but he was enthusiastic in his work. A classic sadist down to his black soul, Goose had found his true niche in life, and the general opinion of the prisoners was that he should rot in hell for it.

The cycle of torturing and questioning, day and night, went on.

After a week of constant torment, Bug made a new request. The prisoner was to write out a statement about the North Vietnamese government that could be read out to the world. He was to say how the people were lenient in spite of his crimes against them, and how humane their treatment was of him and the other American prisoners being held. As he had for so many of the other requests for documentation from him, he refused. And Goose once again went to work.

Making his best effort to resist the inquisition, Dramesi had managed to give up relatively little useful information. Bug knew that he had flown an F-105D aircraft, and the name of his wing commander. That was about it in the way of actual facts. To identify members of his squadron, Dramesi had pulled out names of fliers he had known in the past. Finally, he had said that he was only a captain at the Korat base in Thailand. He didn't make up missions or assign targets. That was the responsibility of colonels and generals, not lowly captains.

But Bug refused to listen to that particular lie. He insisted that Dramesi tell him what the upcoming missions for his squadron would be, where the targets were. This was timely military information. The North Vietnamese knew that the longer they held a prisoner, the less he would be able to tell them about upcoming missions. Bug questioned and Dramesi resisted. And Goose got to enjoy himself. To finally give up something that would sound plausible to Bug, and make the torture go away for a while, Dramesi told about a mission near Hanoi. There was going to be an air attack against a barracks near Thud Ridge. The target was north of the mountain ridge and it would be destroyed. It was also a complete fabrication.

These were the little victories that helped keep Dramesi going through the long days and nights. He hadn't said anything of importance, nothing of value. And he hadn't written anything that could be used against him or his country. He hadn't filled out the biographical questionnaire that Bug kept shoving in front of him. He had even figured out a way to ease the constant pain of the shackles and bar that crushed down on his ankles and feet.

Paying attention to the guards' rotation schedule and when he would have a chance to move at night, Dramesi acted in his own behalf. Crouching down from the stool, he would slide the ankle shackles along the bar until he could reach the table in the corner. He wasn't able to move the shackles off the bar; even if he was caught without the bar on his feet, the punishment would have probably been severe. But there was something he could do to relieve the weight that caused so much pain, something simple and easy to hide.

Feeling around on the table behind him with his handcuffed hands, Dramesi found the screw cuffs that Goose used to secure his wrists together during a torture session, which were made up of wide, thick, solid shackles. Working his way back along the bar until he reached his stool, Dramesi contorted himself until he was able to place the wrist rings of the screw cuffs underneath the iron bar. With the screw cuffs between his feet and the bar resting on top of them, he finally had some relief from the pain of the bar crushing down on the tops of his feet.

There was a danger that he would be caught, but Dramesi paid attention to the sounds in the hallway outside the doors. At dawn, the guards would come down the hall, the sounds of their boot steps echoing loudly enough for Dramesi to hear their approach. He knew that once he heard the bootsteps, he had about thirty seconds before the guards would unlock the door and enter. The door was secured with a padlock and a bolt, so there was considerable noise when the guards used the key to open up.

Thirty seconds; that's the amount of time Dramesi had to get up off the stool, slip his bound arms down past his buttocks, and grab the screw cuffs up from underneath the bar. Pulling his arms back up, he could toss the cuffs in the direction of the table and the noise would be covered by the sound of the door being unlocked and the bolt drawn back. Then he would just be sitting on the stool as the guards came in and another day's cycle began.

The impact of the bar settling back onto his bruised and injured feet was excruciating. But the relief of having the weight eased even for just a few hours was worth it. These were the actions that helped keep him going, helped him maintain the fight for his personal dignity and honor in spite of the conditions he was being kept under.

To relieve himself, Dramesi had to simply pee on the floor in front of his stool a number of times. He did convince one guard to take him out of the room once late in the afternoon. It had been a long session with Bug; the guard didn't wish to foul the air in the room where he had to stand duty any worse than it already was, so he unshackled the irons from the prisoner's feet, untied his hands, and led him from the room.

It was only a short trip to another cell, but he was out of Room 18. That was a boost to Dramesi's morale. The cell he was taken to was a small crypt, only 7 by 4½ feet in size. There were no other prisoners occupying the two bunks stacked one on the other. The only other furnishing was a bucket with a lid in one corner, a filthy rag hanging from a string nearby.

The stench in the windowless room was overpowering, but so was Dramesi's need. He used the horrible bucket in spite of the smell almost knocking him out when he lifted the lid. He stretched out his use of the facility as long as he could. It was a horrible little cell, but it wasn't the room full of pain that waited for him.

His injuries were ignored, other than when Bug asked him if he wanted a doctor to examine his bullet wound. The injury was infected and getting worse. Dramesi always said that he wished to see a doctor, and his request was always denied by Bug.

The questions turned to why Dramesi had tried to escape. His answer was simply that it was a military man's duty to escape. And when a man was tortured, he would certainly try to escape. Turning things back onto Bug, Dramesi asked him if he wouldn't do the same thing, try to escape if he was being held prisoner in South Vietnam.

That answer set Bug off again on how Dramesi had such a bad attitude. Then the questions went back to military subjects. If Bug had learned about the Thud Ridge barracks mission being a fabrication, he didn't show it. But when Dramesi continued to refuse to answer the military questions, Bug went back to asking about the escape. Then the cycle of Goose and the ropes would begin again, with the occasional beating thrown in for variety.

CHAPTER 13

THE DUNGEON

On the eighth day of Dramesi's extended torture session at the Hanoi Hilton, Bug and Goose came into the room and astonished him. The heavy irons on his feet and ankles were removed, and his hands were untied. It appeared that he was being released, at least from his interrogation period in Room 18.

The joy Dramesi felt was strong. He thought he had made it, that he had gone through the crucible and gotten out the other side with his honor intact. He wanted to cheer but held himself back. The fact was, he could barely walk. He went out of that particular chamber of horrors on his own, walking slowly and stiffly on legs that ached and feet that could barely bend. But he walked nonetheless.

Led through the complex by Bug and Goose, Dramesi made mental notes on the interior layout of the building. The group went down three steps into the garden area that Dramesi had caught just a glimpse of earlier. Crossing the garden, they went through a pair of double steel doors, down another corridor, and through another secured door.

The group was in a dark, dank hallway, not much above what might have been found in a medieval dungeon. Lining the walls of the shadowy hall were eight doors, four to a side. Like a scene from another bad old movie, the sound of the lock turning in one of the doors echoed loudly through the hallway. The rusted hinges squealed with the metallic sound of neglected metal on metal as the door was drawn open. Written in black above the door was the number "2."

Shoved into what was little more than a crypt, Dramesi looked about the dreary interior. What he saw was nothing more than a storage place for bodies that weren't quite dead yet. The room was barely the size of a root cellar in an old house back in the States, only a cellar would have smelled a lot better than this cubicle. The bucket in the corner established at least one likely source of the smell. Instead of having two bunks stacked on top of one another, this cell had flat wooden bunks along opposite walls. There was barely a foot distance along the middle of the chamber separating the two sleeping platforms. At the foot end of the bunks, nearest the door to the cell, were a set of wooden and iron stocks, the kind seen in an old movie where the prisoners in the dungeon would have their legs secured.

The stocks were solidly secured to the wood of the bunks. The wooden base of the device had two curved depressions cut into it to accept the prisoner's ankles. A flat iron bar was hinged at one end and could be locked down across the top of the stocks with a padlock. It was another horrible device in a place filled with such things, and Dramesi had a feeling he was going to become intimately familiar with it.

Goose and Bug set the prisoner down on one of the bunks. Shoving his prisoner over, Goose put his legs into the wooden stocks. Then he slammed the iron bar down across Dramesi's already injured ankles and locked the bar in place. The slots in the wooden part of the stocks were small, too small to easily accept the thicker ankles of an American. Bringing the iron crossbar down hard made sure that the stocks could be locked shut. The agony was another plus to the sadistic Goose.

But the binding of the prisoner wasn't completed yet. Grabbing Dramesi's left wrist, Goose put one end of a pair of handcuffs on it. Pulling the prisoner forward, Goose locked the other end of the cuff around the iron bar of the stocks where it went across Dramesi's right ankle. Bent forward to where he could barely breathe, Dramesi only had his left arm free. The screeching squeal of the door's hinges was the prelude to it slamming shut. The lock clicked and the footsteps of Bug and Goose diminished as they walked down the hall. Dramesi was alone in the dingy cell with his misery.

The elation he had felt just a short time earlier was gone. It was apparent that all he had managed to do was survive the torture chamber just to be chained in a dungeon. All he needed was a sweating, muscular, misshaped dwarf to come lurching in with a whip in his hand to make the medieval image complete. Then again, the shuffling insanity of Goose filled that role fairly exactly. Depression and gloom settled across his back like a thick, suffocating cloud.

The question of whether the torture was ever going to end kept running through Dramesi's mind. Bent over the way he was, he couldn't sleep, couldn't rest, and he wasn't even let out of his bonds in order to relieve himself. For twenty-four hours a day, Dramesi remained in that bent-over position. Inevitably, when he soiled himself Goose would arrive to punish the prisoner, pounding Dramesi's head against the cell wall.

The poor food he was given kept him going, but at what cost? Dramesi wondered if death would be the only release from his tortures that allowed him to keep his sense of honor intact. He wasn't even being questioned, just punished.

Before very long, the blood-starved tissues in the feet started to swell. The stocks were so tight that circulation was restricted. There wasn't anything he could do about the itching that continued unabated on his feet; he couldn't reach the point of irritation in order to scratch it.

The only things that were benefiting from Dramesi's position were the insects in the room. Swarms of mosquitoes flourished on his blood, feeding until they were so bloated they couldn't fly. Infection spread from his ankles, and the bullet wound on his thigh remained untreated. He started to wonder not if he would lose a foot or leg, but when it would happen.

Physical escape was pretty much out of the question considering that he couldn't even move off his bunk. Escaping into his mind was possible, but that road would eventually lead to madness. He had to remain rooted in reality. To aid in staying in the here and now, he began to minutely examine the room he was in, or at least as much of it as he could see. Within the reach of his left hand, he found a small bent nail. Just a V-shaped bit of metal, but it fit into the key slot of his handcuffs, and that gave him something constructive to do.

For several days, Dramesi probed and twisted with his pathetic little tool, trying to pick the lock on his cuffs. His physical deterioration was bad enough that even this little activity tired him quickly, and his level of frustration was quick to discourage him. Still, his locksmithing project was all he had to do, and if he succeeded, the reward would be great.

He had been secured in his bent-over position for more than a week. The torture had gone on nonstop for over half a month. For more than two days his world was centered on trying to pick the lock on his handcuffs. Failure and attempt, failure and attempt, try something different, and once again fail. On the third day of his trying, the point of the nail pressed on the proper spot within the mechanism. The new series of probes and movements with the bent nail—that golden key—proved themselves when the cuffs simply fell open.

Astonished, and then flooded with joy, Dramesi was free! Or at least he could straighten his back and sit up. It was a form of freedom, and one that felt good, indescribably good.

Slowly, he straightened his posture, leaned back, and stretched his cramped back. For a moment, the numerous aches, pains, and cramps in his body went away as he luxuriated in just being able to lie back on his bunk. The unpadded boards felt amazingly comfortable for that moment. Then something warned him.

Reacting as quickly as he could, Dramesi sat back up and bent forward into the position he had held for so many days. Grabbing the handcuff with his left hand, he slipped it around his right wrist. Just as he returned to the same appearance he had been showing ever since he had entered cell #2, the cover over the peephole in his door was moved.

An eye showed at the peephole as the guard looked in; all he would see was the prisoner in the same position. The cover slid back and Dramesi breathed a little easier. He had hidden his victory over the handcuffs; that little bit of freedom was still his. Then the keys rattled in the lock on his cell door.

To cover the clicking sound of the handcuff being closed, Dramesi coughed loudly. Sounding sick was pretty easy then, but still the guard came into the cell with a suspicious look. He examined the bound prisoner, found nothing particularly out of the ordinary—just a stinking wretch bound to a board. He turned and left, locking the door behind him.

But the stinking wretch still held the means of his victory. The golden key was still in Dramesi's possession. With it, he was able to open the lock on his handcuffs at will. After some practice—he didn't have a great deal else to do—Dramesi was able to open the handcuffs in only a few seconds.

Paying careful attention to the daily goings-on of the prison helped Dramesi time his periods of freedom from the handcuffs. Sounds of the early morning work by people outside his cell gave him the sign that it was about four in the morning. He could unlock his cuffs and lean back for a blessed few hours of relief. His morning check wouldn't take place until the peephole cover was slid back at about seven. He could quickly blot out the world he was in, the view of his deteriorating feet and legs went away, while he escaped into near unconsciousness.

In spite of being apparently oblivious to the world, a piece of

Dramesi's mind remained on alert. He would find himself sitting up and back into his bound position automatically when there was a warning sound in the hallway outside. The shuffling walk of Goose and the sound of the outer hallway door opening was enough to pull Dramesi up and into position by reflex. His body and mind were protecting themselves as best they could.

But his body continued to suffer as Dramesi remained locked in the stocks. His feet swelled up until his toes stuck up like the nails on an elephant's foot. The hot days and scorching nights combined with the filthy conditions to make his physical state continue to deteriorate. His weight dropped and the pain of his infected bullet wound grew.

The only ally he had assisting him was a rat that went through his cell to gain access to the hall beyond. There was enough room under the door for the rodent to scurry into the hallway, but it always stopped at the door to sense if the way beyond was safe. One evening as Dramesi was preparing to lay back, the rat suddenly turned from the doorway and scampered back the way it had come. Dramesi quickly returned to his bound position and picked up the handcuffs, just as the peephole cover slid back. His rodent sentinel had kept him from being discovered.

It was just over a month since Dramesi had been shot down when Goose and Bug came back into his cell. Unlocking the iron bar on top of his stocks, Goose lifted it away, freeing Dramesi's ankles for the first time since he had come into the room nearly two weeks earlier. When he was ordered by Bug to turn and sit on the bed, Dramesi found that he couldn't lift his legs out of the stocks. The flesh of his ankles was stuck to the wood by dried blood and swollen tissues. He was too weak to pull the legs up himself, but Goose was available to assist.

Yanking the prisoner's legs up, Goose tore the corrupted flesh of Dramesi's ankles as he pulled them free of the stocks. Dropping them to the side, Goose was satisfied that he had "helped" the prisoner to follow the orders of the camp commander. His legs bleeding, the stunned prisoner sat staring at Bug, not certain what would come next.

Another writing period followed, or at least one of Bug ordering the prisoner to write. Dramesi was to detail his missions over North Vietnam. When the prisoner looked at Bug with defiance, he was threatened with going right back into the stocks.

There was no question that Dramesi didn't want to go back into the stocks, but he also wasn't going to write down anything. Playing for time, he agreed to Bug's demands. After shoving ink, paper, and a pen into their prisoner's hands, Bug and Goose left the cell. Dramesi was left with the writing materials and a concern for just what was going to happen next. He was out of the stocks for the moment, but another demand that he couldn't accept had been made of him.

The next morning Dramesi still hadn't written anything, but there was a new guard who came into his cell. The guard was wearing the standard pith helmet that was part of the North Vietnamese military uniform. Either to decorate the bland headgear, or to have an unusual form of camouflage, the guard had tied strands of cloth on his helmet to look like flowers and bits of plants.

The amusing attempt at camouflage caused Dramesi to name the guard Ferdinand, after the flower-loving bull in a children's story. The situation quickly stopped being amusing when Ferdinand ordered Dramesi to clean up his cell.

That amount of exertion was almost impossible for the abused prisoner. As Ferdinand looked on, Dramesi swung his legs off the bunk and to the floor. That was about the only movement he could make, as the pain of putting any weight on his tortured feet and ankles washed through his body like a red flame. Walking was out of the question; Dramesi was barely able to move. His weakness was as obvious as his wounds as he tried to just lift the unused toilet bucket. His injuries left a trail of blood across the floor and he moved across the room in an agonizing shuffle.

His new guard only watched the prisoner for a short time before leaving the cell. It was plain that Dramesi wasn't faking, and that he was barely able to take care of himself, let alone clean his room. It may have been due to the new guard—certainly not because of some change of heart on the part of Goose or Bug—but some type of medical personnel showed up at cell #2 later on that same day.

After an examination of his injured feet and ankles, the "doctor" gave Dramesi a shot of antibiotics. Bandages were secured around his ankles but the doctor left before paying any attention to the bullet wound in Dramesi's leg.

The new guard returned to insist that Dramesi continue with his writing. It was a fairly certain thing that Ferdinand couldn't read English; he didn't speak it to his prisoner, but he didn't have to be able to read to see that Dramesi wasn't doing as told. The pages that had been brought to him were blank, that was plain enough. With a series of insistent grunts, Ferdinand indicated that Dramesi should start writing. Then he left the cell.

Before the day was over, Dramesi had another visit from the doctor and received another shot of antibiotics. There was no way he was going to write down anything close to the details of his missions, but he wanted to buy as much time as he could. Several times over the following few days, either Ferdinand or Goose would look into the cell. Their instructions to Dramesi consisted of little more than an unintelligible bunch of noises, but the tone was obviously that of a warning.

Ferdinand appeared to just consider his assignment a job and didn't go out of his way to injure or harass his prisoner. On the other hand, Goose was a vicious, unstable sadist. It wouldn't do Dramesi any good to antagonize the lunatic who had so much control over his life just then. When the warning sounds echoed through the hallway that either guard was coming, Dramesi would quickly set to work and at least give the appearance of writing on the paper.

The part of the prison where cell #2 was located had been named Heartbreak Hotel by the other POWs. Dramesi had no way of knowing this during his incarceration there since he didn't speak to a single American the entire period. The eight cells along the hallway indicated that there could have been as many as sixteen other prisoners in them if they all shared the double-bunk layout, but Dramesi never heard another voice in the area outside that of the North Vietnamese.

Shouting out, "Is there anyone here?" Dramesi hoped for an answer back. No voices returned his call. From the wall that he shared with cell #1 there came a series of thumps minutes after he called out. There was a sequence to the thumps, but Dramesi had no idea what the code was. He banged back on the wall with his fist, but that didn't garner him a response. There were no answers to his cries. He was only talking to himself.

[CHAPTER 14]

HEARTBREAK AND BEYOND

It was only a couple of days since he had been given the orders to write about his missions that Dramesi found himself under closer scrutiny by the guards. His ability to stall off the guards and Bug looked to be running out. Every time they peeked in, they would pound on the door and indicate that Dramesi should be writing. He would simulate scribbling for a while and the guards would leave. Then it was the time for another interrogation.

It was the fifth of May when Ferdinand opened the door to cell #2. It was easy to see that he wanted the prisoner to come with him, since he had brought Dramesi a pair of crutches. Though the crutches were too long, they did help the still very badly injured prisoner to hobble along and follow where the guard was leading.

The path they followed was out the door and into the main courtyard of the prison complex. On the other side of the courtyard, the pair entered another interrogation room, this one considerably less threatening than room #18 had been.

Two men were in the room waiting for Dramesi to be delivered, one of whom had been an interpreter during Dramesi's first session in room #18. Here in this room he wasn't being threatened, and there were no torture devices in sight. No ropes, chains, shackles, or bars were in the room, just two men who wanted their questions answered. And the subject was a little different from Dramesi's previous interrogations.

The interpreter spoke English well enough and only seemed interested in learning about the prisoner's escape attempt. Mentioning a number of U.S. military sources of information, Air Force survival manuals, and training centers, there wasn't any question that the interpreter hadn't already learned on his subject. He was going to be a very hard man to deal with.

Listening much more than he spoke, Dramesi sat through the interrogation. The main interests of the interpreter were threefold: He wanted to know why Dramesi had escaped in the first place. He also wanted to know how strongly Dramesi felt about the results of his attempt. And finally, the man wanted to convince the prisoner that escape from North Vietnam was impossible, particularly for a Westerner.

The interpreter also pushed the fact that Dramesi was simply a criminal, even though he didn't really seem to be convinced of that himself. What he was certain about was the fact that any further attempts to escape would only result in pain and punishment for Dramesi.

If the first few weeks of his stay at the Hanoi Hilton were any indication of things, Dramesi had no trouble believing that last part. But the conversation didn't change his opinion about escaping, or his desire to succeed at gaining freedom through his own actions.

The session simply ended with the interpreter giving a signal to Ferdinand, and Dramesi was sent back to his cell. That was all: no torture, threats, or anything much. Just a period of conversation, though a fairly one-sided one, and a return to confinement.

That same night, Ferdinand came into cell #2 to wake Dramesi and exchange his clothing. The fouled and stinking black shirt and shorts were taken and he was given a long-sleeved shirt and long pants. Both pieces of clothing were dyed in alternating pale red and gray stripes: unmistakable prison garb.

In the time since he was released from the stock, Dramesi had been trying to catch up on sleep, resting to the best of his ability and getting up only for his meager meals or a guard's knock at the door. The dreams he had while sleeping were an escape, but a strange one. They were among the most vivid he could remember in his entire life. But even in his subconscious, he knew that he had to go back from whatever escape his dreams took him; he had to go back to cell #2 at the Heartbreak Hotel.

The afternoon on the day after his escape interrogation, Dramesi's subterfuge about writing on his missions was discovered. Ferdinand came into the cell and took the pen out of the prisoner's hand as he sat and pretended to write. Crumpling up the papers with barely a glance, Ferdinand took them, the ink, and the pen and left the cell. He hadn't even attempted to read anything on the pages, just crumpled them up as if he knew they were worthless.

Another surprise came as Ferdinand returned to cell #2 later that afternoon. Indicating that Dramesi was to follow him, he led the prisoner down to cell #8. That cell held a shower, which Dramesi was allowed to use. For the first time in the thirty-four days since his capture, Dramesi was clean. Even his long hair was dealt with as Ferdinand cut it with a pair of clippers. The unkempt beard Dramesi was sporting was also shaved, or at least trimmed considerably, with those same clippers.

That evening, Goose came in to cell #2 to take Dramesi out of the room. He wasn't blindfolded and could see that they were going to another section of the complex that was new to him. In another room was the camp commander and something Dramesi hadn't seen in more than a month: a fellow American.

Bug sat behind a table, in front of which was a stretcher on the floor holding a tall, slim American. The man, still wearing his military crew cut, was pale and looked worn. By the appearance of the cast extending the length of his right leg all the way from the waist, he had been badly injured. Chances were good that this man was a new arrival at the prison and probably had only been captured recently.

Before speaking to Bug or the prisoner, Dramesi stood at attention as straight and steadily as he could. But he didn't bow and made no attempt to bow. Bug and Dramesi looked at each other steadily, neither saying a word. It was obvious that Bug was expecting a show of respect. It was just as obvious that Dramesi wasn't about to do what Bug wanted. Looking away, Dramesi gazed at the man on the stretcher.

Finally, it was Bug who spoke, asking if Dramesi wanted to live with the man on the stretcher.

It was an odd question. Given Bug's apparent lack of skill at English, it may have been the only way he could say what he meant. Not sure of the situation, Dramesi paused before answering. It was not unheard-of for other apparent prisoners to be planted in order to gain information. But it was a fairly sophisticated technique, and Dramesi didn't know if the North Vietnamese used such actions. His experience was that the local interrogation techniques tended to lean toward the brutal rather than clever, but he couldn't afford not to consider the possibility. Dramesi had information that he didn't want the North Vietnamese to know about, particularly that he had been a forward air controller with the 4th Infantry Division in South Vietnam.

Still, the fellow American on the floor was injured, and he could be company at least. Finally, Dramesi said yes.

Bug asked the man on the stretcher the same question, and received a no answer. He may not have understood what Bug was asking and the camp commander repeated his question. The man on the stretcher also reluctantly said yes. If he was a plant in order to learn information from Dramesi, he was acting the part very well. It could also have been that the man in the cast considered Dramesi a possible plant.

After the roommates had agreed to each other, Dramesi was quickly taken from the room. Once more he was blindfolded to keep him from learning about where he was going and Goose led him to another part of the complex. They ended up in a part of the Hanoi Hilton the POWs had named the Golden Nugget in Little Las Vegas. The odd names were all taken from places back in the States that were familiar to most if not all of the prisoners, most of whom were pilots or flight personnel. Using the names, they could communicate about locations and if their messages were intercepted, it would be that much harder for the North Vietnamese to understand them.

Now Dramesi was put in room three of the Golden Nugget. The cell was only about a foot wider than cell #2 had been. Again, the furnishings were simple and functional: just the two bunks along the two walls and a bucket. The door to the cell was made of solid wood. There were two others openings in this room, each a one-by-two foot window in the side walls. The windows were barred and closed with shutters. That made things dark and tight as far as the air went in the room.

Before too long, a pair of guards brought the injured man in on his stretcher. They placed him on the other bunk and left. Dramesi soon learned that the other man was Al Meyer, a navigator who had been shot down just a couple of weeks earlier. It may have been his broken leg or his situation; it could have just been his nature, but Meyer was demanding and not very polite about making them. Over the next several days, Dramesi did what he could to help his room-mate in what were deplorable conditions. He did finally have to tell the other man that his name was John, not "hey."

The only consideration the North Vietnamese showed to the injured man was an issue of what they called "special food." The broth he was served was a little thicker, and some slices of potatoes and pork could be found in it. For Dramesi, he only received his usual rice and bowl of thin green soup. The two prisoners also received a banana each. And a real bright spot showed up in the food the day they received some bread with their meal. The bread was an intermittent thing at best. After some time had passed to build up a record, they figured that the chances of getting bread with a meal were nine to one. But a loaf of bread was a real morale booster for the imprisoned men.

One of the other things that raised Dramesi's spirits was the ability to speak to other Americans. He would play word games and quizzes with Meyer to help pass the time. With the ability to move about, Dramesi would exercise, little at first and then gradually more, so as to regain at least some of his strength.

During the "quiet hour," signals had been arranged among the prisoner population to warn of guards approaching the Golden Nugget series of rooms or the Thunderbird cells across the alley. With the windows of the cells open, the men could even see each other. The first fellow prisoner Dramesi spoke to was Dave Gray.

Gray had been shot down in late January '67 and had bad back injuries as a result of his ejection. His F-4C had been shot down after only his fourth combat mission. The enjoyment of the conversation waned when Dramesi said that he didn't think the prisoners would be released for at least a year. Gray was visibly depressed. When the other prisoner finally asked Dramesi what he based his opinion on, the answer was straightforward. U.S. forces were just starting to operate at a high level in South Vietnam. Dramesi felt that the military actions of the United States would take about a year to reach their objectives. Then, the prisoners might expect release when the United States held the upper hand.

Incoming prisoners were the only source of unbiased news for the men already being held. What Dramesi told to Gray was passed along to the rest of the population, even to the prisoner's senior ranking officer (SRO) of the camp, Commander Stockdale. His opinion might not have been agreed with by the others, but it was certainly shared.

Another thing that could lift the spirits of a number of the prisoners, Dramesi among them, was the sound of U.S. air strikes coming in around the city. While in the Heartbreak Hotel, the sounds of the jets and explosions had been muffled by the structure. In the Golden Nugget, the roar of U.S. airpower could be plainly heard. Even the return fire of the North Vietnamese, the green and red streaks of tracer fire, could be seen through the windows as the projectiles climbed into the sky. One night raid was huge, appearing like a Fourth of July celebration to Dramesi.

The guards were concerned about the prisoners when the air strikes took place, but not enough to move them to any real position of safety. When the air-raid sirens sounded, the guards rushed about and ordered the prisoners to take cover under their bunks. More than once, Dramesi ignored the guards and watched the raid, particularly the local air defenses, as best he could. He was gathering information, military information on where the local troops positioned themselves during an attack, how many were armed with automatic weapons, and where the strongpoints might be. It was information that could help when he next escaped.

Other uplifting things happened at the Golden Nugget; at least one took place early on for Dramesi. It was only a few days after his arrival at the facility that he learned an old friend of his was just a few cells down from his. Charlie Greene had been another pilot flying F-105s back when he and Dramesi were serving at Seymour Johnson Air Force Base in North Carolina. He had been shot down along with two other aircraft on March 11 that same year. Greene had gone down about three weeks before Dramesi was shot down himself.

Knowing that there was a fellow flier that he had history with was a boost for Dramesi while spending his time at the Golden Nugget. It was one of the few positive things that helped lighten the dank, dreary mood of the whole place and the situation they all shared.

One of the few bright spots on the average day was when Dramesi was allowed out of his cell for personal hygiene. He had the opportunity to wash himself and his clothes but occasionally the guards cut his time a short. On some days, Dramesi was let out of the cell for as little as ten minutes in order to attend to his needs. Shaving gear in the form of an old razor was issued once a week. The blade was dull and didn't cut a beard very well. Even cut and bleeding a bit, Dramesi always felt considerably better after he managed even a rough shave.

There wasn't much at the Golden Nugget to make the prisoners feel good about anything. As far as Dramesi was concerned, the prison staff treated them little better than animals. He felt he had proof of this in the form of some of the other denizens of the immediate area. Just across from the cell that he shared with Meyer, pigs were being held in an old shower stall. The swine smelled just as farm pigs do everywhere; and the stench was overpowering sometimes. From what he could tell, it was just another tool the prison used to try and dehumanize Dramesi and the others.

Some treatment was a little better than others. Eventually, Dramesi was given an issue of supplies. It wasn't much—two sets of long-sleeved shorts and pants in the alternating stripes that identified prison garb, and a short-sleeved shirt to go with a set of matching shorts. He also received a pair of rubber sandals and a blue sweater. In the heat of North Vietnam, he found the sweater to be an odd item of issue but certainly accepted it. Finally, he also received two hygiene items, a toothbrush and a very small tube of toothpaste. He was told that the toothbrush would have to last him for six months and the toothpaste for three months. But being able to scrub his teeth clean for the first time since he had been captured was a luxury.

There were no periods of intense interrogation such as he had experienced in his first weeks at the prison, but Dramesi knew such things could come at any time. The prisoners were completely at the mercy of the guards, and some of the guards didn't know what mercy meant in any language. Goose was far from being the only sadist the North Vietnamese inflicted on the POWs.

When he was taken one day to a room the prisoners called the Riviera, Dramesi thought that his respite from torture might be over. In the room was one of the five individuals who had overseen his long torture session when he first arrived. The North Vietnamese officer in the room had been one of the interrogators during that first ordeal and he could speak reasonable English.

To his astonishment, Dramesi was informed that he was going to be moved to a better facility; one where his roommate could receive the attention he needed. Dramesi would be receiving this great boon because his attitude had been improving. The Vietnamese also hoped that Dramesi would continue to improve his behavior and remember to do as he was ordered by the guards and staff.

The only answer Dramesi gave was that he understood what was being said to him. He neither agreed nor disagreed with what he had been told, only acknowledged it. Nothing he said could be used against him, his fellow prisoners, or his country. His cooperation was extremely limited. Then the interrogator gave Dramesi a lecture on how badly the war was going for the South Vietnamese and the United States. America was losing and the conflict would be coming to an end soon.

Goose came into the room and led Dramesi away when the interrogator was done talking. But they did not return to the cell right away. Instead, Dramesi was taken to a medic's clinic, a shack really. Was he finally going to receive some medical treatment for the wound in his leg? Over and over again, Bug and other interrogators had said that the infected wound would be treated, but nothing was ever done. This time it looked like things were going to be different.

That was apparently the situation. Dramesi didn't need to see the disgusted look in the medic's face to know the wound was bad. It had never been properly treated since Dramesi had been shot. The treatment was rough at best, not much better than some of the finer points of torture that Goose had delivered. The medic used a pair of tweezers to remove the dead tissue that filled the wound channel. The pain was intense as it rushed through Dramesi's leg and flooded his body. Finally, the worst of the treatment was over when the wound was clean enough for the medic, or at least the dead and rotting tissue had been removed enough for him to wash out the hole with hot water.

Drying the area of the wound had little of the rush of pain that the treatment and washing had held for Dramesi. The medic packed the open wound with what Dramesi thought was sulphur, put a compress on it, and bandaged the whole thing up. The sulphur treatment of wounds was apparently thousands of years old and probably had at least some beneficial effects. At least that's what Dramesi hoped; the fear he had of possibly losing his leg lessened now that he gotten some kind of medical treatment.

CHAPTER 15

THE ZOO

The next night, the guards came for Dramesi and Meyer. The two men were ordered to gather up their meager possessions. Getting on board a truck in the darkness, the men couldn't see enough of what was around them to really identify the area, only that they were remaining mostly within the city.

The trip was a relatively short one, less than four miles to the southwest. The prison camp the truck arrived at had once been a French film studio. The facility had been converted by the North Vietnamese into a prison when they opened it up as only their second POW facility in the late summer of 1965. It was initially a fairly small facility, a walled enclosure only about 100 yards square in size. Later additional areas would be added that nearly tripled the length of the facility grounds.

Of the fourteen different-sized buildings in the compound, none was higher than a single story structure. The most noticeable feature of the place was a large swimming pool in the center of the main area, though it had been abandoned for any recreational use years earlier.

It held only dirty water and garbage as well as some small fish the guard staff raised for their own consumption.

There was livestock wandering around the place, cattle, chicken, and such, so much so that earlier, the prisoners called the place Camp America. A number of the buildings had received farm-oriented names such as "Barn" "Stable," and "Pigsty." The concrete buildings had been converted over from their original purposes into cells, badly ventilated dismal living quarters with only filthy cement floors for the prisoners to sleep on.

The original windows in the cells had been barred over, and then finally bricked up entirely by the North Vietnamese. Doors were heavy wooden slabs secured with padlocks. But there was enough flexibility in the poor-fitting door frames and on the hinges that the prisoners were able to push the wood out and peek into the area beyond. There were also peepholes in the doors; it seemed the local animals looked in as often as the guards. A single dim bulb hung from a wire in each room. Burning night and day, the bulbs cast a dull light across a dreary area.

The North Vietnamese referred to the location as Pha Phim (the Film Studio), among other names. To the U.S. government, the place was identified as the Cu Loc Prison. For the Americans who were held there, it became known as the Zoo around 1966. That name came about partly because of the reversal of the norm; at the Zoo the animals looked into the "cages" at the humans.

After arriving at the Zoo, Dramesi and Meyer were both placed in a single cell in the Stable, one of the buildings along the outer wall of the compound. Their roommate status remained only for a couple of days. Two days after the men arrived at the Zoo, Dramesi was pulled out of the cell to meet a North Vietnamese who seemed to have an inferiority complex.

The little, dark-skinned North Vietnamese whom Dramesi met had strapped to his belt a holster with an American .45 Colt automatic pistol in it. A Colt .45 automatic is a large handgun for just about anyone; on this little North Vietnamese it seemed almost cartoonish. But the way the man acted with the weapon was anything but funny. He was immediately named "Colt .45" by Dramesi.

The pistol-packing North Vietnamese officer informed Dramesi in no uncertain terms that the Zoo was a highly disciplined place. There was to be unquestioned obedience to any orders given by himself, or any one of his guards. Pushing a piece of paper in front of Dramesi, Colt .45 ordered that he sign a statement. As he had back in the Hanoi Hilton, Dramesi refused to sign anything. Colt .45 reacted in a quick and violent manner.

Pulling out the big pistol on his hip, Colt .45 cocked it, the hammer locking back into the firing position with a loud "click." Then he lifted the weapon and put the muzzle up to Dramesi's temple. He stated the obvious, that he would pull the trigger if Dramesi didn't sign the statement. Again, Dramesi refused to sign anything.

This wasn't like the other torture sessions. It wasn't going to be a long, stretched-out period of pain and anguish. If Colt .45 pulled the trigger and the gun was loaded, Dramesi wouldn't care—his brains would be blasted out the other side of his head as the heavy pistol snatched his life away from him.

If the gun wasn't loaded, then Dramesi would have called Colt's bluff, which would probably really piss him off. Then he really would load the gun. Before Colt pulled the trigger or issued another threat, there was another sound growing in volume outside the building.

The increasing wail of an air raid alert siren broke the tension. There was an American air strike coming in somewhere around Hanoi. Guards and camp personnel were running about. Forcing Dramesi along, one of the scrambling guards shoved Dramesi toward one of the buildings near the main gate of the compound. Once inside of the building, it turned out to have been a garage of some kind; the guard pushed Dramesi under the cover of a rough bed. Then the guard ran for cover himself, closing the door to the garage and locking it behind him.

There were two more prisoners under other beds in the old garage.

Ignoring the air raid going on outside, the men lost no time in getting to know each other. One of the men was a big guy, six foot four, who also knew a number of the same people whom Dramasi did from his days at the Myrtle Beach Air Force Base. The big guy was Bill Baugh, and he had been badly banged about when his F-4C had been shot down. One of Baugh's eyes was glazed and white. He could only see some shadows and movement out of it. His punch-out had been so rough that Baugh couldn't remember if he had been injured in the ejection itself or when he landed. Chances were it was on the ejection, since he also had some compressed vertebrae along with a broken jaw and cheekbone.

The other prisoner with Baugh was Don Spoon. He had been the "back-seater" in the two-place F-4 Baugh had been piloting. He had been captured along with Baugh when their plane was shot down on January 21, 1967.

The air raid ended and the guard returned to the prisoners. Together, the three men were marched at gunpoint back to where Colt .45 was waiting for them. Instead of just dealing with Dramesi, the North Vietnamese pushed papers in front of each of the three prisoners.

The demands were simple: each of the prisoners would write out a statement that they would obey the orders they were given by the North Vietnamese. Anything that they were told to do, they would have to do and he wanted signed statements from each of the men attesting to that fact. The first prisoner Colt .45 approached was Don Spoon. He refused to sign, refused to write down anything. Bill Baugh did the same thing. The astonishing change came when Colt .45 turned to Dramesi to write out the statement and sign it.

Picking up the pen, Dramesi quickly scribbled some lines across the paper and then signed it. He then told the two other prisoners to do the same thing. The other men followed Dramesi's example.

The only problem with the capitulation was that Colt .45 could apparently read some English, or he could at least recognize writing, even if it was unintelligible to him. The smile on the North Vietnamese's face faded into a frown as he picked up the pages and tried to read them. There were no words on the paper, just a few scribbled lines. His face growing redder as his rage grew, Colt .45 crumpled up the useless papers and shouted for the guard.

Since the men wouldn't cooperate by writing with their hands, they weren't going to be allowed to do anything with them, including rest. The guard took the prisoners out of the room at the point of a bayonet. Forced into a cell in the building next to the garage, the men were directed to stand in the middle of the room with their arms raised.

The prisoners were not allowed to lower their arms; they weren't allowed to rest or sleep. All they could do was stand in the room with their hands up. Though the guards didn't remain in the room watching the prisoners, they looked in at intervals to make sure the prisoners were standing where they were supposed to with their hands up. To ease their inspection of the prisoners, the guards left the door to the room open.

The prisoners soon figured out where they could stand and see out the open door well enough to tell when the guards were coming. With that warning, the men could move back to the center of the room and put their hands up. As the day wore on, it was Dramesi who suggested that they allow their arms to droop a bit when the guards looked in on them. That way the guards would think they were getting tired, not that they were supermen who could hold their arms up indefinitely.

The trick worked. Guards would look in and shout at the men to raise their lowering arms. When their evening meal was delivered to the room, the prisoners were allowed to lower their hands in order to eat. Then it was back to standing in the middle of the room with their hands up.

For three days the men stood in that room with their arms up. The only thing they could do while watching for the guards was talk. They spoke a lot over those three days, and it wasn't always on subjects that they could agree.

The North Vietnamese had been constantly indoctrinating all of the prisoners that they were criminals, that the United States had not formally declared war on North Vietnam. That made the pilots criminals in the eyes of the North Vietnamese and the world at large. When one of the POWs voiced a question about why they hadn't declared war, Dramesi had an answer.

His experience at the front lines against the Communist Iron Curtain in Europe had taught Dramesi well just what the cost of an all-out war could be. A nuclear exchange would be the inevitable result of an escalation of conflict with the Soviet Union, or Red China, in the case of Southeast Asia. He said that if the United States had declared formal war against North Vietnam, then the allies of North Vietnam, Red China and the Soviet Union, would have been forced to back up their ally and declare war on the United States. A direct confrontation between the world's superpowers would lead to one conclusion that had to be avoided—all-out nuclear war.

The tight rules of engagement the American fliers had to follow also went against the accusation that they were criminals. The pilots endangered themselves so as to avoid possible damage to civilian population centers, hospitals, and schools. Each of the prisoners there was a pretty good example of how careful the men were in their attacks; they all knew how hard it was to conduct an attack under the rules they had to follow. And it was plain that the North Vietnamese knew that the Americans wouldn't attack indiscriminately. The fact that they would hide military supplies and materials in villages and near hospitals and schools proved that. Dramesi had seen the stacks of ammunition and the vehicles hidden in a village himself.

Three days went by as the prisoners dealt with their ordeal. It was only through their own actions that they were able to lessen the torture of standing with their hands raised. Finally, guards came in the room and blindfolded each of the men. Spoon was separated from Dramesi and Baugh. The two of them were placed together in a cell of the building that the prisoners called the Office.

A third POW was in the cell when Dramesi and Baugh arrived. Shot down about six weeks after Dramesi, Don Heiliger had been the back-seater in an F-105F when it was shot down in a bombing raid. The pilot of the aircraft, Ben Pollard, had also survived ejection and been taken prisoner.

The conversations continued as the men tried to keep their own and each other's spirits up. There were conflicts as debates on subjects grew heated. But that was as much a reflection of the constant stress the prisoners were on as simple personality conflicts. Each of the men had his own stories to tell, and each had his own style in telling them. For Dramesi, he told the others what he knew about a variety of sports. From skin diving to sky diving, mountain climbing to boating, he spoke of what they were like, how you did them, and what you could expect to feel, hear, see, taste when you were involved in them. For Baugh, he was more the entertainer. He told a good joke, or a bad one for that matter. And he knew a lot about movies and television, and could mix a good drink too, though the others had to take his word on that. For Heiliger, he spoke of music and religion. But always, the situation the men all found themselves in eventually became the subject of their discussions.

The days had settled into a fairly predictable routine. There were two meals a day, though still very poor rations, and usually included the green soup Dramesi had never positively identified. The men were also allowed a washing period early in the morning where they could clean themselves and their clothes up to some extent. It was also a chance to empty and clean out their room's waste bucket, cutting back a little on the overall stink of the place. For about three hours every day, there was a quiet period where the incessant clanging and noise that was going on behind their building stopped for a while.

There were also the regular indignities thrust upon the prisoners by the guards. There were weekly searches for contraband and information. The prisoners in each cell would have to stand facing the wall, leaning up against it so that they were off-balance. Then the guards would shake them down, searching every nook and cranny of their persons, clothes, and cells.

In spite of the searches, Dramesi always kept one item hidden from the guards: his Golden Key, the bent nail that had first opened his handcuffs back during those horrible first weeks at Heartbreak that was something he kept. The bent nail was hooked into his shorts, up between his legs, and the guards always missed it.

Resistance was a constant struggle. Several of the prisoners along with Dramesi would hold back on any cooperation with the guards or the camp staff. There was the constant demand that the prisoners bow to any Vietnamese they met. Severe punishments could result for the slight bow, the lowering of the head that Dramesi and some of the others did. There were prisoners whose will to resist was less. Among other things, they would bow deeply to the guards, the staff, almost any Vietnamese they came across.

Injuries were treated minimally if at all. Food was consistently poor and insufficient. And there was the constant threat of torture, a threat carried out on a regular basis for what appeared almost any reason. The punishments for simply looking out a window or hole in the wall resulted in tortures such as the prisoners had never heard of during their military training. It wasn't a system that punished simply by the withholding of conveniences and privileges. It was an active campaign of physical abuse, extortion, and retribution. There were those among the staff of the camp, or all the camps in reality, who derived pleasure from the act of inflicting pain. Goose and Bug back at the Hanoi Hilton were far from being the only sadists in the system.

Among the various prison camps scattered in and around Hanoi, the Zoo had developed a reputation as a "bad treatment" camp. None of the places that the U.S. prisoners were kept at were particularly good, but several camps were harsher than others. These were the camps where the more resistant prisoners were kept. In the early part of 1967, there were about 120 or more American prisoners kept at the Zoo. The number of POWs moved up and down as men were moved about; and since they were kept in fairly segregated buildings, an accurate count of the POWs by the prisoners themselves was difficult. But the men resisted their captors, some more than others, and established communication nets throughout the camps.

When the guards and staff learned specifics about the communications, they acted thoroughly and with viciousness. The place was brutal, particularly after the U.S. bombing raids over North Vietnam returned in the spring of 1967. The fact that the summer of 1967 was one of the hottest and driest throughout Southeast Asia also added to the prisoners' suffering. The heat and discomfort were made worse when the walls went up between the buildings in the compound and cracks in the walls and windows were sealed. These actions were intended to cut back on interbuilding communications, but they also served to hold in the heat and prevent air circulation.

Heat was a constant agony to the prisoners. Adding to their misery was the starvation diet intended to sustain them, but little else. Rice that was badly contaminated with impurities and filth made up a major part of the food along with the small serving of pumpkin soup the prisoners received twice a day. There were the occasional fragments of pork fat in the soup, and an unknown meat paste was issued. No one really knew what the paste consisted of and none of the prisoners asked.

Even the water was of poor quality. Illness was a constant companion to the prisoners. Heat rash could drive a man almost insane from the itching and burning pain. Disabling boils were also common, hygiene being limited at best. The heat helped maintain a level of sweating that when combined with the still air of the cells, almost forced the prisoners to rot in place.

Harassment was common. In one series of ten cells in the building known as the Pool Hall, the guards would bring the soup to the prisoners and serve it at a near-scalding temperature. As soon as the last cell was served, the guards would immediately start collecting up the bowls from the first cell—whether the men were finished or not. To eat even their poor meals, the prisoners would have to force themselves to burn their mouths and tongues on soup that already wasn't a lot more than hot water.

One guard, called Magoo by the prisoners for his resemblance to a cartoon character of the time, came into some cells a couple of times a week just to beat the prisoners for no apparent reason. It was as if he had some very strange kind of exercise program for himself, one that just cost him sweat and caused the prisoners pain.

[CHAPTER 16]

COKER AND McKNIGHT

The North Vietnamese government was not simply employing sadists in order to make the lives of their prisoners hell. They knew well of the Code of Conduct and what training the U.S. forces received in it. The Vietnamese well knew that there were sections of the Code of Conduct that prevented American servicemen from cooperating with their captors. They had obtained copies of the Code and studied it carefully. It didn't specify that prisoners weren't allowed to give out more information than their name, rank, service number, and date of birth, only that they had to evade saying any more to the best of their ability.

That ability varied greatly from prisoner to prisoner. The carrot-and-the-stick approach was well known to the trained interrogators. The carrot, privileges, persuasion, and such were tried. But more often than not, the stick approach was used. One of the surprises that the Communists received from using these methods came directly from their own propaganda. They were occasionally astonished at how much abuse the prisoners were able to absorb before yielding to the demands of their captors. Americans were supposed to be weak, but some of the prisoners were strong, very strong. And they resisted torture at the hands of the North Vietnamese to a degree that had not been expected.

One of the ways that the North Vietnamese minimized the strength of the American prisoners was to separate the really resistant ones, the troublemakers, from the general population. There were also a growing number of prisoners to house as the increase in U.S. bombing raids also increased the number of fliers shot down. To this end, several new prison facilities were opened. One of these places was opened in the early summer of 1967. Located near the Yen Phu Thermal Power Plant in northern Hanoi, one of the new camps served a double purpose.

As the prisoners arrived at the Yen Phu prison facility, the North Vietnamese made certain they were seen by large numbers of civilians in the area. In addition to the civilian display of the prisoners, they were shown off to foreign journalists and diplomats as a political ploy. By making the existence of the prison facility so obvious, the North Vietnamese were able to ensure that the United States knew where some of their captured servicemen were. That made the prisoner camp safe from air strikes, and by a coincidence, made certain that the power plant was safe from aerial attack as well.

The first prisoners to arrive at the Yen Phu facility in June 1967 found the place covered with black coal dust, sooty remains left by the nearby power plant. The black dust and incredibly filthy conditions resulted in the prison being named "Dirty Bird" by the POWs. A second holding facility that opened in the vicinity of the power plant received a variety of names depending on the prisoners who were assigned to it, where they came from, and where they were eventually sent to. "Doghouse" and "Foundry" were some of the names given the new facility by prisoners coming in from outlying camps. To the POWs who had been transferred over from the original Dirty Bird, it was the Dirty Bird Annex, or Dirty Bird West.

The dark cells in each of the locations had the original windows bricked over for security. There was no real ventilation, and the summer heat, combined with the dust from the power plant, made the Dirty Bird cells particularly excruciating. The location was so bad that the North Vietnamese allowed the prisoners to be out of their cells rather than have them die of heat and dehydration. The eight-foot-high brick wall surrounding the facility kept the POWs from having much of a view of the surrounding area.

The prisoners were paraded around in the full view of the public a lot more than any of them could remember happening at any other prison. The prisoners were even sent out to the public street, under heavy guard, to perform civic duties such as street sweeping or digging. The extensive "fire drills" made the prisoners realize that they were hostages being held for the safety of the power plant. The problem was that the United States didn't know about the location of the prisoners at the power plant site. There were bombing raids against the plant, but no collateral damage to the prisons or injuries to the prisoners. This was due to the extreme accuracy of the U.S. aircraft and bombs; at least that's what the prisoners told their interrogators. Among themselves, the prisoners thought that they had been lucky indeed.

There was some limited medical service given to the prisoners at Dirty Bird, more than they had received at other camps. The filthy living conditions, combined with the unventilated rooms, very limited washing facilities, and some of the worst food served in the prison camp system offset the medical care and helped underscore the punishment aspects of the camp.

Located as it was in northern Hanoi close to the Red River, Dirty Bird was surrounded by North Vietnamese homes where people worked, lived, and hated Americans. The prison facility was close to Pham Hong Thai Street near Yen Ninh Street. That put the camp in the vicinity of a major roadway, increasing the view of the prisoners to the locals when they were paraded about. It also made it that much harder to contemplate escape by Americans who would have a very hard time blending in with the local crowds.

Navy lieutenant (junior grade) George T. Coker had been shot down the year before, on August 27, 1966, while on his fifty-fifth mission over North Vietnam. Acting as the bombardier/navigator on an A6A Intruder piloted by J. H. Fellowes, Coker and his pilot had to eject when their plane was struck by ground fire. It was either antiaircraft fire or the fragments of a nearby SAM explosion that damaged the wing of the Intruder, putting the plane into an uncontrollable spin and forcing the crew to punch out. Their parachutes were reported by a wingman on the mission. Originally listed as missing in action, both Coker and Fellowes were captured shortly after their landing. When the capture of the men was announced over Radio Hanoi, Coker's and Fellowes's status was changed to prisoner of war.

Having been a tough wrestler during his college days, George Coker was not going to fold easily to the North Vietnamese demands. His youthful attitude was an asset, and he soon developed a reputation as a strong resister. That reputation resulted in his receiving a lot of attention from his North Vietnamese captors, but he remained defiant to the best of his considerable ability.

On November 6, 1965, Air Force captain George G. McKnight was shot down over North Vietnam while flying his Douglas A1E Skyraider. One of the prisoners sent to the hellhole called Briarpatch, a camp in the mountains west of Hanoi, McKnight suffered through some of the most primitive conditions found in any of the North Vietnamese prison camps. Housed in simple brick huts with shuttered windows and no electricity or water, McKnight and a dozen of his fellows were kept literally in the dark. The prisoners at Briarpatch were some of the earliest American fliers to fall into North Vietnamese hands. Because of this, they suffered the longest.

The weather in the mountains during the winter was brutal, the prisoners only having thin blankets for protection from the cold. And they still faced the constant threat of torture at any time. The starvation rations they were placed on were barely enough to keep the men alive and weakened them further. Serious malnutrition became a problem for all Briarpatch prisoners who were forced to spend a long period at the camp. With the beginning of spring, the weather warmed, but the treatment of the prisoners became even more brutal.

In the summer months, there was a concern among the North Vietnamese that there might be a raid on Briarpatch itself. As a result, the prisoners were kept secured: handcuffed or tied to a rope much of the time. Trenches were dug and fortifications put up to help defend the camp and supposedly protect the prisoners. There were even deep holes dug in the dirt floors underneath the prisoners' bunks, supposedly to give the men a bomb shelter in case of an air raid. The holes were also found to be excellent punishments to be inflicted on the prisoners by the guards. McKnight was one of the men forced to remain in one of those dirt holes for a month for trying to communicate with other prisoners. The holes were dark and wet, the walls of the pits crawling with vermin.

In spite of the treatment and living conditions, George McKnight was able to resist the North Vietnamese to the point that they considered him one of the hardliner prisoners, one of the men who set a bad example for the other prisoners. A transfer to another prison camp would be an improvement of sorts for McKnight. He ended up being one of the men eventually sent to Dirty Bird when that facility was opened.

At Dirty Bird as well as all of the other prison camps, the intent of the North Vietnamese was to make the prisoners feel totally helpless in the day-to-day running of their lives. The North Vietnamese intended that the prisoners feel completely under the control of their captors.

The prisoners resisted such control as much as they could. In some of the prisoners, there was still the seed of the ultimate resistance to their captors—escape. Escape from any camp in North Vietnam was hard to even consider. One big problem for the prisoners was specific knowledge about just where they were. For the most part, they had no positive idea of their exact location, which made planning an escape route particularly difficult.

Like so many of the other prisoners at Dirty Bird, George McKnight was allowed into the small yard behind his cell. To make certain that the difficult prisoner would still be there when the guard returned, McKnight was shackled by one wrist to an ankle. Finding a piece of wire, McKnight learned to open his shackles. Close by was George Coker, also a hard case and also shackled. With his own wire, Coker was able to free himself and the two started to meet on an almost daily basis.

Having been one of the prisoners taken from the camp on trips to get water, McKnight told Coker about what he had seen in the local area. There was a large bridge nearby, one made of steel girders with distinctive structural details. It was probably the Doumer Bridge, McKnight had thought. As a navigator who had spent a lot of time flying over the Hanoi area, Coker felt certain that McKnight was correct in his identification. It was the Paul Doumer Bridge in Hanoi (now known as the Long Bien Bridge), and had been a major target. Knowing the landmark of the bridge told Coker how far the camp was in relation to the Red River, the main waterway the bridge crossed. That gave the men their present location with fair accuracy. Dirty Bird was only a few blocks from the river—three or four at the most, according to Coker. Even in the heavily populated area, they might be able to cross such a distance and get to the water without being detected.

The Red River was a major transportation route through North Vietnam. The muddy brown waters ran from the mountains to the northwest and passed along the northern side of Hanoi. From there, the river ran to the southeast, through the countryside of North Vietnam, to empty into the South China Sea at the Gulf on Tonkin. Patrolling in the Gulf waters would be the ships of the U.S. Seventh Fleet.

As a Navy officer, Coker was very familiar with the ships patrolling off the coast of North Vietnam. If they could reach the Gulf of Tonkin, the chances of them being picked up by some U.S. vessel were very good, particularly if they could make their way out to sea to the location known as Yankee Station.

Together, the men decided to escape. The worst thing that might happen was that they were killed in the attempt, but the possibility of freedom made that risk seem a very reasonable one to them. On a practical basis, they knew their chances of success were slim; odds of 1 chance in 1,000 of a successful escape were probably optimistic, but it was still a chance. Dismal as they were, those odds still seemed better than the chances of continued survival in a North Vietnamese prison camp.

There were other aspects of the situation that worked in the favor of the two men. From his time spent at the Zoo, Coker had been shown by another prisoner how to remove the lock from the cell doors. The security arrangements for the doors at Dirty Bird were much the same as they had been at the Zoo. Certain that he could open the doors to the cell, Coker knew that he could get them both out of the building.

Getting over the wall surrounding Dirty Bird didn't strike McKnight as too great an obstacle to their getting out of the camp. Getting past the large number of people he had seen around the outside of Dirty Bird could be the real problem. Then there was the estimated sixty miles of river that Coker figured they would have to travel to make it down to the ocean. The general plan was to swim down the river at night, hole up during the day, and finally steal a boat to take them out to the ships at Yankee Station. Their total travel time was estimated at eight days. They could forage for food; their military training and what they had already been eating in the camps kept either man from being squeamish about what could be considered edible. At worst, they could drink the river water if they had to. It would only take them about three or four nights to get to the river's mouth. There, they could overpower the crew of a small boat, or just steal one from where it was tied up, and head out to sea.

The plan didn't really appeal to McKnight at first. But he remembered a squadron commander he'd had who had always considered the ideas that his juniors brought to him. If an idea seemed impossible, then others wouldn't think it could be done, so give it a try.

The planning stage of the escape lasted only about a week. The date was set for the night of October 12, 1967, Columbus Day back in the States. The day before their planned escape, both Coker and McKnight tested the locks on their cell doors to make certain that they could open them. It turned into a near disaster for McKnight.

The locks on the outside of the cell doors were secure to anything the prisoners could do to them. But the shackle that the locks closed could be attacked from the inside of the cell door. When McKnight loosened the pin on the inside of his door, it got away from him. The weight of the lock pulled the shackle pin through the door before McKnight could get a grip on it. Now the lock was hanging down at the end of its chain, still closed on the shackle. He couldn't open the door and just grab the lock and put it back into place, there wasn't enough slack in the system to allow him to do that.

Prying open the peephole cover, McKnight stretched his arm out and felt for the lock. It was a very vulnerable moment as he knew that a guard could come by at any second and see his arm scrabbling for the lock. The moments passed as McKnight desperately reached for the lock, searching by touch only. Finally, his fingers grasped the errant chunk of metal. In the last moments of his working on the lock, McKnight was certain he would be caught. By feel, he was able to line things up and stuff the shackle back into the hole in the door. With a nail, he secured the lock mechanism back into the door, loose enough that he wouldn't have any difficulty taking it out the next night. Then he leaned back and remembered how to breathe.

The next day seemed to crawl by for both men. The guards seemed to pay particular attention to McKnight. His cell was searched five times. The guards went through his meager belongings without specifying what they expected to find. If the man had made any physical preparations for their escape attempt, gathering food, supplies, and such, the guards would have found them and the plan foiled before it had really begun.

The one preparation McKnight had already sweated through was now causing him more anxiety. He felt for certain that at any moment, the weakened lock on his door would pull off into a guard's hand. But the shackle held. The night finally came. It was time for the two men to make their final preparations and escape.

[CHAPTER 17]

BID FOR FREEDOM

While the nightly propaganda broadcasts were coming out of the speakers in each cell, Coker and McKnight made their final preparations. To help disguise the fact that they were gone, the men had been sleeping under a blanket each night in spite of the heat. The guards looking into the cell through the peephole grew used to seeing little more than a lump in the darkness. When the night of October 12 fell, the men arranged their extra clothing, blanket, and food bowls under the covers. The makeshift dummies were adequate, or at least better than nothing.

The first one out of his cell was Coker. After releasing the mechanism, he put the lock back up on the door after passing through. Once in the outer hallway, Coker went over to McKnight's cell and softly called out to him. Once they had put the lock back up on McKnight's door, the two men slipped off down the hall.

Moving along a tight corridor that ran along the wall of the prison building, McKnight led the escape out into the moonless night. The evening was dark, but the sky clear. With there being so few lights in

Hanoi at the time, there was little to block the view of the stars. The brilliant points of light shone down on the two men making their way to a low wall.

Climbing up onto the wall allowed the escapees to get to a point where they could reach the roof of the building. To help hide their faces and hands from view, they scooped up the handfuls of soot that was everywhere and used it to darken their white skin. Once smeared with the camouflage, they moved across the roof to another wall, dropping quietly down onto it. That wall gave them access to the roof of another building, the far end of which had a pipe leading down into a coal bunker.

Sliding down the pipe and clambering down the pile of coal put the two men up against an outer wall of the compound. On the other side of the wall was freedom, or at least the rest of the city of Hanoi. The barbed wire across the top of the wall was not much of an obstacle to the men who had already dared so much. Holding the strands apart for one another, they climbed up.

The side street that the wall ran along was dark, but not yet completely deserted. There were some locals moving along on their own business, but none of them looked up to see the two darkened men hiding in the shadows. Waiting until everyone had passed, Coker and McKnight dropped off the wall. Remaining in the shadows as much as possible, the two men moved off down the street. Ducking into the doorway of an empty building, the two men stopped to get a better idea of their bearings and to try and calm down their rapidly beating hearts.

The sudden feeling of freedom was exhilarating. McKnight felt as if he could take fifty-foot bounds, but they were still well inside the city proper. The two men could be discovered at any moment so they quickly continued their drive to the river. They had to cross one of Hanoi's main roads that lay between themselves and the Red River, but their luck held as they ran. Crossing the embankments of a wide ditch put them into the wetlands that bordered the river. Just a short distance away was the looming structure of the Doumer Bridge.

Brilliant lights flickered and sparks flew from the girders of the bridge as work crews labored to repair the damage done by U.S. air attacks. The lights of the acetylene torches kept the workers from being able to see into the darkness as the two men slipped along the riverbank to reach a point under the bridge itself. Then there was a sudden movement in the darkness. In the starlight, the men could see the gleam off a round rifle barrel. They had been caught by a man coming out of the shadows. Their bid for freedom was over within minutes of their escape.

Then the "armed guard" stepped further out of the shadows and the men could more clearly see the gleam of light on the horns of the cow. The animal didn't care at all as the two relieved escapees continued with their run.

A train moved across the Doumer Bridge, the clanking, squealing noise of its movement hiding the two men as they moved into the shadows under the bridge. Hidden in the darkness, the men completed their last preparations before entering the water. Using the cord from their pajamalike trousers, Coker and McKnight tied their wrists to each other. From Coker's left wrist a cord reached over to McKnight's right wrist. Now there was less chance the two men would get separated in the muddy waters of the river.

The two men did not want to get separated if at all possible. Working as a team gave them a greater chance of success than if they tried to escape separately. One man could help the other as they went across the countryside; while one slept, the other could stand watch. And there was just the mutual moral support the two men could give each other on their desperate quest for freedom. Slipping into the warm waters of the Red River, they both struck out, swimming with the downstream current.

The channel of the river where the men entered was less than about one hundred yards wide. Once they reached the main channel, the river opened up to nearly a half-mile width. Moving out farther into mid-channel, the men swam with the four- to five-mile-per-hour current as the waters moved to the distant Gulf of Tonkin. There were sampans tied up along both riverbanks, making the idea of eventually stealing a boat seem much more reasonable. The scattered lights of campfires and lanterns also showed that the people of North Vietnam lived along the riverbanks. They would have to hide from the locals when it became light, but for the time being they would just be able to swim with the river.

Now that they had reached one of their major objectives, McKnight felt even stronger about their chances of making it. They didn't need to steal a boat; he felt strong enough to swim all the way across the Pacific to San Francisco.

At the light started to grow in the east, Coker felt that the pair had traveled about fifteen miles from the point where they had entered the river. It was getting to be time to find a lay-up point where they could hide during the day. When they crawled out onto the north bank of the river, they found the area barren. There were no plants or structures where they could hide, not even a large pile of rocks. Getting back into the water, the two men continued to swim downstream as the daylight grew brighter fast.

With the light of dawn coming swiftly, the two men had to make do with whatever hiding place they could find. There were no drifting piles of brush or trees moving down the river, so there was no way they could hide in the water. Two bobbing heads out in an open river would get the attention of anyone in normal times; in a nation at war it would probably get both men shot.

Getting out of the water and climbing up the steep riverbank, the two men made a try at creating their own hiding place. There was no cover, only the claylike soil of the ground itself. With their hands, the two men clawed at the soil, digging away as fast as they could.

Out on the water behind them, the desperately digging men heard a sound. Not pausing in his work, Coker turned to look out into the river. A sampan was going by; the people on board stared up at the two men on the riverbank. The people on the sampan didn't cry out, didn't point or shout, they just stared at the two digging men as the sampan continued on with the current.

With at least some kind of hole dug out of the bank, the two men settled in to the cover they had made for themselves. Only someone looking down from the top of the riverbank would be able to see where they were hidden, and the mudflat that they had seen stretching out from the back of the bank made that seem unlikely. It was hard to rest, but they both knew they had to. While they lay in the trench, Coker told McKnight everything he could about the layout of the river. If something happened to separate the men, he wanted to be certain that his partner could follow the proper course out to the ocean. As McKnight was finally slipping off to sleep, Coker said something a little out of the ordinary. He reminded McKnight that it was the day after Columbus Day, which had fallen on a Thursday that year. It was Friday the Thirteenth.

Woken from sleep by Coker, McKnight was told that the escape attempt was over. Not sure of just what his partner was talking about, he questioned the statement. An old man had come up to fish in the river just a short time earlier. He had stepped up to the top of the riverbank and looked directly down at the two men. Letting out a shout of fear, the old man had taken off, waving his arms and his fishing pole.

That was the time the two men thought would be the most dangerous of their escape: if they were caught by an angry mob of locals. Both men knew very well the orchestrated near-riots that had been caused by the POWs being paraded down the streets of Hanoi. At those times, armed military men had been able to control the worst of the crowd's fury. Out in the open and alone, Coker and McKnight knew that they might be lynched.

Getting up out of their hole, the two men looked around for another escape route, but the land was just as open as it had been when they climbed in. A noisy crowd quickly gathered on top of the river-bank, looking down at the two men. One person in the crowd had a weapon, but he was so shook up by the appearance of the prisoners and the noise of the mob that he couldn't properly load it. With slow, careful movements, the two POWs raised their hands in surrender.

Surviving the shouting mob, Coker and McKnight were turned over to the military, who took them away. They were transported to the Hanoi Hilton, where they both underwent an interrogation about their escape. Open about what they had done, McKnight didn't cooperate with the interrogators as much as he simply told them the truth. Both men expected to die in prison at the hands of the North Vietnamese. The tortures they had faced were ample evidence of what they could expect, and neither of them figured things would get any better. Escape was a tremendous risk, but it wasn't any worse than remaining prisoners.

Astonishingly, there was no real torture applied to either man. There had been no escape committee, no organization of prisoners that had aided the men. It was very nearly a target of opportunity, and the North Vietnamese seemed to recognize that. Only a few days went by before Coker and McKnight were returned to Dirty Bird.

The rest of the prisoners at Dirty Bird knew that something had happened, but had no real information as to just what had taken place. What was obvious was the reaction of the guards and the staff. They were nervous about something, and there were suddenly a number of apparently high-ranking North Vietnamese officers walking about the place.

The first action taken by the guards was to place leg irons on all of the prisoners while they were still in their cells. These weren't the horribly heavy punishment irons, just leg shackles for the most part. In addition to securing the legs of the prisoners, their cells were addressed. The cell doors had reinforcing bolts put through them to hold the locking mechanisms securely in place. Not all of the prisoners had known how to open their doors at will, and now it didn't matter.

There were no widespread punishments, no purges or wholesale torture, just the increase in security of the prisoners and the camp as a whole. Suspecting an escape, the prisoners tried to take a head count among themselves. They noticed a missing man, but he was not Coker or McKnight. One of the prisoners had been far too ill to make an escape attempt, but he was missing. It turned out that the guards and staff had taken the man away to use in a propaganda piece.

The use of the prisoners as hostages to help protect the power plant had proven to be a failure. The U.S. air strikes had continued against both the plant and the nearby bridge. The facility known as Dirty Bird was not a secure one and wasn't worth the bother to improve it. By the end of October, all the prisoners held at Dirty Bird had been placed at other facilities. Most of the prisoners were sent to the Hanoi Hilton, where they ended up in the Vegas location.

It wasn't very long before the news about who had actually made the Dirty Bird escape attempt made it into the prisoner communications net. As the story spread to the other camps, the morale of the prisoners was raised by the news. The two escapees received the admiration and respect of their fellow prisoners for what they had tried to do. It was thought that if the news about what was really happening to the POWs in North Vietnam, the torture, the mistreatment, the terrible living conditions, made it to the people of the United States, the military and the politicians would take action. But for that news to get out, first POWs had to get back to the States. Nineteen sixty-seven was not going to be the year that they did.

For Coker and McKnight personally, they were now considered among the worst of the incorrigibles among the prisoner population. When the Dirty Bird camp was closed, a new prison facility was opened. This was a location where the hardliners among the prisoners could be isolated from the rest of their community. It was a very small but secure location, a courtyard behind the Ministry of Defense building. The place was intended to be a dungeon, and it fulfilled that role. The cells were small and cramped. There was no bunk, only a concrete platform raised up from the floor to act as a bed. Besides the sleeping platform the cells had about a four-foot-square area for the prisoners to stand. Individually, the cells were about nine feet long and less than half that wide. They were all sunken below ground level with no windows. Only a dim electric bulb, estimated at being less than ten watts by one of the prisoners, burned twenty-four hours a day. What ventilation there was came from a small space below the cell door and a few pencil-sized holes through a steel plate above the door.

Ten of the cells were in one building in a small courtyard; a second, smaller building was a short distance away from the first, at a right angle to it. The smaller building had three additional cells; the central one was used as a storeroom. The prisoners' bathing area outside in the courtyard shared the space with a cesspool and a pigsty in the corner next to the latrine. It was a dirty, stinking location. It soon gained the name "Alcatraz" from the prisoners who lived there.

For the men who lived at Alcatraz, the situation for the first few months of their confinement there was not as severe as they had expected. There were normal interrogations, but they were not accompanied by the extended periods of severe torture that all of the prisoners had experienced at other camps. Discipline was strict and the enforced isolation of the prisoners was a punishment in itself. The prisoners were allowed very little time outside of the cells. Solitude took its toll on each of the men in his own way. Boredom and claustrophobia were real problems.

Food was as bad as at many of the other camps. Meals were little more than a bowl of cabbage or pumpkin soup, with a piece of pig fat floating in it on rare occasions. Malnutrition and the accompanying infections, disease, and diarrhea left the men weak and suffering. It was a test of the willpower of each of the prisoners that they were able to remain sane in their wretched environment.

To add to the individual's misery, each man was put in leg irons for additional security. For fifteen or more hours a day, the men were re-strained by the iron shackles put around their ankles. The iron assem-blies weighed from two to twenty pounds and helped keep the men from sleeping even on the poor comfort of their concrete bunks.

Within a few months of the camp being activated, the guards didn't even bother to put the leg irons on the men at night; they just pushed them under the door and expect each prisoner to secure them in place. The guards would watch through the peepholes of the cell door to make certain that the prisoner within donned his restraints. Then they would move on to the next cell. Some prisoners became quite adept at clicking the metal of the restraints so that it appeared they were locked in place. But the padlocks had not been closed se-curely and when the guards left, the leg irons were loosened.

These were some of the small victories among the prisoner popu-lation of Alcatraz. Messages tapped out in a code that all the prisoners knew gave them the ability to communicate between cells. One man would take the message from one wall and transfer it to the cell on his opposite side. Peering under the doors gave some idea of who else was held in the facility, another small fight won against the isolation of the place.

Nearly a dozen prisoners, almost all of them high-ranking POWs, made up the population of Alcatraz for almost two years. Among the POW leadership was a pair of troublemakers, George McKnight and George Coker. They would not be the last POWs to make a serious escape attempt from North Vietnam.

[CHAPTER 18]

THE ZOO ANNEX

Nineteen sixty-eight was a pivotal year for the war in Southeast Asia. President Lyndon Johnson announced in March that he would not seek reelection to the office of president of the United States. As a lure to get the North Vietnamese to cooperate, President Johnson called a partial halt to the bombing of targets in North Vietnam. With the halt, Johnson invited the North Vietnamese government in Hanoi to come to the negotiation table in order to work out a temporary cease-fire to the fighting in Southeast Asia. There was real hope in some circles that the overtures would result in the war soon coming to an end, but the Communist government of North Vietnam simply played the Americans along to gain time and concessions.

To the North Vietnamese, the announcements by President Johnson were interpreted to mean that the Communists were winning the war. That is how the news was delivered to the prisoners. As far as the North Vietnamese were concerned, the antiwar movement back in the United States was what was going to win the war for them. All they had to do was hold out long enough, and the prisoners would remain in captivity for as long as the Communists thought necessary.

There had already been a large increase in the number of POWs being held in North Vietnam. There had been two dozen fliers shot down and imprisoned in August and again in October 1967 alone. To hold this increasing population in secure facilities, the North Vietnamese opened a number of additional prison camps. The Zoo was full to capacity by the fall of 1967. Squeezing additional prisoners into cramped quarters wasn't held up by the North Vietnamese out of a concern for their welfare. Security considerations were a major concern.

An additional facility was opened next to the Zoo in mid-October 1967. The new facility shared a wall with the original Zoo compound, but otherwise operated as a completely separate camp. The new facility consisted of several cellblock buildings facing a central pond along with a number of interrogation rooms and administrative facilities. The cell buildings were separated internally into two fairly large holding rooms, each room being about seventeen by twenty feet in size. The rooms were intended to hold at least four and up to nine prisoners each.

The filthy central pond was soon labeled Lake Fester by the prisoners. The camp itself was called the Zoo Annex. Outside of being able to communicate with the other inmates of a cell, there was little else that gave the Zoo Annex's prisoners a better chance of survival. The food remained poor in quality and limited in portion. Communist indoctrination of the prisoners remained a heavy influence on their daily lives, but the interrogation and torture sessions were relatively light in comparison to past experiences. There were daily activities that allowed the prisoners to get out of their cells and into the daylight. These activities included maintaining a garden as well as general cleanup and trash details.

Most of the population of the Zoo Annex was made up of junior officers, men with a rank of O-3 (Air Force captain/navy lieutenant) and below. This was in part to separate the younger men from the leadership and experience of the older officers. It also disrupted the chain of command that had built up in the camp.

The SRO among the POWs held at the Zoo Annex was Air Force major Konrad W. Trautman. Trautman had been a combat pilot during the Korean War, having flown twenty combat missions in the F-84E jet. On his sixty-second mission over Vietnam, he was shot down while flying close to Hanoi on October 5, 1967. He was a resident of the Hanoi Hilton by that evening.

John Dramesi was in one of the last groups of prisoners to be transferred from the Zoo. Security considerations for the prisoner transfer were simple enough: Dramesi was blindfolded and led from the facility. Having examined the Zoo facility in as much detail as he could, Dramesi was very familiar with the distances within the compound, including the steps it took to get to the southeastern wall; he had considered that wall as a possible exit point for an escape. When he was led from the Zoo, Dramesi paid careful attention to how much time it took to walk him from one place to another. When he heard a gate opening, he knew that they had reached the Zoon Annex. After entering a building, the blindfold was taken off and Dramesi could finally see his surroundings.

In his arrival discussions with one of the North Vietnamese camp staff, Dramesi denied having considered escape. Through a large open door, he could see a high wall topped with strands of barbed wire. When the staff member said that escape would be difficult, Dramesi agreed.

After their discussions were over, Dramesi was told that he would be living with eight other prisoners. As far as Dramesi was concerned, that was fine, but it wasn't as if he could have done anything about it anyway. He knew that the North Vietnamese could do with him as they wished, and he said as much. The tone of the staff member suggested that Dramesi should not be quite as argumentative, but rather grateful. Then the prisoner was led from the room.

The new cell was large and had a pair of iron doors securing it. When he went in, Dramnesi found himself in the center of a large group of prisoners. The men were able to freely talk to one another, something Dramesi hadn't experienced in a while. Recognizing Al Meyer and two other men he knew, Dramesi was quickly introduced to the rest of the men. In an unexpected development, Dramesi found himself the senior ranking officer among the prisoners in the cell. Eventually, a clarification on the seniority policy—that it was based on a man's rank when he was shot down—would make another man SRO for the cell. But for a time, Dramesi was in charge of cell #6.

Only a few days after arriving, Dramesi and the rest of the men from his cell were transferred into another room within the Zoo Annex. While being moved along by the guards, Dramesi paid close attention to the doors sealing off the new cell. They were metal and made up of vertical panels. It looked to Dramesi as if the doors could be made to open by lifting them up a short distance while pushing them away from their frames. If it worked, it looked as if the doors could be opened by actually lifting them free of their hinges.

Considering the possibilities, Dramesi decided to check out the door while it remained open and the guards were away for the moment. His suspicions were correct. In fact, it took too little effort, because suddenly Dramesi found himself holding up part of a door that had slipped completely free of the frame.

Before a guard could come in and discover what he had done, Dramesi's shocked cellmates shook off their startled stares and helped him rehang the door. The door was back in place on its hinges just as a guard arrived.

In very quick order, Dramesi had organized the cell into two-man teams to work together for an escape. The idea behind the teams was to have two men working together who were close to the same height. It would be hard for any casual observer to identify the height of a pair of men walking at a distance, whether they were five-four or six-four, if they were both the same height to start with. Such were the little details he considered to give possible escapees an edge in passing through the Vietnamese community.

The proven ability to remove the door to the cell had excited the men about the possibility of escape. The only one left out of the possibility of escaping from the Zoo Annex was Al Meyer because of the injury to his leg. The idea of an escape was an uplifting one for the morale of everyone in the building. As the suggestion for a planned escape was spread through the cells everyone tended to voice agreement and enthusiasm. Dramesi was now not only his cell's SRO, he was also the head of the escape committee.

As time went by and preparations continued, setbacks plagued the overall plan of escape for the group. To keep the prisoners from organizing and cooperating with each other too much, the North Vietnamese rotated men at random from cell to cell.

Grumbling among the prisoners grew as escape enthusiasm waned. Weekly inspections by the North Vietnamese meant that nothing regarding a possible plan could be written down. It was also very hard to hide any stockpiling of escape materials or supplies. People started rebelling against the assignments given to them by the escape committee, or really just Dramesi as many of the prisoners considered them to both be the same thing. Disagreements grew and the men started working against one another.

A number of the prisoners started to object to the scrounging of materials throughout the camp. They either didn't want to help hide the pickup of an object, such as a railroad spike, iron bars, and such, or they didn't want to smuggle the object into the cells and try to hide it. Many of the excuses given for the failure to cooperate sounded about the same. Things boiled down to many of the men not wanting to risk being caught by the enemy blatantly breaking the rules of the camp. Things had been bad enough when a prisoner was just being interrogated and he resisted. To work directly against the enemy in an active manner, the image of the punishments that might be brought to bear terrified some of the prisoners.

In spite of the initial wave of support, the popularity of an escape lost most of its appeal to the bulk of the prisoner population in the Zoo

Annex. Prisoners who had originally agreed with the planning and preparation were now either just straightforward backing out or putting demands on what they would need in order to escape. Some of the items were excessive to the point of being ridiculous. The worst of the "minimum requirements" included a two-way radio. Some items, knives, a compass, were reasonable and even possible to acquire. Knives could be made from sharpened pieces of metal with strips of bamboo tied in place as a handle. As far as a compass went, the North Vietnamese had unwittingly supplied the means for making one.

In each cell there was a small loudspeaker over which were broadcast propaganda messages, sometimes Radio Hanoi programs, and even music. On the speakers within the easily disassembled boxes were fairly powerful permanent magnets. Simply drawing a piece of steel such as a nail over the speaker magnet would magnetize it. Hanging the nail from a string would be all it would take to turn it into a crude but effective compass.

But the radio was a killer requirement, and the man who demanded that one be available for an escape knew it. It was the fear of torture that made some men grasp at straws so as not to have to escape. Arguments flew back and forth about even the feasibility of an escape. There had been fantasy ideas earlier about killing the guards, stealing a vehicle or an aircraft, and leaving North Vietnam behind. Those had just been the imaginations of men who had no real ability to affect their situation. For Dramesi, it wasn't a fantasy, it wasn't fiction. He had every intention of escaping. And besides, the Code of Conduct required it.

Some of the concerns the other prisoners had regarding punishment torture were very real ones. The Zoo Annex hadn't been going through a lot of active torture during some of 1968, but that wasn't the case in the Zoo. One of the most aggressive of the torturers in the Zoo was not even a North Vietnamese. The stories of what "Fidel" and his crony "Chico" and others did to prisoners were widely known among the populations of both camps but direct experience with the men was limited to less than twenty in the Zoo.

Referred to as the Cuban Program by the United States Department of Defense, Fidel and Chico were Cuban nationals who may have been in North Vietnam to evaluate interrogation methods. As Fidel stated to the POWs who had the misfortune to come under his direct control, his purpose was to obtain the total submission of the prisoners. His intention was to break the men, completely and thoroughly.

Fidel was tall and slim, reportedly a good-looking individual. He had a solid idea of his own importance as he swaggered around the camp. Even the camp commandant deferred to him. The prisoners simply learned to fear the man. Using a combination of heavy torture and psychological pressure, Fidel abused the prisoners to a point where even the North Vietnamese became eventually appalled. His torture sessions were so severe that three prisoners disappeared, reportedly taken away for "treatment" but most likely tortured to near-death. They never recovered. Other prisoners were beaten to the point where their fellows couldn't see how they could still be alive. But they did live, and the story of the Fidel the Cuban could terrify men who had already survived severe torture at the hands of the North Vietnamese.

Dramesi was an active, aggressive fighter; he attacked problems head-on whenever possible, though he always considered his course of action, studied a problem, and meticulously learned everything that he could in order to stack the deck in his favor. He wanted to escape because that was one of the things demanded of a soldier by the Code of Conduct. Many of the other prisoners were much more reserved in their actions. They had already gone through hardships that few outside of North Vietnam would have believed. The threat to the prisoners' lives as represented by individuals such as Fidel were very real ones. Arguments about the possible success, or most likely lack of success, of an escape attempt grew heated among the prisoners.

Actually getting out of a cell was not as great a problem as it first appeared. That argument couldn't be brought up by the prisoners who had seen Dramesi take the door off its hinges his first day. He had also spent a great deal of time working on the wooden outer doors of the cells, practically cutting one free with an improvised tool. In addition to their own efforts, the prisoners could also see the effect of the occasional sloppy attitude on the part of the guards. The door to the cell that Trautman shared with three other prisoners had been left unlocked one night by a guard. The thought of being able to just walk out the door had weighed on the thoughts of the prisoners all night, but none had taken advantage of the situation.

The reservations of the prisoners centered not just on getting out of the cell, but on getting past the population of Hanoi. In a message passed on to the other prisoners regarding the unlocked cell door, Trautman questioned just where they could have gone after leaving the room. The prisoners had some idea of where they were in relation to the Red River and other landmarks but intelligence was limited. The population in the city surrounding them was on the lookout for all Americans; the North Vietnamese government offered a standing reward for a captured flier. A local who caught himself a downed American could receive as much as the equivalent of $1,500 U.S., a significant amount in a country where most lived in poverty.

The one problem that was constantly brought up was the difficulty a Westerner would have in passing though an Asian city. In spite of their poor diet reducing the weight of any of the prisoners to a shadow of what they had been, most of the men were taller than any of the locals. The average North Vietnamese was a black-haired, slender Asian only about five foot two inches tall. No matter how thin, there was no mistaking the height of the average Westerner.

In spite of the protests, Dramesi knew that he could pass by the average North Vietnamese. He had already done so once with very limited preparations. People simply weren't that curious about someone walking by, even if they were taller than average. When they broke out of Dirty Bird, Coker and McKnight had also learned it was possible to pass through a population center such as a city. But the men in cell #6 with Dramesi didn't have that information. Instead, they raised other problems with the cross-country escape.

There was the problem of the local environment escapees would have to go through if they managed to get out of the city. At best, it would be a difficult trek for the malnourished men. Plus the nature of North Vietnam would be working against them. An example of the savage nature of the land was shown very well when one of the prisoners killed a poisonous snake that had slipped into the cell with them. The next day, the snake's carcass was tossed onto a fence when the men went out to empty their toilet buckets. In three hours, the body of the snake was gone; it had been devoured by the insects that swarmed over the feast.

A number of the prisoners had physical disabilities from either their shoot-down ejections, or the treatment they had received at the hands of the North Vietnamese. These were pointed out as being reasons that some individuals wouldn't be able to escape with Dramesi. It was an excuse, but one that he had to accept. Tired of the discouraging attitude of his fellow prisoners, Dramesi asked for a straightforward answer from the men he shared a cell with—Who would be willing to escape with him? One man agreed to go.

CHAPTER 19

PLANNING AND PREPARATION

Air Force captain Edwin Lee Atterberry had been on board an RF-4C photo reconnaissance aircraft during the first air attack on the Paul Doumer Bridge in Hanoi on August 11, 1967. Both Atterberry's plane and an F-105D were brought down by enemy fire during the attack. Ed Atterberry and Captain Thomas V. Parrott ejected from their stricken RF-4C. Captain Thomas Norris also successfully ejected from his F-105D. All three men landed safely but were quickly taken captive by the North Vietnamese. These actions took place only four months after John Dramesi was shot down.

It was several months later that Ed Atterberry became one of the prisoners being held in cell #6 at the Zoo Annex. Out of all of the prisoners held in that cell, he was the only one to stand up and agree to escape with John Dramesi. During many of the arguments for and against an escape attempt, Ed Atterberry had remained relatively quiet. But when it finally came down to a decision to act one way or another, he spoke up.

When it came to making preparations for the escape, it was only

Atterberry who was active in helping Dramesi. Considerations about their physical situation caused Dramesi to make major changes in the plan for getting out of the prison camp. Though the men knew they could get out through the iron doors to the cell, it was the outer wooden doors that were giving them trouble. Dramesi had made cuts along the doors to weaken them, but the work was slower going than it had been originally, even with Atterberry helping. There were other factors that made him reevaluate their possible exit strategy. There was a wall around the courtyard of their building that they would have to get over during the escape, and it wouldn't be their only obstacle. There was a second, higher wall around the entire prison complex. On top of that wall were additional problems for the passage of the escapees: five strands of barbed wire strung on metal poles extended the length of the wall. Besides the barbed wire, there were two bare electrical wires held up one above the other on insulated posts.

The best chance would be if the men escaped through the roof of their building. That way, they would be able to look down into the Annex compound and watch for the two guards who were known to patrol the area at night. Additionally, the elevated position of being on the roof would allow the men to remain well concealed from any observation by people on the ground as they waited for their best opportunity to escape the area.

There were four ventilation holes in the cell's ceiling. The holes were large enough for a man to pass through so the North Vietnamese had blocked them with metal grids. The grids were made up of interlacing strands of barbed wire, five strands in one direction with five or six strands running in the other direction and interwoven with the first. It would normally be a formidable obstacle for men to get through with their bare hands. But Dramesi had more than his bare hands to work with. He had two iron bars and a railroad spike available to him among the materials he had been scrounging throughout the Zoo Annex. It was the risk of picking up some of these materials that had started some of the prisoners actively moving away from

Dramesi and his escape plans. Now that he had them, the ceiling looked to be the way to go. The door panels were abandoned as the avenue of escape.

With the decision made to go out through the ceiling, another problem had to be addressed. The ceiling in the Zoo Annex cell where Dramesi was being held was slightly more than twelve feet high. Even standing on someone's shoulders wouldn't put Dramesi up high enough to get the leverage he needed to attack the barbed wire grid. The problem was a challenge and even the men who had thought the ceiling should not be touched now wrestled with how to do it. One of the prisoners came up with a workable solution.

To get Dramesi up high enough to move the grid away from the opening, four men would hold a pallet over their heads. They couldn't do it for very long, but Dramesi only worked on the escape route about ten minutes each day. The idea worked and he was able to fold the wire grid back and climb up into the ceiling. The tiles that made up the roof of the building could be removed from the inside of the ceiling. Once outside, Dramesi and Atterberry could replace the tiles, covering over their avenue of escape. Anything that would help hide their escape would give the men that much longer to move away from the camp.

The two men continued to work hard to move the odds of a successful escape in their favor. In spite of the poor diet, they started working out in order to build up their strength and endurance. Though their exercise area in the cell was very restricted they both jogged in very small circles until they had run a mile and a half each day.

Though the rest of the prisoners had strong reservations about the possibility of a successful escape, they still assisted Dramesi and Atterberry in their preparations. Cooperation varied with the circumstances. One day several bags of unshelled raw peanuts were delivered to the cell by one of the guards. The peanuts were in addition to the normal ration issued to the prisoners and were a welcome source of protein. As the prisoners in cell #6 were shelling the nuts, one of them pointed out that they would be a good escape food since they didn't take up much room and wouldn't spoil as quickly as other foods would. Two food bags had already been made by Dramesi and Atterberry for the escape. Long and slender with a double lining, the cloth bags could be drawn closed with a string. Within a short time, both Dramesi and Atterberry had filled the bags with raw nuts. The other prisoners grumbled a bit about having to give up a food source but accepted the escape preparations.

When small amounts of roasted nuts arrived with the meals several times during the week, Dramesi decided the cooked items might last longer than the raw ones they had already bagged. This was when some of the cooperation from the other prisoners drew to a close. Asked to trade their ration of roasted nuts for raw ones, the rest of the prisoners refused. Their excuses varied, but the results were the same.

The supply cache for the escape grew and Dramesi had found an excellent hiding place. The walls between the two cells in the building only went up to the ceiling. Above the ceiling, the entire building "attic" was open when Dramesi went up through the ventilation opening. By tying a line to an empty peanut bag, Dramesi would lower the materials into the space between the two cell walls. Attaching the line to a brace made as sure a hiding place as could be expected. Dramesi felt sure the supplies were hidden well enough that they wouldn't be discovered even if someone had to work on the roof of the building.

Though there were lapses in cooperation by the other prisoners, they still helped Dramesi and Atterberry in a number of ways. They continued hoisting Dramesi up so that he could climb through the ceiling opening. On one of his trips, Dramesi checked the roof exit possibilities by lifting up some of the tiles. He could see out across the surrounding area; looking past the wall that surrounded the prison compound, Dramesi could see local children playing in the nearby community. The possibility of escape and freedom beckoned to him.

Gathering intelligence about the camp was a constant job. Dramesi and Atterberry worked diligently to create a map of the compound. Every characteristic of the Zoo Annex was gathered by the two men.

They made notes of each guard shift; the location of every bush, depression, and feature was collected and marked down. Shadows were plotted out as were the location of the guard towers, foxholes, and any other fortifications. Decisions were made as to exactly where they would climb down from the roof, where they would crawl to, and where they could take cover along the way to the outer wall. The problems of the electrified fence on top of the outer wall was addressed by Atterberry, who had prior electrical experience.

Prior to joining the Air Force, Atterberry had been a telephone lineman in Texas. His experience there in handling hot lines and what could happen to them was of great importance to the Party, as Dramesi had code-named the escape attempt. To take out the electrical wires across the top of the outer wall, Atterberry reinforced Dramesi's plan to escape during a rainstorm. It was common for the camp's electrical system to short out during a storm, plunging the camp into darkness. The shorting problem was common enough that the guards would usually ignore them until the morning, when they could work in the daylight.

Rather than try to depend on nature shorting out the electric fence, Atterberry suggested they come up with a pole-and-wire arrangement. By hanging a hooked wire over the top electrical line and letting it hang down, the wire would short out the entire system as soon as it contacted the lower wire. It was a way for the prisoners to "turn off" the electric fence at will. Dramesi even convinced one of the other cells to break the lightbulb out in their courtyard to help keep the area in darkness. When he heard that bulb pop, Dramesi knew they were one small step closer to escape.

Though he had wanted the Party to begin in the fall of 1968, Dramesi was overruled by Trautman, who refused to give his permission for the escape at that time. The SRO also attached some conditions to the escape attempt regarding the time of the attempt and the consensus among the other prisoners in cell #6. Dramesi remained enthusiastic about making the attempt, and he constantly pushed for permission to go. It was when winter came on that he finally relented in holding off on the Party until the spring of 1969.

Though he had reservations about Dramesi and Atterberry even making the escape attempt at all, Trautman had several things to consider as the senior officer of the camp. It was stated plainly in the Code of Conduct that a prisoner would "make every effort to escape and aid others to escape." Dramesi had the right—in his view, the duty—to make the escape attempt. Trautman agreed with this but also had to consider another part of the Code of Conduct.

In the fourth paragraph of the Code, it stated in part that no prisoners would "take part in any action which might be harmful to my comrades." There was no real question that anyone who escaped, whether successful or not, would bring the wrath of the North Vietnamese down on the prisoners who remained. The only way to avoid this was to have all of the prisoners escape, but that was impossible to do in any practical way. Additionally, only Dramesi and Atterberry wanted to make the attempt; no one else wanted to go with them. Enthusiastic as he might be, Dramesi was also a disciplined military man. Trautman had to issue orders, and Dramesi had to follow them.

There was no question that the planned escape was a carefully considered one. Trying to cover all aspects of getting out of the camp, crossing through population centers, and getting down to where the U.S. Fleet could be reached, had been something Dramesi had done meticulously. From gathering intelligence on the camp to preparing their bodies through running and calisthenics, Dramesi and Atterberry were leaving as little as possible to chance. Trautman was particularly impressed with Dramesi's plan and preparations for passing though the local areas.

Having stolen materials to manufacture props, Dramesi and Atterberry intended passing themselves off as simple peasants when going through the streets of Hanoi. The disguises the two men planned to use were ingenious both in terms of their effects and the very simple materials they had to work with.

The North Vietnamese issued very little in terms of medical materials to the prisoners. One of the things they did give out was brown iodine pills to help combat the rampant diarrhea brought on by the poor food and bad water. Having obtained some of the pills, Dramesi found that by grinding them up and mixing them with brick dust and water, they made a reasonable dye to darken the skin of the hands, neck, and face. Several of the pills were held back to also be used to purify water the men would need to locate along their escape route.

To cover up their non-Asian features, both Dramesi and Atterberry had made up face masks: simple squares of cloth that were attached to lines that looped around the ears of the wearer. Such surgical masks were very common among the Asian communities where people used them as a protection against dust and disease. Using strips of bamboo taken from their sleeping mats, the men had woven conical hats also resembling those commonly worn throughout the local community.

The common "black pajama" clothing worn by the North Vietnamese peasantry was made from spare pieces of prison uniforms. They had sandals available to them as well as a few pieces of stage props. Having stolen a few baskets and a longer bamboo pole, the men now had a chogi stick, the very common carrying poles used to transport personal items all over Asia. They even had some simple knives made up from metal strips bound to bamboo handles and carefully shaped and sharpened on chunks of bricks and stone. To help them hide along the way, the men had made up camouflage nets from a number of stolen blankets. Bits of straw from old brooms made up the grass clumps on the nets.

Along with their stash of food, these were the materials that Dramesi and Atterberry would use to make their escape from the Zoo Annex, Hanoi proper, and finally, North Vietnam. It was a daring idea and a dangerous one. Once they got out of the camp, the general plan was for the two men to make their way to the Red River, hopefully completing the trek while there were still a few hours of darkness left.

Once at the river, they would steal a small boat and head off downstream. The plan to escape during a rainstorm would not only give the men cover, it would make the river run that much faster.

With everything working in their favor, the men hoped to be at least several miles downriver before first light. In case an alarm was raised about the stolen boat, they would abandon it, destroying it if necessary so as not to be spotted. Holing up in a hiding place during the day, they would either steal another boat or start swimming if they had to to continue their trip downriver.

The plan was anything but haphazard and nothing was based on a spur-of-the-moment idea. They were very serious about their attempt even though their chances were slim at best. But even a slim chance was worth taking in Dramesi's mind. And Atterberry agreed with him. There continued to be difficulties with the other prisoners in cell #6 regarding the escape preparations as Trautman considered what his decision should be.

Arguments grew more heated among the prisoners as time continued to pass. Having denied permission to escape during the Christmas holidays, ostensibly so as not to ruin any chances of prisoners receiving an early release, Trautman forced Dramesi to move the Party date back at least four months. Demands from the other prisoners that some of the escape supplies be used for everyone's comfort were strongly opposed by Dramesi. The improvised camouflage nets were taken out of hiding and reverted back to being blankets, rotated through the prisoner community for the use of all. And as Dramesi had predicted, as soon as the blankets were found during an inspection, they were taken by the guards. The only thing Dramesi had agreed to fairly easily was removal of the peanut food supplies. The nuts would have spoiled long before the winter was over and an escape would be attempted. A small feast was made of the food.

New food supplies were gathered as they could be over the months. After having cleaned out the bags that had held their nuts, Dramesi and Atterberry looked for other materials to fill them with. There was a small supply of sugar that they were able to put up for the escape. In their creation of clothing items, the hard work by the men had supplied them each with three extra pairs of Vietnamese-style sandals. The two iron bars and the spike were reserved to be used as tools and possibly weapons if necessary. And they eventually gathered enough of the iodine pills to fill two small vials.

In April, Dramesi decided the time for the Party was coming up. Final preparations were made in terms of gathering food. By April 30, the hoarding of perishable food was begun as the men put away some of the few bananas they were given as part of their food ration. Checklists were gone over to make sure nothing was forgotten. The escape would be made on a rainy Saturday night, to help cover the movement of Dramesi and Atterberry through the prison compound. The rain would also reduce the number of people they might come across outside of the camp's walls. On Sunday mornings, the guards tended to be more lax than usual, which could help keep the discovery of the escape being made for another precious few hours.

The first Saturday in May there was no rain and the attempt was put off for another week. The second Saturday of the month, the rain started up just before sunset. It was May 10, 1969.

[CHAPTER 20]

ESCAPE FROM THE ANNEX

Glenn "Red" Wilson was the SRO of cell #6 after it was determined he had seniority of rank over Dramesi at the time of his shoot-down. His F-4C had been shot down on August 7, 1967, and he and Carl Chambers had been quickly picked up by the North Vietnamese Army after their landing. Both men had managed to escape their North Vietnamese captors while they were still within about fifty miles of the Demilitarized Zone. The men had managed to steal a couple of primitive boats, nothing more than hollowed-out logs, but when they climbed aboard them in the water, the nearly waterlogged craft had simply sunk under the weight of the Americans. They were soon after recaptured by the North Vietnamese. Their bid for freedom lasted about twelve hours.

It may have been his own experience that helped color Wilson's opinion on the chances of Dramesi and Atterberry making a successful escape. On the afternoon of May 10, Dramesi asked if he could go up and speak to Trautman about making the attempt that night. Wilson agreed, stating that if Trautman gave Dramesi permission to go, Wilson wouldn't stand in the way of the Party.

Being boosted up through the ceiling opening, Dramesi moved along the attic to where he could quietly speak down to Trautman. It was anything but a private conversation. There was only a hole in the wall that separated the attic spaces of the two rooms where Dramesi could call down to Trautman's room. He had thrown bits of plaster toward the ventilation grid to get someone's attention down in cell #5. Finally, Trautman's voice answered his calls.

It was late in the afternoon and already getting dark as storm clouds gathered. The sound of thunder could be heard coming from the distance, along with the occasional flashes of lightning off on the horizon. It was going to be a serious storm.

The eight other prisoners in Trautman's room had discussed the possible escape attempt for long hours. The men all knew there would be repercussions from the North Vietnamese regarding any escape attempt by anyone. The conflict in the Code of Conduct, regarding the duty to escape and the other clause that stated to do no harm to fellow prisoners, were the fuel for many of the discussions.

An additional obstacle to an escape attempt had been put in place by a senior officer among the prisoners themselves. This obstacle was an order that had been put out by Lieutenant Colonel Robinson "Robbie" Reisner more than two years earlier. In 1966, Reisner had ordered that no POW should try to escape without outside help. It was an effective ban on any escape attempts, since getting help from the North Vietnamese people was considered impossible.

Colonel Reisner had been held away from the rest of the prisoners for an extended length of time. This had happened to most of the senior officers among the POWs, to limit their chances of leading the men by order or example. In the years since Reisner had issued his "outside assistance" order, nothing further had been heard from him by the men of the Zoo Annex. There was a real question as to whether or not his order was still in effect. It wasn't clear at all if an escape by

Dramesi and Atterberry, or any other POWs, would be in direct violation of a senior officer's orders.

Dramesi's opinion was easy enough for everyone to understand: He felt that Reisner's order was no longer in effect. Dramesi made the assumption that Reisner's order had been issued for a specific situation at a specific time. He was definitely not of the opinion that Reisner had issued his instruction as a standing order for all POWs in North Vietnam.

All of this was on Trautman's mind as he considered the situation, long before Dramesi had called down from the ceiling above. All of the rationales for why the men shouldn't be allowed to escape had been voiced, over and over again: limited food, no water, no real plan of evasion, and no outside help. The very real possibility of retribution from the North Vietnamese was also a consideration. Given how vicious the torture of prisoners was as part of their normal interrogations and indoctrinations, the thoughts of what might be done as serious punishments was enough to frighten strong men.

There was really only one reason for Dramesi really having to escape, and being allowed to do so. It was their duty as American servicemen to escape, and the draw of even a slim possibility of freedom was a great motivation. In the final analysis, Trautman decided that Dramesi and Atterberry could not be denied their chance.

Calling up to the man waiting above the ceiling, Trautman asked if Dramesi really thought they could make it. The answer was simple enough: If Dramesi hadn't thought that escape was possible, he would not be asking to go.

Refusing to actually say yes, Trautman said that he could not deny Dramesi the chance. If he wanted to go, it would be up to him.

"We're going tonight," was Dramesi's answer.

"God bless," was all that Trautman could bring himself to say in return.

With the decision having been made, the other prisoners in cell #6 helped lift Atterberry up to where Dramesi waited. The men remaining in the room settled back onto their sleeping pallets and pulled their mosquito nets down around them. They all prepared for a long night, each man alone with his thoughts.

Up in the attic, Dramesi and Atterberry continued with their preparations. Smearing the brown paste they had prepared on one another, they darkened their skin. To complete the last items on the checklist they had, they drank water from the jugs they had pulled up from the room below. Dropping the water containers back down to the other prisoners, they completed the last item on the checklist when they secured the barbed-wire grid back into place.

It was now about 9 P.M. and both men decided the time was right to go. Lifting up four of the roofing tiles and bringing them down into the attic, Dramesi opened up their way out of the building. He climbed out onto the sloping roof, turned back, and Atterberry handed him the tiles he had removed, Once Atterberry was out of the building, all the tiles were replaced and the hole in the roof was covered once again.

The rain-covered roof was slippery and the men had to be very careful in slowly making their way up to the peak. In spite of the care they were taking, one of the roof tiles broke free. Hearts stopped within the chests of both men as the tile clattered down across the roof, shot out into space, and smashed down with a clatter as it struck the concrete floor of the outside washing area. The men were certain that everyone had heard the crash as the roofing tile shattered into a hundred pieces. Before their hearts had started beating with anything close to a normal rhythm again, there was more noise from the direction of the wall between the Zoo Annex and the Zoo itself. A group of North Vietnamese guards were coming.

Certain that the guards had been drawn to the noise of the shattering tile, Dramesi and Atterberry froze in place on the roof and waited to be caught. Readying a replacement camouflage net they had made, the men concealed themselves as best they could on the open roof. The group of guards walked into the central area of the Zoo

Annex, several of them carrying bamboo poles or torches. Suspicious that the poles may be used to push them off the roof, Dramesi and Atterberry watched the guards walk across the compound. It became obvious as the group continued to move along that the guards weren't coming toward the building. Instead, they were heading over to the loathsome body of water that the prisoners called Lake Fester.

It was a North Vietnamese hunting party of sorts, not one looking for escaped prisoners. Standing about the pool of dark water, the guards stabbed down with their bamboo poles. Inside of a few moments, the North Vietnamese took their catch of five large frogs and hung them from their belts. Then the guards just walked back the way they had come. They never even looked up at where the escaping prisoners lay watching them.

The two prisoners regained their composure and started out across the peak of the roof. Not exactly the place to be in an electrical storm, they were heading toward a lightning rod, which stuck up from the otherwise relatively featureless roof. Reaching out to the rod, Dramesi quickly snatched back his hand. He had received a shock. There was so much electricity in the air from the storm that the rod was partially electrified. The men would not be escaping from the roof by sliding down the heavy ground wire of the lightning rod.

Barely slowed in his actions, Dramesi took up the length of hand-made rope he was carrying and asked Atterberry for his. The ropes were another of his escape preparations that were quickly proving essential as Dramesi tied the two sections of rope together. Now the men had enough line that they could secure it to the lightning rod and still have enough to get down to the ground on. Removing a tile overhanging the edge of the roof, Dramesi made sure that the rope would be able to bear down on a section of wood rather than shatter another tile. He went down the rope and took cover at what the men called Station One on their escape route from the compound. He was quickly joined by Atterberry.

The two men now had to cross the single-largest open stretch of ground in their compound, a concrete walk through the garden area. Crawling up to the path, Dramesi stopped. Curled up underneath his camouflage net, he was lying down on his right side in the mud trying very hard to look like nothing more than a misshapen lump. This was Station Two on their planned escape route. As he lifted up the edge of the netting, Dramesi froze in place, scarcely daring to breathe. Not three feet away from his face was a pair of boots worn by a North Vietnamese guard. It would be nearly impossible for the man not to see the huddled prisoner where he lay in the mud literally almost at his feet.

Another consideration Dramesi had made in his escape plan proved incredibly valuable at this juncture. The impossible happened as the guard, wearing a raincoat and a wide-brimmed hat, missed seeing Dramesi. Too wrapped up in his own misery while in the rain, the guard continued on his path to the guard shack by the main gate. Waiting what he considered a safe length of time to allow the guard to join his fellow comrades, Dramesi got up and walked across the rest of the compound, only stopping when he had reached another station in the planned route. He rested next to the outhouse building up against the main outer wall, hidden by both walls and some tall weeds. That spot was Station Three, the last stop inside the Zoo Annex compound. Dramesi was startled when Atterberry plopped down next to him only a few minutes later. It seemed that the other escaping prisoner had been watching Dramesi. When he got up and just walked, Atterberry figured that the coast must be clear and he got up and also walked across the compound. He had never even seen the guard who had so badly startled Dramesi.

It was now that Atterberry's skill was going to come into call on the escape. The men had reached a point where they could scale the outer wall of the compound with the least chance of being spotted. But the electric fence had to be breached and then there was the barbed wire to deal with. As far as Dramesi was concerned, they were going to make it and he told Atterberry as much.

It was about now that the rain stopped coming down, only Dramesi was too focused on what he was doing to notice it. The branches of some trees helped shield the top of the outhouse roof from causal observation. That was where Dramesi intended actually crossing the outer wall. Climbing up to the roof of the small building would put them both within reach of the outer wall and the wires that ran along the top of it.

As the senior officer, Dramesi considered it his responsibility to take the risk of shorting out the electric wires. Following the instructions received earlier from Atterberry, Dramesi had a hooked piece of bare wire in his hand to place over the top line of the electric fence. There were two live wires held up on insulating posts, placed one above the other. Reaching out, Dramesi gingerly put the hook of his shorting wire over the top of the upper line. Then he dropped the wire across the lower line.

Instantly, there was a fat blue spark and a loud pop when the shorting wire touched the bottom line. Sparks flew across the area as the power took the shortest route and overloaded the system. Some distance from where the two men were up on the wall, there was a loud crack as the circuit breaker blew out. Instantly, all of the lights on the north side of the camp went out, plunging the area into darkness.

As guards shouted across the area, Dramesi noticed for the first time that the rain had stopped. Not only was the rain gone, but the clouds were breaking up. The two men would soon be far more visible on top of the outhouse roof than they would have preferred to be.

In the distance, Dramesi could see the guards in the compound gathering around an electrical box on the outside of one of the buildings. The guards had no apparent idea of what to do; they spoke excitedly to each other and kept trying to reset the circuit breaker by flipping the switch lever on the outside of the box. The circuit wasn't going to reset at all, not as long as the shorting wire remained in position. Seeing the guards occupied the way they were was very satisfying to Dramesi. They would be occupied with the electrical box long enough for the two men to cross over the top of the outer wall.

Since he was already up on the wall, Dramesi was going to be the first man to cross over to the outside. The only problem was the barbed wire, which managed to catch him as he was trying to go under it. Calling quietly to his partner, Atterberry quickly unsnagged him. Once on the other side of the barbed wire, Dramesi took the bundles of gear that Atterberry passed to him and dropped them on the pavement on the outside of the main wall. To cut back on the distance he had to drop, Dramesi hung down on the outside of the wall by his fingertips.

It was still a long way down to the hard ground. Trusting in his ability to make a rolling parachute landing fall from the training that had been drilled into him by instructors now on the other side of the world, Dramesi released his grip.

The drop to the hard ground on the outside of the wall was nearly ten feet. In another life, in another place, ten feet might seem like hardly anything at all—the height of a set of household stairs, the branch of a medium-tall tree a child might climb. But in the middle of downtown Hanoi during an escape from a prisoner of war camp, it seemed like a very long distance indeed. If he broke his leg, sprained his ankle, or injured his knee (again!) Dramesi's escape attempt would be over just as he reached the outside of the camp. But none of those things happened. He hit the ground as his jump instructors had taught him. Absorbing the impact easily, he got to his feet and looked up to Atterberry on the wall above him.

With Dramesi on the ground to help break his fall, Atterberry dropped down without incident. Now the men darted over to a group of bushes between two nearby huts. They were free for the moment, but there were a number of things they had to do immediately to remain that way.

Working by touch, the men broke down their bundles of gear. More dye went on their exposed skin to replace that washed off by the rain. The surgical masks went over their faces and the hats they had made were on their heads. With the baskets placed on either end of the bamboo pole, Dramesi shouldered the pole in the same manner as uncounted thousands of Asians did throughout the country. Shouldering the burlap bag holding the rest of their supplies, Atterberry also resembled nothing more than another Asian worker carrying a bundle.

These crude disguises and human nature were all the men had to help them in their escape. Now it was the time to seriously put things to the test as they had to move away from the prison compound.

They were in an area densely packed with local housing. Now that they could see the situation more clearly, Dramesi immediately decided to change their escape route through the area. Believing in facing a problem head-on, Dramesi went along the main local street, right past the gate of the Zoo Annex. Just feet away from the two escaping prisoners were the armed North Vietnamese guards who saw them every day.

But none of the guards saw the two men walking by. Dramesi and Atterberry continued walking down the road heading north to the main road that ran into Hanoi.

The guard shack at the gate was not the only obstacle the men ran into soon after making their way out of the compound. Three North Vietnamese policemen pedaled past the two escaping prisoners. Each officer was wearing a white uniform and mounted on a bicycle, another everyday sight in North Vietnam. The bicycles passed within three feet of the prisoners but their disguises continued to hold. It took some daring for the two men to just keep walking normally with their heads held down. But they had demonstrated their ability to gut things out simply by surviving in the North Vietnamese prison system for the past several years. They would both keep going for as long as they could.

[CHAPTER 21]

FREEDOM RUNNERS

There was no cry from any quarter as Dramesi and Atterberry continued their escape. The pair just kept walking along with their burdens, not looking at all out of place even at the relatively late hour. As they passed by a public watering spot, a local was filling a container from a flowing pipe. There wasn't anything out of the ordinary about the scene, just a bent pipe coming out of the ground with water flowing from the open end and a man filling water jugs. But just as the pair of escapees came up to him, the man finished filling his container and stood up, looking right at them.

Maintaining his composure, Dramesi simply nodded in greeting to the local. All the man did was return Dramesi's greeting and go back to what he was doing. As the two escapees continued on their way, Dramesi was very glad for the surgical masks they had made; not only had the simple disguises passed several tests along the way, they also covered the wide grin that was plastered across his face at that moment. As he looked back at Atterberry, Dramesi figured the man's mask was covering the same kind of smile.

The pair continued on their way with no further incident until they began to approach what they thought was the town of Cu Loc. That was the first time a local tried to speak to the two men directly. As a villager approached them he was waving his hand and speaking rapidly in Vietnamese. Neither Dramesi nor Atterberry spoke enough Vietnamese to say anything that might help them and they couldn't understand what the local was saying anyway. They did the only thing they could in the situation: they ignored him and continued on their way.

Staring at the two escapees as they continued with their burdens, the local just stood in the middle of the street, looking confused. When Dramesi looked back, the local was heading off to some of the larger buildings nearby, and it looked like he was now in a hurry.

Just in case the man suspected anything, the two men sped up to a trot. There was a canal next to the road and Dramesi decided to cross to the other side of the water. Taking off his mask, he indicated to Atterberry where they should go and headed down to the water. The banks of the canal were steep but the two men got across without too much difficulty.

At Atterberry's sudden warning, Dramesi ducked down and took cover. On the opposite side of the canal there was a truck slowly moving along the road. Along the bank of the canal were men walking along shining flashlights at the ground. It was obvious they were looking for something, and the two escapees figured that it could only be them.

It was time to try and find a better hiding place than simply laying down in the mud. There were some buildings nearby so the two men ducked in next to them. In the warm darkness they both heard a familiar sound—the soft grunting of hogs coming from inside the building. Lifting up a barricade intended to keep the hogs in but not humans out, Dramesi and Atterberry were able to slip inside the hut and close off the opening behind them. Now they were both in pitch darkness, their only company the smell and the pigs. The pigs didn't seem to care that the men were hiding with them and Dramesi was glad that the animals didn't get excited and start to squeal.

Outside of the pigsty, the men searching the canal banks continued on their way. Whatever it was they were looking for, neither Dramesi or Atterberry ever learned. The two men just remained hidden in the darkness as long as they considered it necessary. It wasn't practical for them to remain in the pigsty; eventually the owner would come by and discover them. And Dramesi wanted to continue putting distance between themselves and the prison camp.

The farther away from the camp they could get before they were discovered missing, the better. Distance meant that there would be a greater and greater area for the North Vietnamese to cover in their search for the escapees. The population surrounding the Zoo Annex meant there would be little trouble assembling search parties.

Leaving the pigs behind, the two men continued along the side of the canal for a short distance. At Atterberry's suggestion, they turned away from the canal in order to find a good hiding place to wait out the day. They had no sign of the Red River being nearby, so Dramesi gave up on stealing a boat that night.

There was a low stone wall in a bad state of repair surrounding a small church. It had taken much longer to get clear of the city than Dramesi had planned and the churchyard looked to be the best hiding place they were going to find. The building would have been too obvious and searchers would have been sure to check it. But the churchyard had a number of bramble bush thickets scattered over the area, some of them quite thick. Picking one of the thickets next to the broken wall, the two men crawled deep inside.

The large thorns had proven painful to get past. Hopefully, any searchers who might come by would find them too much of a bother and abandon the area. As the two men waited out the morning, Dramesi considered how far they had come and what they had accomplished. No matter what, they both knew that they had made their best pitch for freedom. The North Vietnamese would know that at least two prisoners hadn't given up their will to be free.

The two men had lost track of the time and had no real idea of how long it was until daylight. Dramesi figured that they had come maybe four or four and a half miles from the prison camp. He did suspect that they had made a mistake in timing or something else.

What neither Dramesi nor Atterberry had known at the time of the escape was the exact location of the Zoo or the Zoo Annex in relation to the Red River. The bank of the river had been just barely over a mile from where they had originally gone over the wall. But the river ran to the east of the camp. They had been going in the wrong direction.

As the sun came up, the two men sat in the bramble thicket, the stone wall at their backs. The rain of the night before had washed the air clean and the sun shone down from a clear sky. It felt very good to be free, no matter how much longer it lasted. The sunshine illuminated the churchyard, and the two men could see the groups of North Vietnamese moving across the countryside. These were not people who would be fooled by the simple disguises the two men had. They were armed groups of fifteen to seventeen men and women clearly intent on finding the escapees. They were all armed with rifles or AK-47 automatic weapons.

It wasn't long before one of the search parties came into the churchyard and went up to the abandoned building. Tearing away the barricades that blocked the entrance, the group went inside and thoroughly searched it. It looked to Dramesi as if their luck might still be holding as the group of North Vietnamese came out of the church. Having found nothing, they were gathering up to leave the churchyard when one of the young men decided to examine the thickets in the yard.

In what looked to be almost an afterthought, the young man came up to the thicket where Dramesi and Atterberry were hiding. With a pistol in his hand, he got down on his hands and knees to try to force his way between the thorns. The escapees' luck had run out.

Not more than a few feet from where the two men sat, the young North Vietnamese suddenly yelled to his comrades as he cocked the pistol in his hand. The sound of that one gun being cocked was magnified many times as safeties came off rifles and AKs. The rest of the searchers were running up to the thicket at the yell of the young man.

There was nothing else to be done. Slowly, Dramesi and Atterberry crawled out of the bramble bush as the young man backed away in front of them. Mud-covered, the two prisoners stood in front of the proud group of searchers. The escape was over.

According to later reports, the two men had managed to cover three miles in the twelve hours of their escape. The two men were driven back to the prison camp in an NVA jeep. Atterberry managed to shake hands with Dramesi before the two men were separated.

"We tried," were the last words Atterberry ever said to Dramesi.

Word quickly spread through the Zoo and then the Zoo Annex that the escapees had been recaptured. The luck of the two men had proven false in a number of ways. The original plan for the escape to go out on a Saturday night had been a reasoned one. The guards usually arrived later than normal on a Sunday morning. But the Sunday morning of the escape had proven different than the norm. The prisoners were woken up at 5:00 A.M., even earlier than on a weekday morning. The discovery of the missing prisoners had stirred up a hornet's nest of activity among the North Vietnamese.

Very few of the prisoners had known anything at all about an escape attempt. Normal operational security had meant that only the people who had to know had been told. That was the men in cell #6 where Dramesi and Atterberry had been kept and cell #5, where Trautman and his fellows were held. Other than that, no one else knew of the attempt, even after the escape had been uncovered.

For Dramesi and Atterberry, their ordeal at the hands of the North Vietnamese torturers began almost immediately after their arrival at

A painting by Moki Martin—SDVs launching underwater from the *Grayback*. The flat SDV to the center left is the more modern Mark IX boat. The other two are the Mark VIII, very familiar to the men of Operation Thunderhead. *Philip "Moki" Martin*

Underway with her identifying numbers removed is the submarine *Grayback*. Even without a number on her sail, the unique submarine is unmistakable due to the round clamshell hatches on her large bow hangars. *U.S. Navy*

The very distinctive view of an SR-71 while approaching a refueling aircraft. This bird is tail #980, one of the last flying SR-71s that took part in the Booming the Hanoi Hilton mission. This aircraft has been renumbered as #844 for its research flight missions for NASA. *NASA*

During their platoon training, the SEALs fired their automatic weapons on the range. There is a mix of lightened (chopped) M60 machine guns (right and left ends of the line) as well as the SEALs' favorite, the Stoner MK23 (center of line). *Tim Reeves*

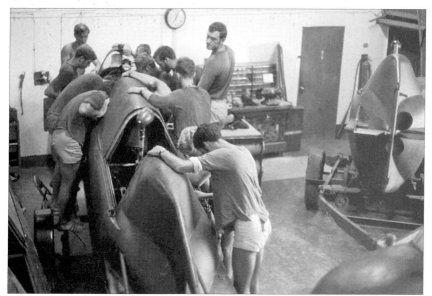

In the hangar on shore, the SEALs of Alfa Platoon familiarize themselves with the SDVs they will operate with. *Tim Reeves*

The SEALs and UDT operators training with the SDVs in the calm waters off Subic Bay in the Phillipines. *Tim Reeves*

During training for Thunderhead, the SEALs of Alfa Platoon paddle a rubber boat toward the *Grayback*. One of the front hatches of the hangars is open as the submarine rests in still waters. *Tim Reeves*

With the *Grayback*'s decks awash, the SEALs paddle rubber boats in toward the open hangars during training. The netting is used to help stop SDV approaching the submarine while recovering them underwater. *Tim Reeves*

While receiving a briefing from Lieutenant Dry on the deck of the *Grayback*, the SEALs of Alfa Platoon listen while shuffling through their gear. The rear of two SDVs can be seen through the open hatch of the right (starboard) hangar. *Tim Reeves*

The incredibly cramped SEAL living quarters aboard the *Grayback*. Boxes of movie films cover the floor while the projector takes up the center of the deck. *Tim Reeves*

Spread out on the deck behind them, the weapons taken by the SEALs on Operation Thunderhead wait to be stowed below. Among the weapons visible are three drum-fed Stoner light machine guns as well as a pair of M60 machine guns. The plan of operation for Thunderhead did not call for direct contact with the North Vietnamese—but the SEALs would be ready for any contingency. *Tim Reeves*

In a lighter moment, Lieutenant Melvin Spence Dry, the last SEAL killed in combat during the Vietnam War. *Tim Reeves*

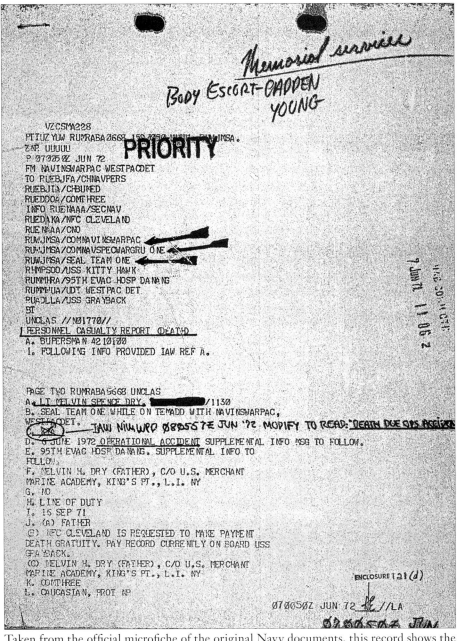

Memorial service

Body Escort—GADDEN YOUNG

VZCSMA228
PTTUZ YUW RUMRABA 2668 159 7250 UUUU MJMSA.
ZNR UUUUU
P 070050Z JUN 72   **PRIORITY**
FM NAVINSWARPAC WESTPAC DET
TO RUEBJFA/CHNAVPERS
RUEBJIN/CHBUMED
RUEDDOA/COMTHREE
INFO RUENAAA/SECNAV
RUEDAKA/NFC CLEVELAND
RUENAAA/CNO
RUWJMSA/COMNAVINSWARPAC
RUWJMSA/COMNAVSPECWARGRU ONE
RUWJMSA/SEAL TEAM ONE
RHMPSOO/USS KITTY HAWK
RUMMHRA/95TH EVAC HOSP DA NANG
RUMMVUA/UDT WESTPAC DET
RUADLLA/USS GRAYBACK
BT
UNCLAS //N01770//
PERSONNEL CASUALTY REPORT (DEATH)
A. BUPERSMAN 42 10100
1. FOLLOWING INFO PROVIDED IAW REF A.

PAGE TWO RUMRABA 2668 UNCLAS
A. LT MELVIN SPENCE DRY.   /1130
B. SEAL TEAM ONE WHILE ON TEMADD WITH NAVINSWARPAC,
WESTPAC DET.   IAW NIWWPQ Ø8Ø557E JUN '72 MODIFY TO READ: "DEATH DUE OPS ACCIDENT
D. 6 JUNE 1972 OPERATIONAL ACCIDENT SUPPLEMENTAL INFO MSG TO FOLLOW.
E. 95TH EVAC HOSP DA NANG. SUPPLEMENTAL INFO TO
FOLLOW.
F. MELVIN H. DRY (FATHER), C/O U.S. MERCHANT
MARINE ACADEMY, KING'S PT., L.I. NY
G. NO
H. LINE OF DUTY
I. 16 SEP 71
J. (A) FATHER
(B) NFC CLEVELAND IS REQUESTED TO MAKE PAYMENT
DEATH GRATUITY. PAY RECORD CURRENTLY ON BOARD USS
GRAYBACK.
(C) MELVIN H. DRY (FATHER), C/O U.S. MERCHANT
MARINE ACADEMY, KING'S PT., L.I. NY
K. COMTHREE
L. CAUCASIAN, PROT NP

ENCLOSURE (21(d)

070050Z JUN 72   //LA

Taken from the official microfiche of the original Navy documents, this record shows the changing of Dry's death from being a killed in action (KIA being crossed out) to a death due to an operational accident. This change was because of the extreme secrecy surrounding Operation Thunderhead and the SEALs' involvement in it. *Kevin Dockery*

In the halls of Annapolis, two warriors finally meet. After thirty-six years, Colonel John Dramesi (right) shakes the hand of Navy SEAL Rick Hetzel (left). *Kevin Dockery*

the Zoo. Initially, Dramesi was taken to the auditorium of the Zoo, a place called the Ho Chi Minh room by the prisoners. His handcuffed wrists were pulled out ahead of him as Dramesi was laid out on a small table. His legs dragged down behind him, heavily weighted with iron shackles.

Both Dramesi and Atterberry had discussed what they would tell the interrogators about the escape. The men had agreed to answer questions but not when. Dramesi knew from hard-learned experience that a prisoner had to ride out a lot of torture to make any lies he would tell sound convincing. That was the rule he had used to survive the first years of his imprisonment with his personal honor intact. It was also the attitude that had earned him the name *dau* among his interrogators. The name meant "pain" in Vietnamese.

One of the items Fidel had liked to use so much the prisoners was called the "fan belt." That item was a strip cut from the sidewalls of a used tire. Originally, the rubber piece had been used as a rope to draw water from the wells of the prison compound. But a broken section of the rope had been discovered to be a very effective whip by an innovative guard. It was with that fan belt that Dramesi was beaten.

Stretched out across the tabletop, the prisoner was held while one of the guards whipped him over and over with the fan belt. It was an extended flogging, one that wasn't going to stop for some time. Men had been beaten with the fan belt before under Fidel's direction. It was these floggings that had resulted in such human wreckage that fellow prisoners had wondered how the recipient of the beating was still alive. Now, Dramesi would be one of those recipients.

In that miserable room surrounded by his enemies, Dramesi started sounding out from the pain of the flogging. He wouldn't allow the sound to come up easily; first there were whimpers with every stroke. The whimpers grew to cries, and then finally full-throated screams of torment. Still the flogging continued until the guards grew tired of lashing at the screaming mass of human flesh in front of them.

The men doing the flogging may have been the regular guards

and staff of the prison camp. But some of the interrogators were new. When the guards had finally stopped the flogging, they dragged Dramesi to another room for further questioning. His back was a mass of bruises and bleeding welts.

In the office were three interrogators, all of them North Vietnamese who spoke good English and whom Dramesi had never seen before. What they wanted to know was why Dramesi had escaped. That was the primary question. Interspersed with the questions were hints that there were those in higher command who wanted a full report on the escape, a personal view on just what had happened.

Through the pain of his situation, Dramesi knew that he had to stick it out as long as he could. Only with his endurance of the torment they were dishing out to him would he be able to outwit the North Vietnamese, hold back on telling them what they wanted to know, lie to them and confuse them. Then he was rewarded with a small victory.

One of the new interrogators screamed in the prisoner's face, threatening him, telling him what his future held. Dramesi was going to be put on a starvation diet, bread and water alone, and not much of either. And he would receive no cigarettes, none at all!

This threat got a quick reaction from Dramesi. He screamed at his interrogator, he begged. They couldn't take his cigarettes away! They couldn't do that.

Once more, the interrogator shouted at the bound man in front of him. Shaking his finger, the man reiterated; *"And no cigarettes!"*

Dramesi didn't smoke.

But the emptiness of the threat didn't keep Dramesi from dropping his head and groaning at the prospect of being forced to quit smoking.

There was a new style of torment used by the interrogators to try and keep Dramesi off-balance. He was forced to sit on a stool in front of an interrogator as he asked his questions. When the flow of questions slowed, or Dramesi's refusal to answer became too annoying, he was snatched up by the guards and dragged over in front of another interrogator. The guards pulled the prisoner along by grabbing up the irons that held his legs together. The rough red tile of the floor abraded the flesh of Dramesi's beaten behind until he felt the blood sticking his shorts to his skin. Again, he was dragged over to another interrogator and the questioning began anew.

As the interrogators became tired, one of them stopped and left the room. The two North Vietnamese who remained were soon joined by the camp commander, who joined in on the interrogation. The guards rotated in and out of the room, but the torture never slacked except for the asking of questions. Goose returned to face Dramesi and the sadist continued with the skills he knew best. Blindfolded, Dramesi was beaten by the camp commander.

Beating went on by the guards who started with slaps, then moved on to full swings with a closed fist. His head rocking from side to side from the blows, the tissues of his face swelled up until he resembled a badly carved pumpkin. For the guards, they nonchalantly just wiped the blood off their hands with a rag; it wasn't their blood.

The ropes were once again brought out and Dramesi was bound in an excruciating position. The interrogators had learned from experience what they could and could not do with their prisoners to minimize damage and maximize torment. When his arms and thumbs were tied together, the man exacting the torture paid attention to the circulation in his victim's extremities. When a finger or thumb was cut and there was neither pain nor bleeding, he knew he had to allow some blood back into the limb or the flesh would die. The return of circulation could be as excruciating as the original torture.

For his time in the room, Dramesi wasn't allowed to sleep or rest. He was secured by handcuffs and leg irons at all times. A bright light was trained on him during the night, the glare meant to keep him awake. The interrogators took time off from their work on the prisoner, but the guards remained alert at all times even when not in the room. When Dramesi looked to be nodding off, the guards would rush in and slap him around to keep him awake. Otherwise, they would just beat on the door at odd intervals to make him jerk awake.

In another room in the compound, Ed Atterberry was going through his own ordeal at the hands of the North Vietnamese. Over the days, his screams could be heard echoing through the prison. Some of the POWs said that the screams were loud enough that you could have heard them several blocks away. But none of the prisoners were that far from the point of Atterberry's torment. The cries of both men rang out across the courtyard, soon joined by the sounds coming from other prisoners undergoing the inquisition of their North Vietnamese captors. It was only a little over a week that the sounds coming from the two escapees were cut back by half.

After their initial five days of torture, the two escapees were moved to new locations. Dramesi ended up back in room #18, the place of his first extended torture session at the hands of Goose and Bug. Atterberry was placed in cell #5, across the Zoo compound from room #18. It was there that his screams stopped eight days after the escape attempt.

Years later, Dramesi was told that Atterberry had died on May 18. According to the North Vietnamese, Ed Atterberry passed away from an illness, probably pneumonia or other virus he had caught while trying to escape. If he had become sick, it had come as a blessed relief to the torment that he had undergone at the hands of the North Vietnamese.

[CHAPTER 22]

ORDEAL

One of the men who had been in room #6, William Baugh, had not agreed with Dramesi and Atterberry's escape attempt. As far as Baugh was concerned, an escapee had to have a reasonable chance of making it all the way out of the country and back to friendly lines, not just getting out of the camp. It did seem to him that Dramesi's attempt was going to be just that, an attempt. In spite of his opinion, he helped Dramesi and Atterberry climb up past the ventilator opening and into the attic of the building.

The men in room #6 knew that the North Vietnamese were going to nail them for the escape attempt. What none of the men realized was the extent to which their captors would go to interrogate and punish the prisoners who had stayed behind. If he had known what was going to happen, Baugh would have been hanging on the feet of Dramesi and Atterberry to keep them from leaving the room.

The other prisoners at the Zoo had witnessed Dramesi and Atterberry being brought back. They passed the information quickly through the grapevine to the prisoners in the Zoo Annex. It was still only a small group of the prisoners who knew for certain that an escape attempt had been made, but now everyone suspected it.

For Dramesi, the punishment was quick and brutal. The initial five days of torture in the Ho Chi Minh room continued without pause in room #18. That miserable place became his cell and torture chamber for more than a month. Placed back onto the stool that he had already spent so much time on years earlier, Dramesi felt the weight and bite of the jumbo leg irons. The two-inch-thick iron bar attached to the shackles bore down on his legs with the unfeeling, uncaring crushing weight of its inanimate mass. The cold iron didn't care about his cries, his pain. It just pressed down on his feet, smashing the arches down flat with relentless pressure. It was just the beginning.

When the irons were firmly in place, the blindfold was removed from Dramesi's eyes. He knew immediately where he was, and he recognized the person he was facing: It was Bug, back again to torment him to the best of his considerable ability. Dramesi recognized in the man a professional level of competence in his job. Bug was to extract information, and he was known to the prisoners as the meanest interrogator in the Zoo. He was now concentrating the bulk of his efforts in pulling information from Dramesi, and he did so for hours.

With the ropes being tightened across his arms and back, Dramesi was questioned as to just who had ordered the escape. When Dramesi answered with the truth and accepted responsibility for the action, that wasn't good enough for Bug. The ropes were pulled tighter, the pain increased, and the guards ignored the screaming of their prisoner. While Dramesi cried out wondering just what it was the guards wanted to know, they left the room.

And it wasn't just his own suffering that Dramesi had to endure; he could hear Atterberry being tortured in another room. Whatever the distance between the two, it wasn't enough to diminish the screams. The sounds of the beatings continued until one night, when they just stopped. There was a dull kind of quiet that fell over the prison for a moment. Listening carefully, afraid to breathe in case he would miss a sound, Dramesi listened for his friend. But there were no more sounds coming from Ed Atterberry, and there never would be.

In the morning, Ferdinand came into room #18 and sprayed the air with disinfectant. Then he went through and sprayed perfume into the air. Lights were centered so that Dramesi bathed in their glare while he sat on the stool, tied and weighted down. A fan was turned toward the chair where the interrogator sat and then started. As the breeze blew, the last player of the grotesque act took his cue as Bug came in and sat in the chair. The day's active tortures then began.

Dramesi was ordered to get up and approach Bug. The horrible weight on his ankles and feet kept the man from being able to move. The pain was so strong that he could barely shuffle a step when it was demanded of him by Bug. It was not enough. It would never be enough.

Twice a day, Ferdinand would stand guard as Dramesi ate his meager meal. The mouthful of bread and single cup of water twice a day was all he was allowed, and his body suffered as much from malnutrition as it did from the torture. The flesh of Dramesi's ankles was swollen and dying from lack of circulation. In a terrible parody of medical care, one day a camp doctor came into room #18. He brought with him a tray of instruments, bandages, and gauze. The North Vietnamese normally used a very brutal and direct form of torture to gain what they wanted; the idea of a sophisticated kind of medical action just didn't seem to fit in with their past treatments. Then the doctor treated Dramesi's ankles and feet, and the treatment was a torture in itself.

The guards took off the heavy irons from Dramesi's ankles, unscrewing the long iron rod and then removing the shackles. When the metal came off, so did clumps of dead tissue from the oxygen-starved flesh of the prisoner's body. There were holes in the skin and deep into the tissues of Dramesi's ankles and the tops of his feet, chewed into by the relentless weight of the irons. The prison doctor used forceps to pull out long bits of dead white flesh from the holes. Left in place, the dead tissue would have eventually rotted, poisoning the rest of the feet and leading to amputation at best.

With a needle, the doctor jabbed his patient with a load of penicillin. The antibiotic would at least help in fighting off the worst of an infection. The holes in the tops of the feet and along the ankles were packed full of the sulphur treatment Dramesi had gone through before. Gauze and bandages went around the wounds.

With his arms still firmly bound behind his back, Dramesi wasn't able to show the doctor the sad state his buttocks were in. Eventually, the medical man could see for himself that the cloth of Dramesi's shorts was fused to the skin of his butt. At first just tugging, the doctor pulled hard and ripped the cloth off, taking skin and tissue with it. The scream that the brutal action tore from Dramesi's throat frightened the doctor's assistant.

With the cleaning and bandaging of the torn flesh of his buttocks done, Dramesi was left alone in the room. The doctor and his assistant left, and Ferdinand took the heavy irons from the room. He returned a few moments later with a lighter pair of leg restraints, which the prisoners called "traveling irons." The lighter leg shackles were normally used to hobble prisoners so that they could move about, but not run or walk quickly. With what seemed to Dramesi to be almost comical care, Ferdinand placed the traveling irons around the bandages on the prisoner's legs. For more than three and a half weeks, Dramesi had been tortured twenty-four hours a day. And his suffering still wasn't over.

Torturing during the day continued, and the enforced lack of sleep went on during the night. Bright lights were turned toward Dramesi at the end of every day and the guards would pound on the door whenever they saw his head nodding. He sat on his stool, but didn't remain alone. The vermin of the Zoo came in to help keep Dramesi company. Just about every night, a large rat crept into the room, looked about, and took whatever poor scraps the prisoner hadn't been able to finish. On one night, a large black spider came into the room. The huge arachnid was about the size of one of Dramesi's hands, and he watched it make a circuit of three of the room's walls.

Slowly coming up to within a few feet of the prisoner's still badly swollen feet, the spider stopped. Dramesi was afraid that the big arachnid would make a meal of the many mosquitoes feeding on his nearly immobile feet. If it did, there was nothing the bound man could have done about it. But the spider turned and moved away, finally taking up residence underneath the interrogator's table. Dramesi had high hopes that the creature would take it upon itself to try and eat Bug, or at least give him a nasty bite.

The tortures went on after Ferdinand completed his daily ritual of making room #18 smell a little better. Bug wanted Dramesi to write confessions, and finally to make a tape recording reading from papers that were put in front of him. Before he could say no, Goose had given the ropes binding his arms a savage pull. Screaming with the pain, Dramesi acquiesced to Bug's demands. But he still made a mess of trying to read the documents. Stumbling in his speech and barely speaking coherently at times, Dramesi was given sugar water to drink in order to soothe his throat, hoarse from screaming. After a long day, the prisoner was inwardly satisfied that nothing he had said would make a good piece of propaganda. Bug packed away his gear, and the tape recorder was not seen again.

After even more torture sessions, Dramesi felt that he was down to weighing only 100 or maybe 110 pounds. For more than a month, he had suffered daily beatings with fists and the fan belt. The rope tortures had gone on fifteen times. He was no longer bothered by living in his own filth. For thirty-eight days, the little stool in room #18 had been his home, bed, and toilet. He felt that death might not be very far away. In the end, he had told the interrogators some of what they had wanted, but he hadn't written anything of use to them. Neither had he given them a propaganda tape. So much of what he had said were lies and distortions; none of the interrogators could be certain of the use of anything that he had told them. It was a victory.

For the other prisoners who had not taken part in the escape attempt, the nightmare started only slightly later than it had for Dramesi and Atterberry. Some of the first men to undergo the inquisition at the hands of the North Vietnamese were the men who lived in room #6. The punishments and interrogations were quickly spread out among the rest of the population of the Zoo Annex and then the Zoo itself. For weeks, all of the men from room #6 were tortured for information on the escape attempt. Unlike the Coker-McKnight attempt, which had been very close to a spur-of-the-moment situation, the North Vietnamese were certain that the Dramesi-Atterberry attempt was the result of an organized plan. They refused to believe that the escapees had done most of the planning and preparation for the escape themselves. The North Vietnamese wanted to know what the organization was inside the camp, which prisoners were in it, and how to break it up.

The North Vietnamese were able to disband any possible prisoner organization without any information from the prisoners. Tortures were doled out in wholesale lots. For months, the screams of men undergoing extreme torments echoed around the Zoo compound; then, the tortures spread outward.

To ensure that their prisoner population was secure, the North Vietnamese interrogated men at other prisons in the system besides the Zoo compound, First it was the prisons in Hanoi itself, then the ones around the city. Finally, even the prisons out in the country employed the torturers full-time. Many of the prisoners were suffering with no knowledge of any escape attempt. They had nothing to tell their interrogators to help make the pain stop.

Through their vision spots under doors and through cracks, the prisoners in the Zoo watched other prisoners being taken out of their cells and moved along to the torture rooms. Floggings with the fan belt became so common that the North Vietnamese established a standard procedure for employing them. The prisoners would be stripped of their trousers and forced to lie on the floor. Two guards would alternate rushing in from a corner of the room to swing the fan belt down and strike at the bare buttocks and legs of the man on the floor. By alternating, the guards were able to keep up their exertions for a longer time and the running up to the prisoner helped build up the impact of the weapons.

The technique reduced to a bleeding mass the lower back, buttocks, and thighs of a prisoner undergoing a flogging. The punishments didn't stop there; they only changed. Bamboo clubs were used to break all of the cartilage in a prisoner's lower legs. Guards would feel along the shins of a screaming man to see what parts they hadn't broken yet, then lean back and strike at anything solid they found.

The reprisals and interrogations went on from that first Sunday after the escape and well into the summer. Twenty-six prisoners were taken from the Zoo and the Zoo Annex to undergo extensive tortures and interrogations. The ropes were used on all of the men with some variations in the techniques. Men were tied in excruciating positions, with their arms secured behind their backs and then they were lifted from the ground by the ropes that were securing them.

One cell in the Zoo compound was discovered by the North Vietnamese to be the primary means of communications between the Annex and the Zoo proper. There was a window in cell #1 of the Zoo that overlooked the wall of the Zoo Annex. Because of that window, the men inside could see the hand signals of the prisoners in the Annex. That window was quickly sealed off by the North Vietnamese on the day Dramesi and Atterberry were brought back to the Zoo. To the North Vietnamese, the three prisoners inside that cell must have known everything that was going on in regard to the escape and many other activities in the camp. That singled the men out for particular attention from the interrogators.

Second only to the suffering undergone by Dramesi and Atterberry were the tortures given to those three prisoners from cell #1. Because of operational security, Trautman had not told anyone in the Zoo about the escape. The men in cell #1 hadn't passed on any messages about the escape. In the Zoo were the bulk of the senior officers among all of the prisoners. There couldn't have been a plan without their approval; the North Vietnamese were certain of this and they intended to learn all of the details.

The window of cell #1 being shuttered was only the first step the North Vietnamese took to minimize communications among the prisoners. Every hole, window, and ventilation port in the Zoo and the Zoo Annex was closed off. The heat of the coming summer made the cells stiflingly hot. The lack of circulation made it hard to breathe. But the sealed-off openings weren't enough to keep out the screams of the tortured men.

From cell #1 Red McDaniel, Al Runyan, and Ken Fleenor underwent tortures straight out of Dante's *Inferno*, only these tortures were worse because they were real. McDaniel suffered more than seven hundred lashes during floggings that went on for more than two weeks. There were thirty-eight bleeding wounds opened up on his back, legs, and buttocks during a single flogging. Beatings were common as the prisoners were struck with fists, shoes, sandals, and clubs. Electric shock was used; power from a battery coursing through the twitching muscles of a prisoner left him a mewling travesty.

Tied in ropes and irons, McDaniel suffered a compound fracture of one arm. While McDaniel was suspended in the air from a rope, a guard tried to push the bone sticking out from the torn flesh back into the arm.

All the senior officers were tortured, some to the point of near insanity. Men were beaten into unconsciousness; others wished they could "go out" to escape the pain. Larry Guarino was the SRO of the Zoo and had had no prior knowledge of Dramesi and Atterberry's escape attempt. If he had, he would have ordered the men not to go. He thought that there was no chance of success of any plan that did not include outside help. Guarino also considered any plan that did not have such help to be in direct violation of the order issued by Reisner years earlier. Dramesi had been right in considering Reisner's order to have been for a specific incident. But Guarino had been right in thinking that any attempt, successful or not, would cause the remaining prisoners to suffer a brutal retribution by the North Vietnamese.

Men suffered their tortures and then were stuck into solitary confinement for extended periods. Dramesi was finally released from the ropes on June 17. The stool, ropes, and lamps were taken away by Ferdinand and the prisoner was allowed to collapse to the floor. For the balance of that day and the night that followed, Dramesi was left alone; no guards came in to see him. He lay on the cool tiles of the floor in a near swoon, too crushed to really sleep and too exhausted to stay awake.

Ferdinand came back into the room with a mosquito net and hung it from four chairs spaced on the floor. For two nights Dramesi slept there; it took everything that he had left in the way of strength just to creep under the mosquito net. Now he was receiving a small bowl of soup as well as more bread. A cup and container of water were placed close at hand.

By June 20, Dramesi was taken from room #18 and placed in another cell across the compound. He was barely able to move, even with the lighter set of leg irons having been removed from his ankles. He had to carry his waste bucket, and even that effort took everything he had left in the way of strength. Left inside the cell block, Dramesi sat on his bucket while Ferdinand was out of sight. Reaching down, he put his hand under the door of cell #1. He had no idea who was inside the cell, it didn't matter. What he wanted to do was tell someone in the prisoner population that he was still alive. That was the message he tapped out against the bottom of the cell door. There was no answer from inside.

As he started to tap out the message again, he stopped. There was a touch against the palm of his hand. The fingers of whoever was inside cell #1 were gently stroking the palm of Dramesi's hand. Whoever was inside that cell either did not know the tap code, or they just didn't know what to say. But it was a gentle touch from another human being, a fellow sufferer in the prison of the damned.

As Ferdinand returned, Dramesi pulled his hand back. On the other side of the cell door came a whine and scrabbling sound as the occupant also knew that a guard was approaching. In his mind's eye, Dramesi could see whoever was in that cell retreating to the farthest corner of the room, huddling and staring at the door in fear.

But Ferdinand hadn't come up to punish anyone. Instead, he took Dramesi to a shower and allowed him to clean himself for the first time in over a month. After just trying to absorb the feeling of water running over him, Dramesi was taken back to room #18. For months, he remained there in solitary confinement. He was kept in the lighter traveling irons but fed soup and bread twice a day. Once a week, he was allowed to go and clean himself in the shower and empty his bucket of waste.

In September, a change took place throughout North Vietnam. The guards and officers whom Dramesi could see were wearing black armbands. He heard people crying. Then came the sound of artillery booming. It was a twenty-one-gun salute given in honor of the death of Ho Chi Minh. The leader of North Vietnam was dead and the lives of the prisoners would be changed because of it. It was September 1969.

[CHAPTER 23]

SEALS, FROGMEN, AND DARK WATERS

There were a great more U.S. Navy forces in Southeast Asia than the ships of the Seventh Fleet at Yankee Station in the Gulf of Tonkin. These forces ranged from the massive carriers that had launched many of the aircraft that penetrated the skies over North Vietnam, to the small, fiberglass-hulled boats of the Brown Water Navy, which traveled the rivers and canals of South Vietnam. There were also troops that were part of the Navy. These Navy troops were not just the United States Marine Corps that had served with the ships of the U.S. fleet since the earliest days of the country. There were also new units of fighting men, some so unique that their kind had never been seen in the world before.

In 1962, President John F. Kennedy recognized that the world had changed greatly, and the styles of conflict had changed with it. The days of huge armies conducting great campaigns of fire and movement were limited in the world of possible nuclear annihilation. In the early years of his administration, President Kennedy knew that wars would increasingly be fought in the shadows. Many of the conflicts of the future would be wars fought by guerrilla armies. Men would hide in the darkness, to strike and bleed an enemy, and then return to the shadows to wait for their next opportunity.

It would take a new kind of American fighting man to take on these new enemies, to fight the war against them in their own arena. The new fighting forces envisioned by a young president would be counterguerrilla units, and each branch of the military would have their own groups of these special-operations soldiers. For the United States Navy, these men would be the SEALs.

Organized in 1962, the SEALs were commissioned as two teams: SEAL Team One on the West Coast at Coronado, California, and SEAL Team Two on the East Coast at Little Creek, Virginia, and named for the three environments in which they would operate: the sea, air, and land. The men of the SEAL Teams were recruited directly from the Underwater Demolition Teams (UDTs).

Created during World War II to chart and attack the obstacles on enemy-held beaches, the men of the UDTs became known to the public as the Navy Frogmen after the war. The men of the UDTs were among the fittest and most extensively trained troops in the U.S. Navy. From their ranks, volunteers were accepted into the new SEAL Teams. As SEALs, the men learned counterguerrilla warfare, airborne (parachute) insertions, land combat, and what it would take to fight in any environment on the planet. They would fight an unseen enemy on their own turf, wherever that turf might be.

In 1966, the first direct action platoons of Navy SEALs were deployed into South Vietnam. Working in the swamps, jungles, canals, streams, and rivers of South Vietnam and particularly the wet morass of the Rung Sat Special Zone (RSSZ) outside of Saigon, the SEALs started taking back the night from the Viet Cong. Within a year of their first combat deployments into Vietnam, direct action platoons from both SEAL Teams One and Two were fighting a counterguerrilla war, and they were fighting it very well.

The primary enemy forces in South Vietnam were initially the Communist guerrilla army of the Viet Cong (VC). Working to overthrow the government of South Vietnam and unite the country under the Communist leadership in Hanoi, the Viet Cong were a difficult enemy to come to direct grips with. Very rarely would they take on the U.S. military in an open battle. The leadership of the VC and their masters up in North Vietnam recognized that directly fighting the strength of the United States and their supported allies of South Vietnam was only a way to ensure the destruction of the Communist cause. Instead, the VC fought from ambush, attack small units when and where they could. Strike and withdraw into hiding. And the jungles and swamps of South Vietnam, particularly the Rung Sat and rich farmland of the Mekong Delta, offered unlimited hiding places. They chose when and where to fight, and would withdraw to safety when threatened. It would take forces that could go into the difficult areas and demonstrate to the Viet Cong that no place would remain safe for them.

In spite of the very secret nature of the units during the 1960s, the exploits of the Navy SEALs in Vietnam quickly became something of a legend, both among the American military and public back home, as well as in the huts and jungle camps of the Viet Cong. Called "the men in green faces" by the enemy for their extensive camouflage makeup, the SEALs made the Viet Cong terrified of the night. Instead of being able to move in the dark, travel the canals and waterways of South Vietnam almost at will, the Viet Cong were now facing men who would silently appear and attack, then fade back into the shadows and black waters.

Very quickly, the SEALs became masters of the night ambush. A group of SEALs would remain hidden in the darkness, sometimes submerged in muddy water up to their noses, waiting for an enemy force to pass down a known trail or waterway. The sudden blaze of gunfire from a SEAL unit would overwhelm an enemy force, surprised by the lethal rain just appearing out of the night. Intelligence materials were gathered up from the bodies, survivors would be gathered up as prisoners, and the SEALs would withdraw from an area.

Becoming absolute masters at hiding in whatever terrain they might be operating in, the SEALs could remain undetected in an area for as long as necessary. Observation and listing posts along known or suspected enemy routes could be manned by SEALs for extended times. Even a SEAL platoon or squad might stay in a single spot for up to forty-eight hours just to observe. If a target appeared, the SEALs could strike suddenly even after two days of hiding in the mud, snatch up an enemy, and withdraw just as unseen as when they arrived.

A platoon of SEALs eventually became fourteen men led by two officers. The platoons were further broken down into two squads of eight SEALs each, each squad being a pair of four-man fire teams. No SEAL worked alone. This was a lesson solidly implanted in every SEAL and UDT operator during the earliest training experiences in training. Every teammate had a swim buddy, and a swim buddy was never left behind.

The actions of the Navy SEALs had already been felt in North Vietnam even before the direct-action platoons entered combat. In the mid- and early 1960s, the SEALs operated mobile training teams (MTTs), which helped teach and advise South Vietnamese naval commandos how to conduct operations against North Vietnam. Working from U.S.-supplied armed high-speed boats called "Nasty" boats, the South Vietnamese naval commandos conducted raids along the North Vietnamese coast, ripping up shore installations with gunfire and planting explosive charges. They learned some of the waters off North Vietnam and the capabilities of the North Vietnamese Navy. The SEAL advisers who worked with the Nasty boats also learned these lessons, and reported them up the chain to higher commands.

The SEALs amassed a long list of successes during their operations in South Vietnam. They also had their losses, teammates killed during the five years of direct-action missions against the Communists. Though each man lost was a heavy blow to the SEAL Teams, the enemy paid an even heavier price for each operator loss. Conservative estimates have more that two hundred enemy personnel killed for each of the forty-nine SEAL and UDT operators killed in Vietnam. The actual number of enemy soldiers taken out by the men of the teams could be very much higher. In all of their hundreds of operations against the enemy in Southeast Asia, not one operator was ever left behind. In spite of their working deep in enemy-controlled areas on operations where they were often outnumbered, a SEAL was never taken prisoner.

Within a year of the SEALs putting platoons into Vietnam they were conducting a very special type of mission. As individuals and as a group SEALs considered the most important mission to be the rescue of Americans POWs. In South Vietnam, it was the Viet Cong who held POWs, both from the American forces as well as those of the South Vietnamese military. These prisoners were sometimes captured in combat when cut off from their units. Some were targeted for kidnapping by the Viet Cong and others just had the bad luck to be in the wrong place at the wrong time.

However they were captured, prisoners being held by the Viet Cong were often kept in horrible conditions, even worse than those inflicted on POWs in North Vietnam. It wasn't that the Viet Cong tortured their prisoners to a greater extent than their Communist brothers in the North; it was that the conditions in the jungle prison camps were primitive at best.

Prisoners in the hands of the Viet Cong suffered badly from disease, exposure, malnutrition, and exhaustion. To keep their prisoners from the hands of possible rescuers, the Viet Cong moved them about from camp to camp at almost a moment's notice. There was a wide network of temporary prison camps set up all through some of the most inhospitable areas of South Vietnamese jungles and marshes. Both American and Vietnamese prisoners would get moved about almost at random, usually bound and hobbled in some way and always under close guard. For these reasons, combined with the severe abuse and neglect they suffered at the hands of the Viet Cong, more POWs disappeared or died while in captivity in the South than their brethren in North Vietnam.

All of the American forces would do anything they could to rescue POWs. For the Navy SEALs, the desire to rescue prisoners held by the enemy was taken as almost a personal vendetta against the Viet Cong. With their deeply ingrained philosophy of the importance of the group above the individual, and to never leave anyone behind, the SEALs would feel it necessary to drop everything when the information became available on where prisoners might be held. The possibility of liberating American POWs caused the SEALs to bring all of their considerable skills and resources to the mission.

During the years SEALs had been operating in South Vietnam, they developed their own sources of intelligence, their own means of evaluating that information, and the ability to rapidly act on it. This gave the SEAL units a speed of reaction that was much faster than any of the traditional military organizations. On one occasion in August 1970, a prisoner who had escaped the Viet Cong was able to give specific, timely information on the location and manning of the prison camp where he had been held. This was the kind of information that the SEALs were quickly able to react to, especially when the unit was being run by a very competent and aggressive officer.

On mid-morning, August 22, 1970, Lieutenant Louis Boink of SEAL Team Two, 6th Platoon, moved his men out on a raid on the reported VC POW camp. Boink had organized a major operation in a very short time, bringing in an Australian aircraft bomber group, Navy assets to provide gunfire support from offshore, Army helicopter units, the Navy Seawolves and their helicopter gunships, and a regional company of South Vietnamese into a coordinated effort to take down the POW camp with minimal casualties.

While the Australian B-57 bombers began an air raid on a jungle and canal area to block the Viet Cong's movement, the SEALs moved in. Having inserted by helicopter nearly four miles from the location of the camp to avoid detection, the SEALs rapidly moved across very rugged terrain to get into position prior to the Australian air strike. A quick shot fired by the SEALs took out a Viet Cong guard as he headed into a bunker. U.S. Army helicopter gunships opened fire, sending 2.75-inch high-explosive rockets blasting into the jungle to the north and west of the camp. The jungle erupted with high explosives and spinning bits of steel fragmentation as the bombers and the gunships left the Viet Cong with only a small avenue of escape. In the terrible confusion of the attacks, the hope was that the Viet Cong guards would not have time to open fire on the POWs and might just run for their lives.

Following the lead of the escaped POW who guided them to the camp, the SEALs tore through the area looking for POWs but found nothing. The trail the Viet Cong had left through the jungle in their near-panicked withdrawal from the camp was relatively easy to follow. The helicopter gunships, particularly those of the Navy Seawolves, came in for close-air support of the SEALs on the ground. Accurate naval gunfire from the five-inch guns of the USS *Sutherland* offshore also kept the pressure on the fleeing Viet Cong. Though the maelstrom of fire, the SEALs kept chasing the enemy, always keeping the pressure on and watching for the slightest chance of rescuing prisoners who might be left behind or make a break for it themselves in the confusion.

Moving rapidly through the swampland all around the area, the SEALs chased the Viet Cong for more than two hours. Finally, the men of 6th Platoon came upon a group of twenty-eight Vietnamese prisoners who had finally been abandoned by their Viet Cong captors. On-call helicopter transport was quickly brought in to evacuate the prisoners, some of whom were suffering from malnourishment and abuse at the hands of their captors. In spite of the success of a very complicated and nearly perfectly executed operation, the SEALs felt some of the bitter taste of failure. In the stunned and then joyous group of Vietnamese prisoners, there had been no American POWs found.

The possibility of rescuing American prisoners held by the Viet Cong was considered so important it was specifically addressed by all of the United States intelligence agencies. Material relating to the location of prisoners of war would come under the code name Bright Light. That material would be given expedited handling and quickly put in the hands of direct-action units such as the SEALs. Priorities were set up so that assets would be placed at the disposal of Bright Light operations so that no time would be lost in trying to react to information. The location of POWs and Viet Cong prisoner camps was information that had a very short shelf life. Good, solid intelligence had to be acted on quickly and competently to give a mission the best chance of rescuing POWs.

In the swampy Mekong Delta provinces of South Vietnam, intelligence officers often asked to have a SEAL detachment made available to them for action on Bright Light missions. There were a number of raids on suspected prisoner camps. On several missions, a number of South Vietnamese prisoners were liberated, some of whom had been prisoners of the Viet Cong for years. But the main prize so desired by the SEALs and the people they worked with, the rescue of American POWs, always seemed just out of reach. During the early years of the 1970s, as U.S. involvement in direct combat operations was ending, some of the last SEAL detachments deployed to Vietnam were intended to help conduct POW rescue operations. Other combat operations continued, but became the missions of the South Vietnamese rather than American units.

Detachments of SEALs remained active in the Southeast Asia area, though not necessarily in Vietnam. Mobile training teams of SEALs conducted operations with members of the Thai special operations units. There were also SEAL training operations being conducted out of Subic Bay in the Philippines, a base for the United States Navy since the end of World War II. Along with the SEALs at Subic were detachments from the UDTs stationed at Coronado in California.

While it was the Navy SEALs who garnered the bulk of the attention when it came to combat in Vietnam, the UDTs had also maintained a presence incountry throughout the war. The primary missions of the UDT detachments tended to match the meaning of their name. Underwater work was conducted, particularly along the shores of South Vietnam. Working from specialized submarines, the UDT operators (the term *frogmen* was only used by the general public and was not popular in the Teams at the time) conducted reconnaissance missions that resulted in detailed charts being made up of much of the South Vietnamese coastline. Many of the areas surveyed and charted had never been mapped before.

Demolition operations were also conducted by UDT detachments in Vietnam. Navigable canals were blasted through the marshes, and obstacles placed by the Viet Cong were blown free of the streams, rivers, and canals by high explosives. Underwater skills were learned, new equipment tested and trained with, and mission capabilities were increased.

On January 10, 1972, Alfa platoon of SEAL Team One was deployed to the U.S. Naval Base at White Beach on Okinawa. The unit was to act as the contingency platoon for the SEAL WESTPAC DET (West Pacific Detachment). The SEALs were led by Lieutenant Melvin "Spence" Dry as their officer in command. They were to operate as missions came up.

[CHAPTER 24]

NEW TIME

The world changed for the prisoners in North Vietnam with the death of Ho Chi Minh. The worst of the tortures was over and the treatment of the men in general improved. For Dramesi and much of the prisoner population leadership, they remained in isolation. Improvements came, but their arrival was gradual.

Through his own tricking of one of the guards, Dramesi was able to finally sleep in his cell without the weight of the iron shackles on his feet. Once a week he was taken from room #18 and allowed to clean himself and his clothes in a shower. On return to the room where he was kept, Dramesi was once again put in ankle shackles and a heavy iron bar was threaded through them. Then a large iron padlock was snapped on the bar to prevent it being removed again. The guard he called "Kid Crazy" or more often just K.C., would simply toss Dramesi the heavy lock and then stand at the room door waiting to hear the sound of the lock being snapped shut. Figuring out how to make a noise with the metal pieces that sounded like the lock being shut wasn't too hard for Dramesi to accomplish. When K.C. heard the sound and left the room without looking back, that was hard for Dramesi to believe, but only for a moment. Then the grin spread across his face. After the last inspection of the evening was done, Dramesi was able to spend a night sleeping without the heavy weight of the irons across his legs.

An attempt to jam the lock with lead taken from a toothpaste tube almost resulted in disaster. With a few small bits of lead Dramesi had jammed up the lock mechanism so that it could be closed and look secure, but wasn't actually locked. That way he could remove it at will. But when a guard tried to open the lock with a key, the lead caused the whole mechanism to jam. Through some luck, Dramesi was able to get the lock open and cleared before his sabotage was noticed. The guards had been concerned with the situation but in the end they did not punish the prisoner. Dramesi's freedom from the leg irons had only lasted for a short, but satisfying, time.

It wasn't until past the middle of November 1969 that Dramesi was finally released from room #18. It was nighttime and dark, but he was blindfolded when finally taken to a location at the Hanoi Hilton complex known to the prisoners as the Stockyards. Placed in an unlit, filthy room, Dramesi was allowed to move about in the darkness to try and settle himself in to his new cell. The stench of the barely ventilated place was strong and he was still wearing his leg irons. In the end, he was able to escape in the only way that was left to him at the moment: He slept.

It was a week before things improved, and they did so fairly rapidly. There was an issue of clothing, some comfort items including some well-received soap, and even a pair of sandals, which helped protect Dramesi's badly abused feet. What was truly astonishing was how suddenly the quality and quantity of the food improved. At first, there was so much food that he couldn't eat it all. But his body quickly grew used to getting the materials it needed to try and heal itself to some extent. One of the things that really helped Dramesi improve was being issued all the water that he wanted and needed.

But interrogations were not over. It wasn't long before Dramesi found himself back in front of Bug in a new interrogation room, though the torture that had spotlighted so many of the other meetings with Bug was not employed. Instead, Bug used a different ploy, telling Dramesi that other prisoners had been released from captivity. They were home in the United States while he was still in Hanoi.

The demands to write continued unabated. One of the things demanded of him was a request in writing that the camp commander have his leg irons removed. But Dramesi refused.

The structural security of the door to his new cell was so poor that Dramesi knew that he could get out if he wasn't wearing the leg irons. As he slept one night during a tropical rainstorm, Dramesi dreamed about a successful escape. In the dream, he ended up at sea with Ed Atterberry, floating about and waiting to be found by the U.S. Navy. He was still the man he had been before the ordeal of torture he had just gone through. And John Dramesi was not done trying to escape.

On December 9, Dramesi was told he had been forgiven by the camp commander. The leg irons finally came off and the miserable little cell was left behind. He was moved to an area of the camp the prisoners called Little Vegas and the cell blocks located there had been identified by the names of a number of casinos in Las Vegas. Dramesi was sent to the Mint and secured into cell #1.

Cell #1 was even smaller than the one he had left behind, but the Mint held something Dramesi hungered for: company in the form of fellow prisoners. In cells #2 and #3 were George Coker and George McKnight. For as long as they could, the prisoners communicated with each other. The North Vietnamese had put the three escape attempt survivors next to each other in the same cell block. The men had a lot to talk about.

Talking was still something that would quickly earn the angry attention of a guard. In the solitude of their cells, the men leaned into the walls in order to hear the tapping sounds made by the other prisoners. The tap code was simple and words were just spelled out by the sound of soft strikes against a wall. For hours, there remained the haunting image of men listening in the darkness and rapping.

On occasion, Dramesi would meet face to face with another prisoner, the first one being George Coker. The freedom to speak was a very welcome one, but the long tap conversations remained a standard for communications between the prisoners while in their cells.

When caught trying to pass a written note to other prisoners, Dramesi was taken into one of the interrogation rooms and threatened with torture. It was May 10, 1970, exactly one year since he had tried to escape. He was forced to stand facing a wall for several days, but there were no long sessions with the ropes or the return of the leg irons. It wasn't very long before Dramesi was looking out of his cell window, examining the camp compound, and making mental notes on things like the guard rotations, the one guard tower visible to him, and the makeup of the compound wall. Such information would be valuable for another escape attempt.

Moved to a new cell block, this one the Stardust, Dramesi was in a solitary room—but George McKnight was now in the cell across from his. Life was continuing to improve very gradually for the prisoners, though communications were still limited. Small gift packages had arrived from back home for some of the men, and they were allowed to receive them.

There were discussions on the plausibility of escape attempts between Dramesi and his immediate group. But the plans were never practical enough to be considered seriously. There were rifts between groups of the prisoners in the compound and throughout North Vietnam. Some of the prisoners cooperated with the North Vietnamese to different degrees; some remained as solid as they could in their resistance. For Dramesi, the Code of Conduct was not as flexible as it was for others and he remained as adamant as ever in his decisions. There were other prisoners who also stood as Dramesi did, but not all the POWs were as firm in their resolve.

On Christmas Day 1970, all of the prisoners received something of a gift from the North Vietnamese: the creation of Camp Unity. The men were taken out of their cells and searched thoroughly before being sent out in small groups to stand in a nearby alleyway. Prisoners who had been communicating with each other for weeks now actually met face-to-face for the first time. Many just ran about shaking hands; some hugged and some cried. It was a major reunion of people who had suffered together and now could share friendly human contact.

But the delivery of the presents was not over. The North Vietnamese gathered the men up, blindfolded them, and moved them in groups under armed guard. In a short time, the men arrived at the new location. For Dramesi, he found himself in a large room with what seemed to be a huge group of POWs. Forty-seven prisoners would now be sharing the living space of a single room more than seventy feet long and over twenty feet wide. And they could talk freely with each other.

The camp rules were not really relaxed to any extent. But the men could interact openly, and that was something they had never been able to do before. There were still interrogation sessions, mostly involved with the North Vietnamese trying to gather propaganda materials of one kind or another. Writings were demanded and tapes desired, but Dramesi and a number of others still refused to cooperate to varying degrees. One thing that appealed to Dramesi in particular was the re-creation of a certain prisoner organization, an escape committee.

With the large gathering of POWs in the single room, there were now a number of senior officers available to lead the prisoners in a cohesive manner. One of these officers was placed in charge of the escape committee and Dramesi was told that he would have to clear any plans through them. Dramesi was held in a position of respect by a number of prisoners, including senior officers, in part because of his hard discipline and personal strength that had allowed him to survive severe torture without bending to the will of the North Vietnamese.

The present lack of torture and what were considered improving conditions for the prisoners caused a large number of them to disagree with Dramesi on the idea of escaping. It had not been long since the summer of torture following the escape attempt of Dramesi and Atterberry. The men remembered those horrendous days and were not anxious to relive them. The threat of reprisals frankly terrified many of the POWs. But for Dramesi, there was no question of whether any of the prisoners should attempt to escape; it was just a matter of when. It was their duty, their honor, and their right to be free.

There were a number of prisoners who would talk to Dramesi and to whom he would listen. One of these men was Major James H. Kasler. Not only was Kasler an ace pilot from his more than one hundred missions during the Korean War, he had been a tail gunner in B-29 bombers during World War II, flying missions against the Japanese in the Pacific. Now he too was a POW, having been shot down over North Vietnam on August 8, 1966. The North Vietnamese had recognized what a prize they had in holding Kasler as a prisoner and had given him particular attention during questioning. He had also been one of the prisoners to go through long sessions with Fidel, and had still come out without cooperating with the enemy.

The resistance of the prisoners against the authority of the North Vietnamese had to be maintained, if not increased. But many of the prisoners were worn down. The ultimate in resistance would be an escape, but almost none of the other prisoners were interested in even hearing about such an idea. But several people did want to keep the idea of escape alive in Camp Unity, and one of these people was Colonel Reisner.

After some conversation with Dramesi, Reisner admitted that his earlier orders about not escaping without outside help had been directed toward a single situation. Dramesi had been right to try and escape when he did, and now Reisner wanted him to establish a committee to research, plan, and organize another escape attempt. There was one control that Dramesi had to accept, though: There would be an officer unknown to him who would have the final say on any escape attempt. Someone else would give the go or no-go order.

That situation was not the one Dramesi would have preferred, but he did accept it. He was to plan an escape, but was not the head of the escape committee. That position was held by Colonel Hervey Stockman. Within a short time of Dramesi's conversation with Reisner, Stockman had approached him for a talk. In spite of his enthusiasm for a freedom bid, Dramesi was able to critique what had gone wrong during his attempt with Atterberry. He could accept the mistakes made and plan against repeating them. One thing that Dramesi was able to quickly identify as a problem was the lack of ability to tell the time.

Dramesi and Atterberry had been able to get several miles from the camp, walking through a populated area and not drawing a great deal of attention. It was the fact that they had not gotten far enough, been outside what Dramesi called the five-mile security zone, that had allowed them to be so quickly captured. But the thing that was most important in making an escape attempt was the will to succeed, having the determination to make the attempt in the first place and actually carry out the plan.

Colonel Stockman felt he could agree with Dramesi's opinions on what an escape would need. And he told Dramesi that the escape committee would be meeting and work out a plan. Along with Dramesi and Stockman, the committee would include George Coker, George McKnight, Jim Kasler, and Bud Day. Of the six men in the committee, half of them—McKnight, Coker, and Dramesi—had already made escape attempts from camps. Immediately following his shoot-down and ejection, in spite of being badly injured, Bud Day had gone through a period of escape and evasion from the North Vietnamese. It was a very good pool of determination, knowledge, and experience with which to plan and execute a possible escape.

Time continued to pass for the prisoners at the camps. Apathy and fear had taken hold in a number of the men, though there were periods of defiance of the North Vietnamese. Feeling that a symbol would help draw the prisoners together, Dramesi set out to create the most powerful one he could think of. With a needle formed from carefully sharpened copper wire and scrounged materials, he set to work. On a white handkerchief, he stitched. The blue field came from a sweater that had been supplied by the North Vietnamese, but not for the purpose that he employed it. White thread came from a towel, red stripes from a set of underwear sent in another prisoner's Care package. Yellow thread from a blanket provided a gold border. Working for nearly two weeks sewing quietly every night, Dramesi made an American flag. It was what he considered the ultimate symbol of freedom. It was early 1971 and he had been a prisoner for nearly four years. It was longer than any American POWs held during World War II, and there were many other prisoners about him who had been held by the North Vietnamese for much longer.

Through the movements of prisoners dictated by the North Vietnamese, the makeup of the escape committee changed. By the late spring of 1971, the committee was made up of Dramesi, Coker, McKnight, and Kasler. As the ranking man, Kasler took over the command of the committee and he still wanted to see an escape go forward. The men planned for an attempt to be made in August 1971, six months away.

A planned escape would require supplies, which would have to be gathered and hidden from the guards. The discovery of some plastered-over drain holes gave Dramesi the possibility of a secure hiding place. With some excavation and working with scrounged and materials stolen from the North Vietnamese, Dramesi found that his drain holes were indeed very good hiding places. With that hurdle covered, the plan went forward to the next major obstacle, this one among the prisoners themselves. It was time to explain the plan in general and what the escape committee wanted to do to the senior ranking officer in the room.

With the removal of most of the senior officers from the room, there was a new SRO in command, and he was anything but agreeable to an escape attempt. During the discussion with the SRO, Dramesi pointed out many points of the escape plan in general and several parts in particular detail. He had found a pathway out of the room and the building again through the ceiling as during his last attempt. The rope that needed to be used for the escape could be manufactured from what was available; the committee had already made up a section and tested it for strength. Materials for the escape, food, disguises, and most important, information, were available in much greater quantity and quality than Dramesi and Atterberry had available to them during their attempted escape nearly two years earlier.

Again, the pathway to freedom was going to be the Red River. Instead of immediately stealing a boat and possibly alerting the North Vietnamese as to just where the escaped prisoners were heading, Dramesi had come up with an alternate plan. The escapees would use plastic bags, of which they already had a satisfactory supply, to make life preservers and waterproof their gear. The swimming approach had already been tried by Coker and McKnight; it would be even better with prior preparation. The plan was not foolproof and it never could be. But it was a good one and had a better chance of success that the previous attempts.

In the end, the planning fell on deaf ears. The new SRO wouldn't approve of an escape plan and he wouldn't allow anyone to make the attempt. That escape effort was ended and the date in August came and went without action. The end of the summer of 1971 was a very down time for Dramesi, but he still wasn't going to surrender. The Code of Conduct insisted that prisoners make every effort to escape, and he was going to continue following that directive to the best of his ability.

[CHAPTER 25]

OPERATION DIAMOND

In the last months of 1971 the North Vietnamese again moved a number of prisoners about the compounds. In response to the prisoners' activities—some of which were no threat to the North Vietnamese or the security of the camp—the guards removed a number of the senior officers of room #7. Among the people taken from the room was the SRO who had refused the escape committee permission to continue with their plan.

A few days before the shakeup, the SRO had given Dramesi some very unwelcome information. The order was simple: There could be no escape without outside assistance. The SRO said that such was the policy and it was going to stand. The statement was also a complete reversal of what the SRO had told to Dramesi close to when the two had first met in the beginning of Camp Unity.

While he had been held in solitary confinement after his punitive torture session in room #18, Dramesi had been visited by a number of North Vietnamese. One of these individuals had been a high-ranking senior officer who told Dramesi in no uncertain terms to not escape again. If he escaped a third time, the officer had said, "That will not be good for you." Dramesi had been the only prisoner to have already escaped the North Vietnamese twice before. The officer was assuring him that a third attempt would be the end of John Dramesi.

In spite of that threat, Dramesi had been going ahead with preparations for another escape. The North Vietnamese had threatened him with death, and the implication that it would be a particularly gruesome one. Now his own leadership was putting roadblocks in his way. But that did not stop Dramesi or the others who wanted to make their bid for freedom. A new escape committee formed and considered a possible plan of action. The rotation of men in and out of room #7 resulted in a new SRO. To maintain operational security, Dramesi and the newly formed committee did not bring the new SRO into their confidence. They were facing enough difficulties with the new escape orders from the senior SRO of the entire camp.

The first in a series of new orders issued by the camp SRO was that no one could escape unless he could show their plan had at least a 90 percent chance of success. All of the men knew that even a well-planned, fully supported mission over enemy territory didn't have those odds of success most of the time. The requirement was so ridiculous that the men laughed out loud after hearing it. It was obvious to everyone concerned that such an order was impossible to meet.

The 90 percent order showed that the camp SRO was simply trying to give lip service to the demands of the Code of Conduct. It was so obvious a dodge that he soon issued a new order to override the demands of his earlier one. Considerations for an escape could go forward, plans and preparations could be done, but only if the men planning the escape could show they had outside support.

There had been new developments in the preparations for an escape unknown to the camp SRO or even the SRO of room #7. Dramesi and other members of the escape committee had been working to establish that they did indeed have outside assistance. Very covert lines of communications had been opened to the prisoners, allowing the almost unthinkable to take place: The men could actually get a message to higher command back in the United States. Outside help was not necessarily available from among the local population of Hanoi, but there could be arrangements made for a pickup of the prisoners once they reached the ocean.

The camp SRO issued another order that appeared to end the question of escape while still remaining within the directives of the Code of Conduct: The SRO would not make the final decision as far as the go or no-go on an escape attempt was concerned. That decision was to be deferred to the highest available outside authority. Only if an escape committee could get permission from the United States could they carry out their plans. It was a requirement the camp SRO could not see being met on any practical basis. He hadn't considered Dramesi's determination to reach freedom, or die in the attempt.

The men of the escape committee had been making preparations and plans that would not have met the 90 percent rule put out earlier by the SRO, but it was the best plan developed to date. The greatest advantage they had over earlier attempts was the amount of intelligence that had been gathered on the surrounding area. A map had been supplied to the escape committee, one that showed Hanoi in finer detail than the men had seen before. Wrapped in plastic to keep the paper from being damaged, the precious map had been stuck inside a hollowed-out twig. The twig had been sent down the gutter in the camp, where Dramesi had been waiting. It wasn't long before the guard had been looking the other way and Dramesi was able to take the innocuous-looking object out of the water.

The map held the kind of information that could have changed the outcome of Dramesi and Atterberry's earlier escape attempt. One of the valuable points of information was the exact location of the prison where the men were in relation to the surrounding area. The Red River was off to the west, a relatively short distance considering how much ground Dramesi's previous attempt had covered. In addition to significant locations, the map also had notes detailing what kind of traffic could be expected on which roads, and what would be the easiest and fastest path to follow to the river.

Many of the plans and some of the preparations intended for the August 1971 escape plan were still available. Dramesi had confirmed the hiding places available in the plastered-over drains were still there. Supplies could be stashed away and the disguises put together. They had even stolen some mirrors, materials they would need to signal American forces. The men of the escape committee had everything they needed for an escape, as well as a very good idea of what would and would not work. Hard-won experience had shown that a Caucasian could move through the local Asian population and not be noticed. It would only take audacity, bravery, and leadership to make a plan work.

In spite of the lack of support from some of the other prisoners, Dramesi and the rest of the escape committee went ahead with their preparations. There was no sign from the North Vietnamese that there would be any change in prisoner status for the foreseeable future. They were pawns in the international game being played out between the North Vietnamese and the government of the United States. The only sure way Dramesi could see to change the situation would be to take an active role in determining at least his own fate. And that active role meant escape. But he was first and foremost a military officer. He respected the chain of command, no matter what he thought of those above him. He would obey orders and follow the requirements put forward by the SRO of the camp.

The covert communication system worked both ways. A message could be gotten out by the prisoners that would eventually make its way to U.S. authorities. In addition, the prisoners could receive information, and materials, though in Dramesi's opinion, the kinds of things that came in were not worth the risk or difficulty to receive them.

What was known as the three "S's" made it to the prisoners on a fairly regular basis: sympathy, snack packs, and sports. That meant that the incredibly valuable communications system managed to deliver messages of sympathy from home, as well as sports results. The information was a morale booster, as were the foodstuffs that came in. In some cases, the sports and sympathy information was contained within the snack packs.

Dramesi was not the only one to not really give a damn about who was winning the World Series. He considered such things to be a terrible waste of space, time, money, and effort. But the people who had established the communications link felt that such things were important, and to the prisoner population at large, they were a link to home—in spite of very few people at the camp even knowing that the link existed.

These were the kind of things that came in to the camp despite the scrutiny of the North Vietnamese. The delivery of the messages and materials could be spotty. Delays in the system were inevitable, and they couldn't be foretold or prevented. When the request for permission to escape went out, the return message would have to come in by the most timely and positive method available. It would be a very brief message, as required by the delivery system. There would be one signal for yes, and another for no. What the return message would be was suggested by the prisoners; the specific means of its delivery was left up to the outside authorities.

To help ensure that the incoming message was received it would be repeated. And it would come from a source that would prove authorization from the highest source. For security purposes, only the escape committee knew that the message would be coming in. But everyone in the camp would know it was delivered.

The men of the escape committee realized what the results of their planned escape could be. It could mean a great deal more than just the freedom of those who got to the far side of the wall. They knew that their request could be turned down. Because of the political implications of the resulting escape, the decision to go or not go could only be made by the highest authority, the commander in chief himself. The effort to support the escape would very likely be a tremendous one. When the message came to the prisoners, it was unmistakable by those who knew what it was.

The U.S. intelligence community received the message that Dramesi had sent out and immediately recognized its importance. While still maintaining the highest levels of security, the proper authorities were notified of the decisions that had to be made. The basic plan of the prisoners' escape was given a code name. It was to be called Operation Diamond.

[CHAPTER 26]

BLACKBIRDS BOOMING THE HANOI HILTON

One of the most exotic aircraft of the Vietnam War was also one of the most rarely seen. Shot at a number of times, but never hit, the SR-71 Blackbird (named for its special black paint) was at its heart simply a reconnaissance plane, but an extremely sophisticated one. It carried no armament, but the cameras and sensors it had on board could do more damage to the enemy than anything short of a nuclear weapon.

The SR-71, and its CIA-operated single-seat predecessor, the A-12, barely resembled an aircraft on first glance. The huge black jet appeared to be more of a spacecraft or at least a winged missile than one of the greatest high-performance production jets in the world.

Developed as a replacement for the U2 spy plane, the SR-71 was designed from the beginning to be able to outfly anything put up against it—be it aircraft or missile—for at least several decades from its first introduction. As a strategic reconnaissance aircraft, the SR-71 has yet to be bettered more than fifty years after its introduction. It is a high-performance camera platform, even more effective than an orbiting spy satellite for some missions. With its two-man crew, the cameras of an SR-71 can cover an area of 110,000 square miles per hour of flight at 82,000 feet. That gives the craft the capability of photographing the entire United Kingdom in less than an hour while on a single mission. And the detail the cameras can make out is such that a golf ball can be resolved on the ground from 80,000 feet—about a 1.7-inch sphere seen from more than 15 miles up.

To protect itself, the SR-71 operates on the very edge of space; altitudes of over 82,000 feet are normal for an operational flight. The speed that the craft can move at is also a major part of its success; the SR-71 is capable of cruising at Mach 3 to Mach 3.5—three to three and a half times the speed of sound, or from 2,280 to 2,660 miles per hour. At top speed, the Blackbird covers a mile on the ground in less than one second, over 3,300 feet per second, literally faster than a speeding bullet.

At 82,000 feet altitude, the air is a killing –69 degrees Fahrenheit and is so thin that it only exerts a pressure of 0.4 pound per square inch, as compared to 14.7 pounds per square inch at sea level. The environment would kill an unprotected human being in seconds if they were exposed to it. The SR-71 was designed to operate at its best in this same environment. But special problems had to be addressed when designing the craft to make sure it worked at its intended flying speeds.

In spite of the thin air and subfreezing temperature at altitude, structural parts of the SR-71 can be heated to 600 degrees Fahrenheit by just the friction of the plane flying at a modest Mach 2.4, which equals one mile every two seconds. Because of this and other factors, the bulk of the SR-71 was built of titanium alloys. The titanium skin of the jet helps protect the aluminum airframe components from the heat that would otherwise melt them in flight. It was the first aircraft ever to be built of such special materials, the fuselage being 93 percent titanium alloys and composite materials. It paved the way for the future family of stealth aircraft.

The SR-71 itself is basically a flying fuel tank with engines, except for a little room allowed in the design for sensors and crew. The most dominating outside feature of the craft, besides its sinister black shape, are the two huge Pratt & Whitney J58 engines that each develop 32,500 pounds of thrust. The huge engines were specially designed in the precomputer age of slide rules and pen-and-paper engineering to operate effectively at high altitudes and speeds and made the SR-71 the fastest and highest-flying air-breathing jet in the world for most of its operational life.

The craft that would become the SR-71 was first flown on December 22, 1964, and entered service with the U.S. Air Force under the Strategic Air Command in January 1966. Just fewer than thirty of the craft were built in the 1960s; at the time, the cost per copy was $34 million.

The crew for an operational SR-71 was made up of a pilot in the front seat and a reconnaissance systems operator (RSO) in the rear. Though a fully qualified pilot himself, the RSO did not operate the aircraft. The rear seat in the cockpit did not have a set of flight controls, through there were a number of instruments there that enabled the RSO to assist the pilot in managing the SR-71's systems. Instead, the RSO ran the cameras, radar suite, and the rest of the sensor systems to carry out the basic reconnaissance mission of the aircraft.

Prospective crewmen who wished to serve in SR-71s had to have at least 2,500 hours in the air on standard aircraft before they would be allowed to volunteer for the training program. The cost and rarity of the aircraft meant that only the most technically proficient people were allowed to operate the unique craft. Additionally, the secrecy of almost every operational flight of an SR-71 meant that those who manned one of the great black birds had to be among the most trustworthy in the Air Force. The physical demands of flying on the edge of space in a high-performance aircraft also required a high level of fitness to survive the missions and bring the bird, and the crews, back alive.

The required near-perfect professional performance reviews of prospective volunteers would be carefully examined while the men themselves underwent a battery of medical tests and deep-background checks. Even after all of these requirements had been met by those wishing to serve in SR-71s, they still had another high hurdle to pass. The selection board that interviewed each volunteer was made up of people who already actively manned the aircraft. They knew best just what the demands were on a person, both physically and mentally, when flying Blackbirds. Because of this unique knowledge, the opinion of the selection board was given a good deal of weight when it came time to finally allow a specific volunteer into the training program.

An initial deployment to Asia of the A-12 proved the value of such an asset in obtaining photographic intelligence of enemy sites. In May 1967, it was put out in high-level intelligence briefings that the North Vietnamese were going to be fielding missiles that could greatly escalate the conflict. The director of the CIA stated that the A-12 was invulnerable to Soviet-made antiaircraft missiles and would be the proper aircraft to conduct surveillance of North Vietnam. The plan to deploy the craft was approved by President Johnson himself and A-12 aircraft were quickly deployed to Kadena Air Base on Okinawa as Operation Black Shield. The first operational flight over North Vietnam took place on May 31.

The A-12 and subsequent SR-71 both proved too difficult to hit by any of the dense North Vietnamese air defenses. Over the most heavily defended airspace in the world, the closest any of the aircraft came to being hit was when a very small piece of brass from the fuse of an SA-2 "Guideline" missile was discovered imbedded in the aircraft's skin in an after-flight inspection. The SA-2 missile has a maximum range of about 31 miles, an altitude ceiling of 80,000 feet, and a maximum speed of Mach 3.5. The 287-pound high-explosive warhead of the missile caused no damage, but left the pilot with a very interesting souvenir. It was the closest thing to a hit on an A-12 or SR-71 in more than 1,000 flights over enemy territory.

The SR-71 took over from the A-12 aircraft at Kadena in early 1968. The CIA-run overflight program was closed and the Air Force in the form of the Strategic Air Command (SAC) took over the reconnaissance mission previously done by the Agency. As an SAC overseas reconnaissance station, the Kadena SR-71 detachment became known as Operating Location 8 (OL-8).

The stationing of the SR-71s at Kadena resulted in something that followed the crews and aircraft for the rest of their existence—besides their amazing record of accomplishments. Though referred to publicly as the Blackbird, crew members preferred the nickname that was conferred on the craft soon after their arrival in the Okinawa area: Habu. The Habu is a dark-colored poisonous snake indigenous to the islands that make up the Okinawa area. Locals referred to the strange black aircraft as "Habus" because of its general resemblance to the reptile, and the name stuck. For both the SR-71s and the crews, they referred to themselves as Habus, and the reconnaissance missions conducted off the OL-8 base were referred to as Habu missions.

The Soviets already knew well of the unusual aircraft being launched from Kadena, as they had one of their "fishing trawlers" standing radar picket duty every time one of the CIA A-12s had taken off. A string of Soviet spy ships continued the procedures along the China coast, tracking the high-flying aircraft on their way to Vietnam. Coordinated tracking of the flights was conducted with Chinese surveillance radars and the information sent on to North Vietnamese military officials, and SA-2 target acquisition radars would lock on to the approaching SR-71s.

The long black craft could cross the entire country of Vietnam in eight minutes, and the SA-2 crews were able to do little about it in spite of the early warnings from their Communist allies.

In June 1970, a special mission planning board was created to look at the possibility of conducting a rescue operation for POWs held in North Vietnam. The target of the mission was going to be the Son Tay camp, located twenty-three miles to the west of Hanoi. The SR-71 crews knew the Son Tay area well, since they had been conducting recon flights over the area since 1968. Their mission was to try and determine the number of POWs held at the camp at any given time. Few other assets were available to maintain the level of quality surveillance over the Son Tay camp necessary for the rescue mission without attracting the attention of the North Vietnamese.

While U.S. Special Forces volunteers trained diligently to rescue American POWs, the SR-71 overflights continued. Enough intelligence was gathered to suggest that a rescue could result in the freeing of as many as sixty-three U.S. servicemen held at the Son Tay site. Using some of the information gathered by the SR-71s from Kadena, a mock prison camp was set up at Hurlburt Air Force Base in Florida. The camp layout was exact and the Special Forces men rehearsed all phases of the mission, code-named Operation Kingpin. Specific parameters were required for the operation, including clear weather and a quarter-moon a given distance (35 degrees) above the horizon for maximum visibility of the area for the nighttime operation. The windows for the operation that met the mission parameters were October 21–25 and November 21–25. The decision was made and the mission a go for November 21, 1970.

In the last weeks leading up to the execution of Operation Kingpin cloud cover prevented a view of the Son Tay area from the SR-71 flights. Low-flying drones were tried twice to gather the last-minute intelligence but they were never recovered. The mission went forward without the intelligence being available regarding the last few weeks around the camp.

President Nixon gave the final approval for Operation Kingpin on November 18. A coordinated strike against North Vietnam was conducted by Navy aircraft coming in as the Kingpin transport helicopters were moving into the Hanoi area. Because of a suspension of active bombing missions against North Vietnam at the time, many of the Navy aircraft were not carrying any offensive ordnance, but they did distract the North Vietnamese.

At 2:18 A.M. on the morning of November 21, an HH3 Jolly Green Giant transport helicopter crashed-landed according to plan in the center of the Son Tay prison compound. The operation went flawlessly with a short, vicious firefight taking out one hundred to two hundred of the North Vietnamese Army soldiers who tried to repel the invaders.

In spite of the success of the raid against the NVA troops, there was a major problem with the mission as a whole. There were no prisoners at Son Tay to be rescued by the Special Forces troopers who had come so far and risked so much. In spite of an intensive search, no POWs were found. There were no losses among the Special Forces troops and only one man was wounded during the engagement. They successfully extracted after slightly less than thirty minutes on the ground.

It was learned later that the sixty-five POWs who had been at Son Tay had been moved in July because of the threat of flooding in the area. The mission was declared a tactical success but an intelligence failure. It was only the day before the raid that intelligence estimates had suspected that the POWs had been moved to another prison site about fifteen miles away from Son Tay. That estimation was later proved to be the correct one. Since all of the planning for Kingpin had centered on Son Tay, command decided to continue with the mission as originally laid out since moving the objective at the last minute would have put all of the raiders and supporting assets at too great a risk.

Only a short time following the raid at Son Tay, SR-71 overflights brought back photographic evidence of the damage done by the Special Forces troopers. These pictures became famous back in the United States, though it would be years before the public knew the full story of Operation Kingpin, and even longer before the involvement of the Habus from Okinawa became known. But the Son Tay raid would not be the only time that the SR-71 aircraft and crews would be involved in trying to rescue their fellow servicemen in North Vietnam.

The relatively few SR-71s available and their operating expense of $30,000 an hour during flight time made their mission tasking one that took serious consideration. Major intelligence and command organizations, such as the Defense Intelligence Agency, National Security Agency, and the Commander in Chief Southeast Asia, all had to have their tasking assignments for the SR-71 prioritized and approved, sometimes by very high offices. Missions could not be done just "off-the-cuff," as extensive preparations to the aircraft and its navigational systems were needed beforehand.

Approval for missions could come from very high sources depending on just where the SR-71s were intended to fly. Violating the sovereign airspace of foreign countries was not something to be taken lightly. Mission approval would have to come down from the State Department, a select secret committee of the National Security Council, or the president of the United States, depending on the operations parameters. Once that approval had been received, the SAC Reconnaissance Center would send the tasking on through the command chain, setting events in motion that resulted in the Habus moving into the air.

SR-71 missions had expanded from one a week during their early years at OL-8. During the later years of the Vietnam War, missions were being flown on an almost daily basis. But some operations stood out from the others, not just for where the great black aircraft were going, but for what they were going to do—and why.

Even for holders of high security clearances, such as everyone involved directly with the SR-71 flights, information was given on a need-to-know basis. Two missions conducted during the early part of May 1972 were so secret that the pilots and RSOs involved knew what they were going to do and how, but not why.

A flight of three SR-71s was assigned to fly from Kadena to North Vietnam on a daylight mission. The operation required two of the aircraft, the primaries, to overfly Hanoi at a specific time and "lay down" a sonic boom. The crashing thunder of the booms could be heard throughout the Hanoi area.

The mission had come down from the highest command source. There was no question that the pilots and crew would conduct the operation; they did not know the specifics of their signal, only that it was intended for the most important people they could think of in North Vietnam—their fellow fliers and others who were being held as prisoners of war.

The name given to this operation was "Booming the Hanoi Hilton." The signals were to be given by the primary aircraft at noon on May 2 and 4, the sounds to go out within fifteen seconds of one another. The two booms signal was so important that a third SR-71 was assigned to the mission as an immediate spare. If anything was to go wrong with one of the primary aircraft, the backup would come in and conduct the operation immediately. Timing was so critical that the spare aircraft would follow the primaries all the way to the target zone, well into the very hostile airspace over North Vietnam and the most heavily air-defended city in the world.

Major Tom Pugh was piloting SR-71 #968 (the last three digits of the serial number of the bird); Major Ronnie Rice was his RSO in the rear seat. Theirs was the lead aircraft for the flight. The second primary aircraft for the mission, bird #980, was piloted by Major Bob Spencer while Major Butch Sheffield pulled RSO duties. In the backup aircraft was Lieutenant Colonel Darrel Cobb as the pilot and Captain Reggie Blackwell. Theirs was a somewhat unique SR-71, one of only four to receive its own nickname. On the tail fin of #978 was painted the head and ears of the Playboy rabbit. The aircraft itself was the Rapid Rabbit and had been the second SR-71 delivered to the Air Force.

On this series of missions, the three aircraft split up as they came up to the target area over Hanoi. On one of the operations, #968 approached the target area from the south, coming in at 75,000 feet. The other primary aircraft, #980, came in to the target at 80,000 feet from the southeast. Though not used actively in the operation, #978 would have come in at 70,000 feet from the west.

When the agreed-on code word was transmitted from the primary aircraft, #978 broke off its run short of the target area. Now only Pugh and Spencer were piloting their birds over Hanoi while Rice and Sheffield were conducting some of the most precise navigation and timing of their careers. The planes slowed in their approach, giving up one of the greatest defenses of the SR-71, its tremendous speed, in order to make their signal loud and clear. As the time approached, the pilots let out their throttles and the mighty exhaust of the Pratt & Whitney engines roared out. At noon on May 2, a sonic boom rang out in the air over Hanoi. Fifteen seconds later, a second boom rolled through the air. Two days later, the same actions took place in the air over a puzzled and frightened Hanoi population.

The Booming the Hanoi Hilton missions had been conducted without a hitch, in spite of some very tight time parameters placed on the flights. The missions were successful, but the crews never knew why. For decades after, none of the men involved really knew what their message had been intended to convey. They knew that their mission had been an important one, but it was a seemingly small thing among all of the other accomplishments of the SR-71.

The dangers of flying such sophisticated and demanding aircraft came up less than two months after the Hanoi mission. SR-71 #978, *Rapid Rabbit*, came down in severe crosswind conditions at the Kadena airfield. On the second landing attempt, the undercarriage gave way as one set of the main wheels hit a concrete obstruction. The crew came out of the landing safely, but the *Rapid Rabbit* was a writeoff. The bird was stripped down for spare parts to help keep other SR-71s flying, and the remaining hulk was buried at the airfield.

The amazing career of the SR-71s continued on for years following the end of the Vietnam War. The Air Force in general, and fighter pilots in particular, never "took" to the great black birds and their reconnaissance missions. The birds were retired in the 1990s, the last ones flying having been turned over to NASA. Now they exist primarily as display pieces for the public at museums.

The lead bird for the Booming missions, #968, is the centerpiece of the Virginia Aviation Museum in Richmond, Virginia. Set up just outside the main doors to the museum, the SR-71 was dedicated to the public in November 1999. During the restoration of SR-71 #975 at the March Field Air Museum in California, it was discovered that the left tail fin on that craft was one of the pieces salvaged from the *Rapid Rabbit* after its crash. It is the only part of #978 known to be on public display.

SR-71 #980 continued to fly after life with the Air Force. It was assigned to NASA for research and received the new tail number 844, painted on its upright fins in large white numerals. On October 9, 1999, the last flight of an SR-71 took place. That craft was NASA #844.

Together, these craft and the dedicated men who made up their crews delivered the most expensive two-dot Morse code message ever sent. Those two booms, the letter "I" in International Morse Code, had no real meaning to the pilots of the birds that sent them out. But it meant the possibility of freedom to one of the prisoners below.

[CHAPTER 27]

OPERATION THUNDERHEAD

In the Yokosuka Naval Shipyard in Japan, U.S. Navy lieutenant commander Edwin L. Towers, a staff officer with the Seventh Fleet, was not expecting any major life changes to take place anytime soon. Even though he was aboard the *Oklahoma City*, the flagship of the U.S. Seventh Fleet, major adventures were more along the lines of completing everyday duties. So he was in for a surprise when he was called down to his captain's office.

There was a lieutenant commander in Captain McKenzie's office when Towers arrived. The new man was introduced as Earle Smith from Washington, D.C., and he had some highly classified information he wanted to discuss with Towers—information that had only been shared with two other people on the ship, Captain McKenzie and Admiral Holloway, the operational commander for all of the naval assets of the Seventh Fleet.

That statement from Smith was startling enough, but it didn't hold a candle to what Towers heard next. There was going to be an escape of POWs from camps in North Vietnam, sometime between June 1 and

June 15, 1972. The number of escapees wasn't known and no other details of their plans or pathways to freedom were revealed but one: The men would be making their way to the Gulf of Tonkin and continue on out to sea to the best of their abilities. The Navy was to help identify the escapees and recover them from enemy waters. Authorization for the mission had come from the higher command and Earle had been ordered to come and help put together a plan and execute the mission.

It was an astonishing statement, and the most limited information possible on which to plan a mission. But that was exactly what the higher command had wanted, and that desire had come from the Chairman of the Joint Chiefs of Staff, Admiral Thomas Moorer, Chief of Naval Operations. The only higher authority would have come from POTUS—the President of the United States and Commander in Chief of the U.S. Military, Richard M. Nixon.

This was pretty heady stuff for a middle-ranking officer. The suspicions were that Lieutenant Commander Earle was from some service besides just the Navy, most likely one of the intelligence services: the Central Intelligence Agency itself. That didn't really matter at the time. His authorization was real, the mission was a serious one, and the planners had almost nothing to go on at all.

All that Towers could learn from a private conversation with Earle outside the captain's office a short time later was that the information on the escape had come from the POW camp itself. The methods of communication were classified and weren't open for discussion. Earle was a bit surprised that Towers even knew of such techniques, but he had learned of them during a training school he had attended years earlier. The other news that was given was the deadline. The plan for the mission had to be ready for submission and approval by the admiral inside of forty-eight hours.

It was a daunting task, one that Towers realized would take maximum commitment. But the possible rescue of prisoners of war from North Vietnam was something that just about every member of the U.S. military dreamed of in one way or another. It hadn't been very long since the amazing Special Forces raid had been conducted against the POW camp at Son Tay. In spite of a nearly flawless operation, no American prisoners had been found. On this operation, the information had come from the prisoners themselves. All possible aid had to be given to these men without concern for personal sacrifice or cost.

There was a scramble for information by Towers on just what assets would be available for the mission, and just what their capabilities would be. Operational security was paramount. Only a very minimal number of people could know the object of the mission. If anything leaked out to the North Vietnamese, the repercussions to the prisoners could be terrible. There was no question of just how the North Vietnamese treated the prisoners under their control. A few men had been released and in spite of all of the North Vietnamese efforts, some of the truth had come out. Torture was a very real threat; so was death. And there were the intelligence assets in place that had to be protected. Whoever had helped get the information out of North Vietnam would have their lives snuffed out or worse if the Communists even suspected their existence.

They had to have very brave men who would conduct a difficult mission under extreme conditions of danger. For air assets, there were the combat search-and-rescue crews and the helicopters they flew. For even more special assets, it wasn't long before Towers learned about the Navy SEALs, the UDTs, their capabilities, and a very amazing submarine.

The USS *Grayback* (LPSS 574) had begun her life in the 1950s as part of the most important of the United States military assets, the nuclear triad. To defend against an all-out nuclear war, there had to be a guarantee that some nuclear-capable forces would survive even an effective first-strike by the major enemy of the age, the Soviet Union. The bomber force of the Strategic Air Command was one part of the triad of U.S. forces; ballistic missiles were another. But the most effective of the forces, the one most difficult for the enemy to detect, target, and destroy, were the nuclear missile–launching submarines.

The first of the missile-launching submarines employed by the U.S. Navy did not use a vertical firing missile, as is seen so much today. Instead, the first nuclear-armed missiles fielded by the Navy were winged ones. Resembling a rather small jet aircraft, the Regulus guided missile was very close to what is called a cruise missile today. The weapon was carried with its wings folded and had to be assembled for launch. When fired, the more-than-thirty-foot-long missile launched from a cradle with rocket boosters. A turbojet engine would push it and its 3,000-pound nuclear warhead to a range of over fifty miles. The Regulus II missile had even greater capabilities.

It took a very unusual submarine to carry the Regulus weapon. The sub would have to have a deck hangar that could transport the missile in a dry condition and allow it to be removed, prepped, and launched from the deck of that same submarine. The first boats to carry the missile were modified World War II diesel-electric boats. Soon, they were joined by two purpose-built boats, the *Grayback* and the *Growler*.

For her era, the *Grayback* and her sister ship, the *Growler*, were the two largest conventionally propelled submarines in the world. The huge diesel-electric boats were that size for a reason; their bows were made up of two large bulbous hangers. Regulus missiles could be accessed and serviced from inside the submarine while it was underwater. In just under seven minutes, the submarine could surface, launch its missile, and be back underwater to prepare for another launch. From the late 1950s to 1964, the *Grayback* and her fellow submarines patrolled as part of the nuclear deterrent force of the United States.

In the mid-1960s, with the adoption of the Polaris-launching submarines, the *Grayback* and others of her general type were removed from service. The two World War II fleet subs that had the large hangars on their decks became amphibious transport submarines and operated with the Underwater Demolition Teams, U.S. Marines, and Navy SEALs for a number of years. The *Grayback* also underwent refitting to become the first large transport submarine capable of carrying up to sixty-seven men and their equipment, with the facilities to feed and berth the men without difficulty. In particular, the *Grayback* could transport special miniature submersibles, what were known as Swimmer Delivery Vehicles (SDV), in the two bow hangars that had previously carried missiles.

The bow hangars on the *Grayback* were massive structures, each one a cylinder about eleven feet in diameter and sixty-six feet long, large enough to carry a single Regulus II missile. During her refit into a special operations transport, the hangars on the *Grayback* had a major change in their design, when a bulkhead was fitted in each one. Now the hangars each had a dry and a wet side. Personnel could operate in relative comfort on the dry side, preparing and maintaining equipment. The wet side of the hangers could now be flooded while the submarine was under way. The aft end of the wet side could be opened to the sea to release swimmers, rubber boats, or SDVs.

The SDV was a small, black fiberglass craft that could carry a crew and Navy SEALs much farther and faster than the men could possibly swim. And the little submersibles could be launched from the hangars of the *Grayback* while she was still submerged. The wet side of the hangars was about twenty feet long and could hold two SDVs on their launching cradles. A transfer lock on the bow bulkhead of the wet-side chambers could hold two personnel and flood or drain to allow passage between the wet and the dry side of the hangar while undergoing operations. The dry side of the hangar was an area about twenty-five feet long where equipment was stored. There were bunks for the special operations personnel, deployed SEALs using the port-side hangar, and the UDT detachment using the starboard-side hangar. The starboard-side hangar was fitted with a ten-foot-long decompression chamber for use during underwater operations. The port hangar held additional storage areas in the same space. Both hangars were connected to the interior of the *Grayback* through waterproof hatches.

Stationed at Subic Bay in the Philippines, the *Grayback* was constantly in use practicing and training with the SEALs and a UDT detachment assigned to her. There were additional operations conducted with both Army Special Forces and Marine Force Recon units off the unique boat. And she was only a relatively short cruise to the waters of the Gulf of Tonkin and the shores of North Vietnam.

The suggestion for the use of the submarine had come from Earle, who also knew the skipper of the boat, Commander John Chamberlain. At that moment, the *Grayback* was in port at Subic Bay. It was a relatively easy matter to just call down to the boat. The problem came with just what could be said in the conversation. Within a matter of only a minute, the only thing Chamberlain could say over the open line was that there was a question of whether the *Grayback* would be available for the specified time period.

The remaining details that had to be discussed with the skipper of the *Grayback* would have to wait until there could be a face-to-face meeting between him and Towers. At the local Submarine Ops office, Towers was able to learn a little bit about the *Grayback*, but the specific capabilities about the submarine, the SDVs, and the men who would operate them had to wait until the scheduled meeting at Subic Bay on May 22.

The planned escape time for the prisoners was for sometime between June 1 and 15. Whatever watercraft the escapees would be able to secure, they knew to signal with either a red or a yellow flag during the day. At night, the signal would be an arrangement of red lights.

To ensure that there would be assets on site to assist the escaping prisoners, there would be at least several days' overlap for the mission on either end of that window. The basic mission profile that was put together by Towers centered about the conduct of surveillance operations running from May 29 to June 19.

The surveillance area for the operation was very large, covering nearly fifty miles long and including both the mouth of the Red River as well as all of the estuaries of the secondary rivers and waterways that connected to it downstream of Hanoi. The size of the area was large in part due to the suspected lack of navigation capability on the part of the escaping prisoners.

Back at the Hanoi Hilton, Dramesi planned to follow the Red River to the ocean waters, but to account for the various tributaries and forks in the flow of the river, the escapees would consistently take the right-side choice to continue on their way.

The primary units conducting the surveillance would be HH-3A search-and-rescue helicopters and the SEAL units deploying from the *Grayback*. The helicopters would operate off of their parent carriers, but almost no one on the surface ships of the fleet would know about the SEALs' involvement; nor would they be told that there was an American submarine operating in the area.

Only a small handful of officers were briefed on what was really the objective of the operation. A cover story was used to brief all of the other personnel who had to have some knowledge of the mission in order to conduct their parts of the operation: The mission was to recover defectors from North Vietnam, people who had held high government offices. Even if by some means the North Vietnamese heard about such a mission, they would be spending their time trying to locate who the defectors were rather than increasing the security of the prison camps.

The primary ships used in Operation Thunderhead were relatively few in number. The USS *Long Beach* (CGN-9) was a nuclear-powered guided missile cruiser with a complement of nearly 1,000 officers and men. She would be the command ship for the operation, and her captain would be one of the men given a full briefing on the actual target of the operation. The USS *Harold E. Holt*, a Knox-class fleet escort ship, would be part of the supporting units for Thunderhead. The *Holt* had a hospital unit on board so it would receive the POWs once they were recovered and transport them to Subic Bay. The ship carried a primary armament of one forward Mark 42 mount with a single five-inch gun. The cannon could put out a more than seventy-pound high-explosive shell to a range of over fourteen miles.

Detachment 110 of Helicopter Support Squadron Seven (HC-7) was assigned to operate off the aircraft carrier USS *Midway* as a combat search-and-rescue (SAR) unit. The HH-3A Sikorsky Sea King helicopters of the HC-7 detachment were armored and armed with a 7.62mm minigun as well as M60D machine guns. The minigun is a rotating-barrel, high-rate-of-fire machine gun that can spit out rounds at a gunner-selectable cyclic rate of 2,000 or 4,000 rounds per minute. On board the HH-3A helicopter, the minigun fed from a 2,000-round box of belted 7.62mm ammunition and was mounted at the starboard-side hatch. The two other machine guns on board, the M60Ds, fired the same ammunition at a much more sedate cyclic rate of 550 rounds per minute and were mounted at the port side and stern. The SAR helicopters were the primary surveillance platforms for the operation and would perform the rescue/extraction of the escaped POWs once they were located.

The only naval assets that were assigned solely to Operation Thunderhead were the submarine *Grayback* and the UDT and SEAL detachments aboard her, and Lieutenant Commander Towers, the officer in charge (OIC) of the operation. All the other naval craft and crews would be conducting their regular missions, taking the war to the North Vietnamese. During the time period that Thunderhead would be active, there would be air strikes conducted against targets in North Vietnam. These ALFA strikes would also be conducted on and around Hanoi itself. It was hoped by Towers and the other officers involved with Thunderhead that the ALFA bombing around Hanoi would help give cover to the POWs for their escape attempt.

The search and surveillance for the POWs would be conducted by SAR helicopters in addition to their regular duties. There would be two to four flights a day through the target area, varying in the time they spent in the air and when they passed through the area. No matter when or how long the helicopters flew, they would cover 100 percent of the search area, which extended from west of the "Hourglass" River to north of the Red River—a coastal area that ran from 19 degrees 58 minutes North/106 degrees 02 minutes East at its southern end near the Hourglass River to 20 degrees 30 minutes North/106 degrees 35 minutes East at the far northern end past the Red River.

The flights would be on watch for any small craft waving a red or a yellow flag. The SAR helicopters would operate under the call sign "Big Mother" while conducting their surveillance mission. Any identified small craft would be immediately reported to the OIC (Towers), identified by the call sign "Hernandez." Once the flag was reported, the helicopter crew was authorized to do whatever was necessary to further identify the occupants of the craft. If fired upon, they could return fire and call in fire support as necessary.

The SEALs would have a much more difficult and dangerous mission to perform: A two-man SEAL element would be landed on an island known to be held and occupied by the North Vietnamese. The island was located at 19 degrees 54 minutes North/106 degrees 05 minutes East and was in a central location to observe the primary site where the POWs were expected to appear. Once in place on the island, the SEALs would man a twenty-four to forty-eight-hour observation post. The SEAL element would be rotated by slipping in a new team by SDV and removing the previous team back to the *Grayback*. All of these actions by the SEALs, the SDVs, and the *Grayback* would be conducted within North Vietnamese waters. The details of just how the island observation portion of the mission would be conducted were left in the hands of the SEAL officers and the commander of the *Grayback*. The *Grayback* had the call sign "Panther," and the SEAL element would be identified as "Tom Boy."

Daily situation reports on the conduct of the operation would be sent by Towers to the Chairman of the Joint Chiefs of Staff, the Commander in Chief of the Pacific Fleet, and the Commander of the Seventh Fleet, Admiral Moorer, Admiral Gaylor, and Vice Admiral Holloway, respectively. The messages would be sent Top Secret SPECAT (Special Attention).

After meeting with Commander Chamberlain and briefing him

on the details of Operation Thunderhead, Towers had the capabilities of the *Grayback*, her SDVs, and the personnel of Naval Special Warfare explained to him.

The SDVs were the Mark VII Mod 6 models, known to the men who used them as "Six Boats." Each of the black-hulled craft were wet-type submersibles. That meant they flooded with water and each person aboard had to wear breathing apparatus while operating. The Six Boats carried a crew of two, a driver and a navigator, and two fully equipped SEALs. The fiberglass Six Boats were more than eighteen feet long, almost three feet wide, and less than five feet tall. Operating and riding in one meant a long, cold trip underwater breathing air from the eight ninety-cubic-foot tanks on board. The air was enough to supply the four men on board with breathing gas for three hours at a normal usage level. That time underwater could be extended by the men breathing from their own personal breathing systems normally used for entering or exiting the craft. The six silver-zinc batteries on the SDVs could move them through the water at a maximum of four knots for up to eight hours.

Each SDV weighed over a ton before including the crew, passengers, or their equipment. The craft were normally operated by crews from the UDT detachment on board the *Grayback*; the SEALs were the passengers. The central buoyancy tank of the SDV could be pumped out or water added to adjust the craft in the water. Sliding hatches covered the front and rear compartments of the SDVs, leaving the men within in a dim, wet environment. Lighting was held at a minimum to cut down on battery drain, and the cramped quarters meant that all of the men on board couldn't move about to keep warm. It was a claustrophobic, dark, difficult way to swim through the water unseen. But the SEALs and the UDT operators were trained to work with the Six Boats, and the *Grayback* had two of them available for Thunderhead.

The Grayback herself was more than unusual and had other aspects besides her bow hangars that made her particularly fit for the operation. As a diesel-electric boat, the Grayback could move silently through the water when required. Operating from batteries, the electric motors and other systems of the *Grayback* made her quieter than even the best nuclear submarines of the day. Her crew was expert in getting the very best performance from the sub they were all very proud of. There was an additional specification of the *Grayback* that would allow her to conduct the twenty-two-day-long planned observation mission.

The seawater intakes and outlets for the *Grayback*'s machinery were not along the bottom of her hull, as they would be on most other submarines. The openings were up along the side of the *Grayback*'s hull, where they could be run while the sub was sitting hull-down on the bottom. This meant that the critical machinery of the boat could remain running while the *Grayback* was sitting on, or more usually floating just above, the sea floor. Only when she needed to recharge her batteries would any part of the *Grayback* have to rise above the surface. At those times, she would rise up to just below the surface and extend an air-breathing snorkel. With her snorkel raised, the *Grayback* would quietly run her diesel engines, recharging the batteries until she submerged once again.

Like a huge steel alligator, the Grayback could wait silent and unseen underwater, only coming up to breathe at long intervals. Unlike a reptile, the Grayback could launch her SDVs while remaining submerged, the small craft coming out of the bow hangars as the great clamshell doors opened slowly. While inside the bow hangars, the black-hulled Six Boats could be serviced and prepared by men traveling in and out of the submarine through the bow hatches connecting the hangars to the interior of the boat. Once mission-ready, the SDVs would be winched out on wheeled dollies by men wearing underwater breathing gear and launched from the deck.

CHAPTER 28

LAUNCH

Alfa Platoon of SEAL Team One was on deployment as the Naval Special Warfare Western Pacific Detachment (WESTPAC) on Okinawa when Operation Thunderhead was being laid out. The platoon of twelve enlisted men and two officers of Alfa platoon were the first contingency element sent out by SEAL Team One, there to conduct special operations in support of the U.S. Navy as the need arose. The deployment was supposed to be a normal one for the men of SEAL Team One, particularly now that the Vietnam War was winding down and the Navy was beginning to change its operational tempo from wartime to a peacetime footing. Alfa platoon was tasked with setting up the SEAL quick-reaction base facilities at White Beach on Okinawa as well as conducting training with special operations units of American allies in the area. The U.S. Navy base on White Beach was a large one, but there were no support facilities available to meet the SEALs' particular needs. Among the structures prepared by Alfa platoon was a diving locker and paraloft for the maintenance and preparation of parachutes. Several members of the platoon proved that their carpentry skills equaled that of their weapons-handling abilities.

The men of the SEAL platoon were all combat veterans, some with multiple tours of duty in Southeast Asia. They had already been conducting training operations in Korea during their deployment and the SEALs had already experienced time on the *Grayback*. In mid-February, the platoon was picked up by the submarine at Okinawa and cruised to the Philippines. There, they operated with the detachment from UDT Eleven as well as spent time in jungle and survival classes before conducting training with the Philippine Navy special operations units. In March, the platoon began heading back north. During their initial time on the *Grayback*, the SEALs and the crew of the sub enjoyed a short stay in Hong Kong as a break from their duties. It was soon enough that the SEALs returned to their training.

The mountain climbing Alfa platoon experienced in Korea was not going to be among the skills used when they received orders to report to Subic Bay. They would be a significant portion of Operation Thunderhead and were being involved with some of the earliest Navy preparations for the mission. Alfa platoon arrived at the huge U.S. naval base well before the SR-71s conducted their mission high across the skies of North Vietnam.

On April 10, Alfa platoon was once again picked up by the *Grayback* from Okinawa for a three-day cruise to the Philippines. Once the platoon arrived at Subic, the SEALs started training almost immediately after receiving briefings on their new mission assignment. In spite of each of the members of Alfa platoon holding a high security clearance, none of the men was told the real objective for the upcoming operation. Instead, the SEALs were eventually told that they would be conducting a demolition operation in retaliation for a North Vietnamese strike against U.S. naval assets in the Tonkin Gulf.

In mid-April, the USS *Buchanan* had taken fire from North Vietnamese 152mm gun batteries located in the Do Son Peninsula at

Haiphong Harbor. The shelling had resulted in one seaman being killed and seven wounded. The SEAL operation would reportedly be conducted against the gun battery on the Do Son Peninsula. The general plan called for the SEALs to launch from the *Grayback* in Z-birds (inflatable rubber boats). A pair of swimmer-scouts would go onto the beach and conduct the initial reconnaissance. Depending on what the pair found in the immediate area, the rest of the force would be called in by infrared signaling devices concealed in the hands of the scouts. The men were told that there was a North Vietnamese Army garrison for the guns, and the whole platoon knew that an all-out fire-fight was something they should avoid if at all possible. On the peninsula, the SEALs would patrol to the gun batteries and destroy them, then withdraw and return to the *Grayback* in the rubber boats.

Though some of the SEALs wondered why the mission against the gun batteries was being conducted in a ground operation rather than by aircraft or naval gunfire, they trained for the operation thoroughly and professionally. The men who would be conducting the swimmer-scout insertions conditioned themselves by swimming miles every day. Two of these men were Frank Sayle and Tim Reeves. They swam for hours in the waters off Subic until they reached a level of fitness close to that of Olympic-class competitors.

Using their rubber boats, the SEALs conducted launch-and-recovery operations from the *Grayback*. Rendezvous with the submarine were conducted in complete darkness, utilizing specialized infrared signaling and detection equipment. The men paddled their rubber boats with the strength of their arms driving the small craft across the water. There were also outboard motors that could be used on the rubber boats. One of the motors, a specially silenced fifteen-horsepower motor, never seemed to work properly and was considered unreliable. Paddles always worked, and the men of the teams had learned their use very early on their initial training.

As a practical exercise, the SEALs conducted a number of full-dress nighttime insertions and patrols. Fully camouflaged and armed, the

SEALs followed their swimmer-scouts onto land and went incountry, passing local villages whose occupants had no idea they were about. With a suppressed shot from a Mark 23 9mm Hush Puppy pistol on one patrol, a duck was killed before it could make a sound in alarm at the approaching green-faced men. Not even the quiet thud of the shot caused any alarm in the villagers as the SEALs continued their exercise. The men were silent in their movements, little more than dark shadows passing through the jungle. Their confidence in their own abilities was very high; they knew what they were capable of.

There was very limited training with the SDVs aboard the *Grayback* during Alfa platoon's time at Subic Bay. A detachment of men from Underwater Demolition Team Eleven was assigned to the *Grayback* and would be operating the SDVs. For most of the SEALs, their experience with an SDV consisted primarily of a walk-through, an examining of the boats while they were on their transportation trailers prior to being loaded on board the submarine. During the training at Subic Bay, there was no mention to the men of Alfa platoon about utilizing the SDVs in any upcoming operation. The SEALs knew that if they were involved with SDV operations, it would be as passengers rather than active crews of the small underwater craft. All they would have to do with the craft was get in and out, and that involved little more than opening the sliding hatch cover.

The UDT operators continued their training with the SDVs separately from the SEALs. Along with members of the *Grayback*'s crew, the UDT operators practiced launching and recovering the SDVs. The bow hangars had a wet side and a dry side. The wet side could be pumped out and the SDVs worked on while sitting in their launch cradles. This way, the batteries could be recharged and the pressure in the breathing air tanks brought up to peak. There was also the necessary maintenance of the equipment—an everyday fact of life in the Navy, and particularly in the SEAL and UDT teams. When you worked underwater, your life depended on your breathing equipment. If you didn't maintain that, death was a certainty. So the philosophy of constant maintenance was an easy one to connect with every facet of their operating in the teams, whether on dry land, in the air, or underwater.

Training could be long, dull, and repetitive during the more than six weeks that the SEALs prepared for their upcoming mission. But the men of the teams were professional in all of their actions; they conducted the training until they were perfect at it, and then worked to improve on that.

After Lieutenant Commander Towers had come and gone from the *Grayback*, all of the men were taken back on board and the submarine made sea-ready. The twelve enlisted men of the SEAL platoon were being led by two officers: Lieutenant Melvin S. Dry was the officer in charge of the platoon, and his assistant was Lieutenant Robert J. Conger Jr. The chief petty officer of the platoon was Philip L. "Moki" Martin. All of the leadership of the platoon had multiple combat tours behind them and knew what to expect of their men in any conceivable circumstance. In spite of the trust they had for each other, there was a limit imposed from higher command on just what all of the SEALs could be told, even when their mission briefing took place after the submarine had left port.

There was no place on board a submerged submarine where a secret could be leaked out to the enemy. But Operation Thunderhead was a unique situation in more ways than one. Only the officers and a couple of the enlisted men were told the entire mission profile. All of the rest of the team were told what they needed to know in order to conduct their part of the mission. And the mission sounded like it would be a hairy one, or at least there was the very real possibility of a raised pucker factor if things went south in a hurry.

The story of the demolition operation against the gun batteries was now abandoned, in spite of the men having loaded volumes of explosives and demolitions into the special magazines on board the submarine. Now the men were told that they were to go out and land on an island near the mouth of the Red River. Eventually they were told that they wouldn't be conducting the operation from the rubber boats they had trained with. For the utmost in secrecy, they would conduct the infiltration by launching an SDV from the *Grayback* while she was submerged. Moving underwater at night, the SEALs and the UDT operators would head for the island where the SEAL element would exit the SDV. With only light weapons with which to defend themselves, the SEALs would conduct an observation post, looking for the red flag or red light on any local small watercraft. Using their own judgment, the SEALs would make contact with the indicated small craft after reporting in to higher command. The object of their attention was going to be high-ranking Chinese or North Vietnamese defecting to the United States.

There was no mention of escaping POWs; originally only a few members of the platoon and UDT detachment, primarily the officers, were even informed that their original mission had changed from one of demolition to that of recovery. The rest of the platoon was brought up to speed on the new mission, or at least some of what the new mission would be. There were strong suspicions among members of Alfa platoon that they were not being told what was actually going on.

While the SEALs were on the island, the *Grayback* would remain submerged at a distance of only a few thousand yards from the island. The specific location of the submarine layup point would be dependent on the best judgment of Commander Chamberlain regarding the safety of his boat and crew.

Presented in those terms, it didn't seem like an excessively difficult mission. The real danger came in the fact that the entire operation would take place in the national waters of North Vietnam. On top of the threat of enemy detection, the SEAL element would be conducting their observation post on an island known to be occupied by North Vietnamese. But the existence of a North Vietnamese naval base, and even the small native fishing village on the island, was kept from the SEALs not directly conducting the initial parts of the operation

The basic mission was one that the SEALs were very experienced with; the observation and listening post mission had been conducted hundreds of times on deployment in South Vietnam. It would be nothing new for the men to work behind enemy lines, possibly surrounded by hostile forces. It was through missions like that and even more hazardous ones that the SEALs had developed a reputation of a unit to be feared by the Viet Cong and NVA. But this operation would be taking part so far behind the lines that they couldn't even be seen over the horizon.

It was the fear of possible capture and interrogation of the SEAL element on the island that had caused higher command to order the compartmentalization of mission information. If they were captured and made to talk, if the men didn't know that there was going to be a POW escape, they couldn't tell anyone about it. That would at least help minimize the North Vietnamese suspecting and looking for a possible intelligence net involving the prison camps. The cover story about high-ranking defectors was a plausible one and would also help deflect a North Vietnamese search for hard-won intelligence assets in their own country.

As the *Grayback* traveled underneath the U.S. Seventh Fleet, there was time for a small distraction from the pressure of the upcoming operation. In a message received shortly before their leaving port, Moki Martin had been informed that he would be promoted to the rank of warrant officer. The close-knit makeup of the SEALs made for a certain level of familiarization between the officers and the enlisted men. They were far more casual in their interactions than most of the rest of the Navy. An example of this was that Lieutenant Dry was known as Spence to his men, in spite of his being a commissioned officer and a class of 1968 graduate of the U.S. Naval Academy.

There are traditions in the Navy, and they were not going to be ignored on board the *Grayback*. Martin's orders had read that his promotion would be effective the first of June. On that day the wardroom of the *Grayback* was cleared out and a small celebration took place. With a cake baked for the event, Philip Moki Martin was welcomed by the officers of the *Grayback*, SEAL, and UDT platoons, to the ranks of the Officer Corps of the United States Navy.

The trip to the operating area off the coast of North Vietnam was an uneventful one for the SEALs. They had nothing to do in regard to the operation of the submarine and it was far too crowded to conduct the near religion of the SEALs: physical fitness exercises. Lieutenant Dry was the son of a Navy submarine skipper and he was more than relaxed among his men aboard the *Grayback*. To pass the time, the SEALs gathered up the movies they had brought on board from the base at Subic. The seventy-five films were watched over and over again in the SEALs' living quarters. Davis was the man whose bunk was closest to where the projector was set up, resulting in his becoming the platoon's projectionist. Some of the favored films of the platoon included *Vanishing Point*, which highlighted a long, high-speed car chase across the American West. To make the films more entertaining after having seen them repeatedly, they were run backward. Instead of a fiery crash ending a scene, a racing car was born from the consuming flames. Moki Martin had a particular liking for two of the movies, *Vanishing Point* and *Two-Lane Blacktop*. But even he started to think that all of the films were just kind of blurring together as the sub continued on toward North Vietnam.

Distractions were needed by the SEALs to help keep them from noticing some of the details involved in living effectively as passengers onboard the *Grayback*. The living quarters in the hangar spaces were constantly damp; there was no real way to dry them completely while the submarine was under way. The humidity resulted in a mildew smell that permeated the compartment. But the mildew was not the only noticeable smell; when the submarine surfaced her snorkel to run the diesel engines, the air was also used to vent out the boat. The only trouble with venting the boat was that the air circulation system resulted in the forward head venting through the SEALs' compartment. The announcement to "vent the boat" made many of the unconventional warriors practice their breath-holding abilities as they looked for sources of fresher air.

But even just watching movies all day couldn't be done by the SEALs during the entire cruise. The submarine was so quiet in its silent operation that the noise of the movie projector was considered enough to get the sub detected. When operating in the silent mode, a crewman would come up to the compartment and tell them to turn off the movie projector.

The concern for silent operation of the boat was a legitimate one—the *Grayback* was passing under one of the largest concentrations of U.S. Navy ships since the Korean War. More than seventy vessels of the fleet's ships were in the waters of the Tonkin Gulf at that time. Only the USS *Long Beach* had anyone on board with the knowledge that an American submarine was operating in the area.

On the surface and in the air above the *Grayback*, Operation Thunderhead was already ongoing. As the submarine crept undetected beneath the Seventh Fleet, HH-3A helicopters were already conducting searches for the escaped POWs. Having decided to take as active a role as possible in the operation, Towers was riding along as an extra set of eyes on some of the helicopter flights.

On Saturday, June 3, the *Grayback* arrived on station at the point where she would launch and wait for the SDVs to return. The crew was excited about the mission taking place. They all knew that it was something big even if they didn't know the details. The specifics didn't matter; they were there to do a job and they would conduct themselves to the best of their considerable abilities.

The *Grayback* settled to the bottom, where she would rest for the extent of the operation. She preferred to stay in at least eighty feet of water to be certain of remaining undetected during the day. The boat was more than three hundred feet in length. In eighty feet of water, she could easily lay with her bow down almost on the bottom and raise her stern to the surface. But for the mission, they were willing to run in slightly shallower water since the Red River tended to make the local waters murky.

Rising only enough to lift her snorkel to the surface and recharge her batteries, Chamberlain got on the radio to the *Long Beach*. The message was a simple one, short as submarine skippers prefer them to be. Panther was on station. She would begin operations that same night.

It was at 2:00 A.M. on June 4 when the first SDV launched from the *Grayback*. It was a nighttime lockout and launch, meaning there was very little light for the men swimming about the submarine's deck to see what they had to do. In the darkness all about them would be the occasional sparks and glows of the phosphorescent marine organisms floating in the water. Concentrating on their work would help keep the men from looking about them into the shifting darkness, and it would keep them from thinking about just where they were.

Crewing the boat were the men from the UDT detachment, Lieutenant (Junior Grade) John Lutz and Petty Officer Tomas Edwards. The SEAL element on board the SDV, and who would be spending the next two days on an enemy-occupied island, was Lieutenant Dry and Warrant Officer Martin. The SEALs were wearing their camouflaged combat uniforms, web gear, and weapons. For his choice, Moki Martin was armed with a Swedish K 9mm submachine gun. Spare magazines, supplies, and other gear were strapped all about him. It was crowded in the SDV at the best of times. With their combat gear, the SEALs were in a particularly tight situation. The hatch covers were drawn shut and there was nothing they could do but ride out the trip.

The trip was turning into a very long one. The launch time for the SDV had been planned by Chamberlain to take advantage of the maximum amount of slack water that would be at the end of the flood tide. The SDV would be going in against the current of a freshwater river emptying into the Gulf of Tonkin. Moving a four-knot-capable SDV against a two-knot current would be difficult in the best of circumstances. The planning of the launch to coincide with slack water would help cut down on some of the current the men would have to fight.

It was a minus tide that passed through the Gulf of Tonkin that night. A minus tide is one where the tide level goes down to a point significantly lower than a normal tide. That meant the current coming from the mouth of the river was greater, which meant trouble for the SDV.

The Six Boats were fitted with all of the most modern systems available for them at the time; those systems, combined with the experience of the men on board, told them the mission was in real trouble.

Prior to launching the SDV, all the normal mission preparations had taken place. The men knew that the transit would cover between three and four thousand yards, for a maximum trip time of two hours. On the return trip, the boat would be running with only the two UDT crewmen on board, so the boat air should last well enough for the mission. But the SDV was churning on without getting anywhere. Lutz, the driver, got on the communications system that allowed the men in the SDV to speak to one another even while underwater. As far as he was concerned, they had not covered very much distance and were bucking a much greater current than expected. They had also made some navigational errors that resulted in the men not being able to sight the island.

Finally, near first light, the batteries of the SDV gave out completely. There was a contingency plan in place to cover this situation. If they had to abandon the SDV, they would scuttle the boat and swim as far out to sea as they could, where the men in the water would activate their radios. The signals from the waterproof radios would bring in the search-and-rescue helicopters hovering nearby. All the men had to do was to tread water and wait for pickup.

The message came in to the *Long Beach* from the *Grayback* that morning. It was a short coded one and contained the words *Briarpatch Tango*. Those two words were enough to send a chill through Towers when he heard them. Thunderhead personnel were in trouble. The fact that the message had come in from Panther meant that it was either the SEALs, the UDT, or the SDV that was in trouble. In this case, it was all three.

While the SAR helicopter was in the air, the radiomen on board the *Long Beach* were tracking the signal coming from the water and the SEALs' radios. The plot from the *Long Beach* put the signal from the SEALs about four miles from the island where they were supposed to have set up. The helicopter was also flying within six miles of the coast of North Vietnam. It was not a comfortable place to be for an aircraft armed with only a pair of M60 machine guns and a single minigun. But the SAR crew had been in much tighter situations before, performing combat rescues while taking enemy fire. They prepared their weapons and kept an eye out on the water. With directions helping to vector them in, they spotted the group of four men in the water and the large black bulk floating nearby.

The rescue hoist that was at the starboard side of the helicopter was easily able to raise the men in the water into the bird. Festooned with gear and weapon, with water pouring off of them, the men from the SDV got into the hovering helicopter and considered their next move. The SDV in the ocean below them was still floating, just barely awash. The only item that had been salvaged from the boat was the expensive and critical communications system. All of the rest of the boat was still floating below them. It couldn't be left; a North Vietnamese fisherman or even a naval vessel was sure to find it. And that was if the SDV didn't eventually wash up onshore of its own account.

As the commander of the boat, Lieutenant Lutz made a decision. The SDV would be sunk with gunfire from the helicopter. The first bursts from the minigun ripped into the sea. At the high rate of fire, the spinning barrels of the weapon were kicking out projectiles at a rate of more than sixty a second. For several long seconds the roar of the minigun sounded out and shook the helicopter. The power of the gun's vibration was nothing when compared to the spray kicked up by the dozens and dozens of high-speed projectiles splashing all about the SDV. Raked from bow to stern, the black hull finally started to sink.

Looking at where their SDV had disappeared, the SEAL and UDT operators just stood and dripped saltwater down on the deck. Having made a decision, Towers had the helicopter head out toward where the *Long Beach* was located. They would set down on the ship and keep the men from the submarine there, sequestered so that the crew wouldn't see them and start asking questions about the heavily armed combat dressed commandos who had suddenly appeared on board. In the radio message that was sent out from the helicopter, it was requested that all of the crewmen on the *Long Beach* remain be-lowdecks while only necessary personnel witnessed the helicopter coming in and unloading.

Both Dry and Lutz could see the logic about where they were go-ing and why when told by Towers over the helmets that had been handed to them. And they emphatically said that they wanted to get back to the *Grayback* as soon as possible. As the helicopter approached the *Long Beach*, there were no crewmen in sight on the decks. Once the bird set down, Earle came out to lead the SEALs and UDT men away. The helicopter lifted off almost immediately to conduct the morning sweep of the search area. Operation Thunderhead was still going forward.

[CHAPTER 29]

DEADLY WATERS

There was no question that the men from the SDV wanted to get back to the *Grayback* at the earliest opportunity. The submarine was not coming up for long enough messages for the SEALs and UDT operators to explain what had happened on the first infiltration attempt. The *Long Beach* was a safe fifty miles from the coast of North Vietnam. The *Grayback* was well within enemy waters. The vital information the SEALs and UDT operators needed had to be transferred to the submarine before she launched her second SDV.

With an earlier radio message to the *Long Beach*, Chamberlain had been assured of his men's safety. For the moment, he didn't concern himself with them. He still had a mission to perform in support of Thunderhead. An observation post had to be established on the island to cover the mouth of the river, a blind spot blocked from seaward view by the island itself. The second SDV would be launched that night, the same time as the first had been.

The message to the *Long Beach* had included the disposition of the crew and passengers of the first SDV. The submarine would conduct abbreviated ops that night, shining to the north of the *Long Beach's* location. The *Grayback's* human assets needed to be returned by helicopter that evening.

The language used by Chamberlain took some translating by the SEAL and UDT officers in order for those on the *Long Beach* to understand. The meaning wasn't too difficult: The *Grayback* would continue her mission and launch another team in the second SDV. The shining term in the message meant that the submarine would raise its snorkel above the surface and shine an infrared light mounted on top of the mast. The invisible beam of light could be easily seen by night vision devices available to the pilots of the SAR birds. That would allow a helicopter to approach the *Grayback*, and the men would insert from the bird while it was still airborne, conducting what the teams called a "cast."

The insertion meant the SEALs and UDT operators would jump from the helicopter and just plunge into the water. From the surface, they would swim down to lock into the submarine while it remained submerged. The casting technique seemed more than a little unusual, but the officers assured the staff at the *Long Beach* that it was a technique they trained with and continually employed. As long as the helicopter pilot did what they told him to, everything would be fine.

Warrant Officer Martin would be the jumpmaster for the cast. He had a great deal of experience with the technique as well as more than eight hundred parachute jumps to his credit. The pilots of the helicopter they were jumping from had never conducted such an operation before; the briefing that Martin gave the men was a carefully detailed one to prevent any mistakes.

The one most basic rule of the helicopter casting technique was called the 20/20: the maximum forward speed for a cast was twenty knots, and the maximum altitude was twenty feet. The SEALs were tough, but anyone could get broken. They had learned the 20/20 rule through hard experience and training. The pilot stated that he would try to get as close to that speed and altitude as possible. Martin said that lower and slower were fine, but no higher. He was going to call the cast from the door of the bird. If Martin thought they were either too high or going too fast, he would signal the crew chief, who would then alert the pilot over the intercom. Once the other three men had cast from the bird, he would jump himself.

The winds were high as the men boarded the helicopter and lifted off. The plan was to make the cast at about 11:00 P.M. The sea state was running about one to two; that put waves reaching a maximum height of four feet across the waters speeding by below them. It was also an overcast night, which caused problems for the helicopter pilot. That kept him from seeing the horizon. Not having a solid reference point for his flying, the pilot was depending on his instruments and experience, but he had never flown a cast before.

Arriving at the *Grayback*'s last reported position, the helicopter flew a crisscrossing search pattern but failed to see the shine of the infrared beacon. On board the bird with the men from the SDV was Towers. He had decided to accompany the men to their jumping-off point and witness the action. Hooked into the intercom system, only Towers and the crew chief of the bird could speak to each other.

While the men from the *Grayback* prepared to jump, the helicopter was searching frantically for the signal from the submarine. At one point, the pilot had his attention drawn to a bright light through his infrared goggles. But the lights were only the lamps in a North Vietnamese hut. They were passing over North Vietnam itself, having crossed the coast by following the wrong signal.

As the fuel situation in the helicopter started to grow serious, Dry took up a helmet and communicated directly with the pilot. As far as he could tell, the bird was moving too fast and at too high an altitude for a safe insertion. There was a 15-to-20-knot tailwind pushing the helicopter and throwing off the instrument readings for the pilot. At one point, the pilot dropped the bird so low to the water that the tail section of the hull was actually in the water. The crew chief screamed into the microphone, warning the pilot of the situation before the helicopter swamped and went down.

The situation was growing critical. At his position in the door, Martin could not see the telltale spray that would be kicked up by the helicopter if they were at the right altitude. Dry was saying very little, his face set in grim determination. The last thing he said to Martin was "We've got to get back to *Grayback*."

Now the helicopter crew finally made out a flashing light and knew it must be the *Grayback*. No longer trusting his automatic equipment, the pilot made a manual approach for the drop. When he was in position, he called out the signal "Drop, drop, drop." It was dark and the wind was blowing hard at the tail of the helicopter as Martin looked out the hatch. He could just make out the salt spray kicked up by the helicopter on the dark water below them. It looked much farther away than he was comfortable with. But the search-and-rescue swimmer who was a member of the crew had a number of water jumps to his credit. He trusted his pilot and gave Dry the signal to jump by slapping him on the shoulder.

The final decision was his, but Dry knew how important it was for the mission to return to the *Grayback*. He and Martin were the two most experienced SEALs on the operation. And the current information they had was vital; the launch time of the second, and last, SDV had to be changed. Without hesitating, he stepped off into the darkness and plunged to the seas below.

The other three members of the team immediately followed their officer out on the cast. The last man off the bird was Martin, and he remembered counting the seconds as he fell toward the water. Instead of the one or two seconds he should have been able to say before impacting with the surface, he made it to three before cursing just before impact.

The strike against the water was very hard, as the helicopter was moving much faster than the twenty knots it was supposed to be going.

The tailwind had pushed the bird to almost twice the maximum speed for a safe cast. And Martin figured they had been at least double, maybe triple, the maximum safe altitude when he exited the bird. The impact with the water was stunning and Martin was badly shaken up by it. So was John Lutz, who had injured his back and knee. Lutz was the first member of their team whom Martin came across as he started to call out and swim about the insertion point. He had managed to retain his swim fins after the impact, along with his web gear and Swedish K submachine gun. Putting on the fins, Martin was able to move about in the water as he searched.

The next man Martin came across was Edwards. The man's moaning drew the attention of the SEAL as he was swimming in the darkness. Edwards was floating facedown when he was found by Martin and had to be flipped over to keep him from drowning. After inflating the other man's life vest, Martin could see that he was badly hurt. But there was nothing that could be done for him as the men floated in the ocean.

Visibility in the choppy seas was maybe ten feet or less. In spite of repeated calls into the darkness, there was no answer from Dry. As the least injured man and best able to swim, Martin gathered Lutz and Edwards together as they continued the search for Dry. Then they spotted the flashing lights that had drawn the helicopter pilot to signal the drop. It wasn't the infrared beacon of the *Grayback*; it was the emergency strobes of the second SDV crew and passengers.

As they found out later, the second SDV was launched at an earlier hour than the previous night's. Lieutenant (j.g.) Robert Conger and Petty Officer Sam Birky were going to be the SEALs conducting the observation post. Lieutenant (j.g.) Tom McGrath and Seaman Steve McConnell were the UDT operators who had been the crew of the second SDV. Conger, McGrath, and McConnell were floating in the water, and both Dry and now Birky were missing. The mission had gone downhill at a thundering gallop. Martin was becoming more than a little disgusted with the situation.

The men were all floating together as they heard the engines of what could have been North Vietnamese patrol boats starting up in the distance. They couldn't have been more than two thousand yards from shore—not a very comfortable distance from enemy territory. The weight of the Swedish K hanging down from Martin had been of little reassurance. But against an enemy patrol boat, it would do little or nothing.

The water was home to the SEALs and frogmen of the UDT. It hid them, protected them, and they were all more than used to it. The other thing they had all learned from the first days of training was that you never left a teammate behind. And now Martin and the others had the missing Lieutenant Dry and Petty Officer Birky weighing heavily on their minds.

They had been in the water for hours when one of the men complained about someone sticking their foot in his face. It wasn't one of the swimmers in the group; the foot belonged to Spence Dry, floating facedown in the ocean. Pulling the body up to himself and flipping it over, Martin could see that Dry was dead. There appeared to be blood on his nose and face, but there wasn't anything they could do for their officer. The men inflated Dry's life vest and kept his body with them.

The group of men kept swimming all through the night. It was about 5:00 A.M. when they managed to raise the *Long Beach* on their waterproof radios. At 7:00 A.M., the welcome sight of an SAR helicopter coming in over the horizon greeted the weary eyes of the swimmers. Then the bird went down to the surface and hovered, some distance away from them all. Were they going to have to swim over to get picked up?

Then the men in the water could see that the helicopter was picking somebody up from the surface: Sam Birky. Everyone who had gone into the water, whether from the *Grayback* or the helicopter, had been found. Edwards was badly injured and Lutz wasn't much better. But both men was still alive, which was more than could be said for their officer. With Towers again on their pickup bird, the men were winched up from the sea and taken to the *Long Beach*.

Dry and Edwards were moved onto the aircraft carrier *Kitty Hawk*, which had much better treatment facilities. On board the *Long Beach*, the remaining SEALs and UDT operators were debriefed about what had gone so wrong in the operation.

The second SDV had been launched early to give the maximum amount of darkness for the men once they got to the island. If there had been a mechanical or electrical problem with the first SDV, they could recover the men from the island and at least some of them could return to the *Grayback*.

The crew of the *Grayback* were working to help launch the second SDV in the dark water and operating against a fairly heavy current. The sub was moving slightly, and the deck crew indicated the SDV should put on more and more ballast. The plan was to keep the SDV within homing beacon range of the *Grayback* during the launch so that the small craft could turn back to the submarine if it ran into difficulty. The problem wasn't one of currents this time. Instead, the SDV was overweight, and when launched it immediately foundered and sank to the bottom.

Struggling with the sunken SDV, the crew and one of the SEALs worked hard to try and get the boat under way. The *Grayback* was nearby but unseen in the darkness. The men all knew that the big boat was only slightly buoyant so that it wasn't resting hard on the bottom. At any moment, the submarines could come crashing down on them in the darkness. Taking a final breath of air, the men abandoned the SDV and made a free ascent to the surface as the current drove them past the hull of the *Grayback* and out to the open sea.

Waiting in the back of the SDV, Birky was separated from the rest of the men as they worked on the boat. He remained in the rear compartment, breathing boat air as the minutes ticked by. Finally, he left the compartment and moved forward, breathing from a little bail-out bottle each man had for just such a purpose. Surprised to find no one at the SDV but himself, Birky made his ascent to the surface. The SDV remained abandoned on the floor of the gulf.

The SEALs and UDT operators on board the *Grayback* knew that something had gone very wrong with the SDV launch. The sound of the pinger, the sonar device on board the SDV, kept banging away close to the side of the big submarine. Inside the steel hull, the men could hear the pinger, and it just kept going, never sounding as if it were moving away. It was obvious that something had malfunctioned, but no one knew what.

It was sometime earlier that day, while Dry, Martin, and the rest were still on board the *Long Beach*, that the remaining leading petty officer of Alfa platoon, Rick Hetzell, was called to the submarine's wardroom for a briefing. John Chamberlain was waiting in the wardroom along with several other men, including the intelligence officer who was wearing a sterile Navy officer's uniform—one without any identifying insignia. They had called for the next-in-command of the SEAL platoon, and that was Rick Hetzell. He knew the situation was a serious one as soon as he entered the compartment.

The officers told Hetzell that they wanted him to pick out some of his men and prepare for an insertion. They would be the next unit to go in to the island after the SDV had launched. He was to go in to the beach and pick up some indigenous personnel. The insertion would be done with a rubber boat. That was just about all of the information that he was given. But it was enough.

Going back up into the SEALs' compartment, Hetzell chose his men. Having trained as a swimmer-scout for the operation, Tim Reeves was one of the men to go; so were Eric Knudson and Doug Hertsic, one of the UDT operators aboard who had been assigned as an SDV driver. Doug had transferred over to the UDT from SEAL Team One within the last year and Hetzell knew him well. Since there wasn't another SDV available, neither Hertsic nor Scotty Shaw, who was an SDV navigator in UDT Eleven, had an active assignment.

After working up an operations order (op-order) for the mission,

Hetzell took the other men into the diving locker for some privacy and briefed them on the mission. Then he asked if anyone had any suggestions to add to the op-order in case they ran into any problems or contingencies on the mission. That was the way things were brainstormed within the teams; the had been polished over years of actions in South Vietnam and ensured that all possible scenarios had been covered. In this case, everyone in the dive locker agreed that it sounded like a good plan, so they were done.

The basic plan was a simple one: Four men would take the Z-bird with the twenty-five-horsepower Mercury outboard motor on it. They would go in to the island and stop about two hundred yards off the coast. At that point, Tim Reeves would swim in to check out the area. If the beach zone was safe, the men would paddle the boat in for continued silence rather than use the outboard motor. They would park the boat and wait for the indigenous personnel to show up. Once contact was made, the personnel would be picked up and extracted back to the submarine.

In his original wardroom briefing, Hetzell had been told to expect from two to four indigenous personnel to show up for evacuation. If it were just two people recovered, there wouldn't be any trouble fitting all of them on board the rubber boat. If it were four people, Hetzell and Reeves would give up their places and swim back to the submarine. That was just the way it was: a simple and straightforward plan. But trouble began when the officers returned to the wardroom.

Once Hetzell and his chosen team arrived at the wardroom, he was immediately questioned as to just who the other men were. The answer was that they were the men going on the op. It was immediately questioned as to just how much information Hetzell had given to the rest of the men. When he told the officers that he had fully briefed the men, the reaction was unexpected.

The officers were angry that Hetzell had breached security when he informed his men. That was unacceptable to the SEAL and he said plainly that it was how they operated in the teams. Everyone had to be on the same page for an operation; it was how they worked and it had proven successful. The officers reluctantly agreed.

Once everyone was seated in the wardroom, Hetzell went over his warning order for the benefit of the officers and asked for changes. One of those changes involved the use of the fifteen-horsepower silent engine on the rubber boat in place of the more powerful Mercury. The intelligence officer was adamant that the silent engine be used. Finally, Hetzell told him that the motor just didn't work, that it had never worked, and he had never seen one of them run for more than fifteen minutes before breaking down.

The officer mumbled a concern that the other motor would be picked up more easily on radar. Hetzell countered that they would all be picked up on radar anyway so the rubber boat might as well be moving when it happened. As far as Hetzell was concerned, the only reason for using the silent motor was that the name sounded cool. The only reason that it was silent was because it wouldn't run, and that it might immediately sink to the bottom when it was tossed overboard.

There was another man in the wardroom who had not been there during the earlier briefing. The new man was the diving locker chief for the boat. The officers wanted the chief to go along on the mission because he knew how to communicate with the boat. And the chief stated that he wanted to go on a SEAL operation.

The situation did not sit well with Hetzell, though he didn't immediately voice his concerns. He did point out to the officers in the compartment that he was trained in communications. He also felt that he and his men could do whatever had to be done in order to maintain contact with the sub. Then he had some pointed questions for the chief.

The man wanted to go on a SEAL operation. Did he know how to clear a Stoner when it had a spinback? Did he know where Reeves kept his medical kit? How about where Knudson carried his pop flares?

It was pointed out that each of the men in the platoon had the answers to those questions. If one man was wounded in the dark, he knew where to reach on his teammate right next to him to get what he needed to stay alive. The platoon had trained so long with each other that they knew how each other moved in the dark, how any man would react in an ambush, enemy contact, or breaking enemy contact. And the final question asked of the chief: Just how far could he swim? If they picked up more defectors than they had room for in the boat, some of the SEALs were going to swim back to the submarine. Could the chief do that?

With his face fallen, the chief admitted that he couldn't answer any of the questions.

One of the SEALs finally asked point-blank if the reason the chief was supposed to go along on the operation was because they didn't have an officer to go on the op.

"Yes," was the blunt answer from the intelligence officer.

The officers were not very happy that there wasn't a SEAL-qualified officer to go out on the mission. But all of the other officers, both UDT and SEAL, had yet to return to the *Grayback*. It was pointed out to the officers that of the four men, three were cadre instructors in the teams and the fourth man had been on numerous combat operations—including a POW rescue operation that released nineteen South Vietnamese prisoners, but that specific information wasn't known to Hetzell and the others at the time.

The point was made that the men who were going on the mission as it stood were the men who had actually trained the two platoon officers, Dry and Conger. The experience was there to conduct the mission; that wasn't a question.

It was during this meeting that Tim Reeves, who considered himself something of a linguist, asked a question that should have received a direct response. He was concerned about what language he should refresh on so as to be ready to communicate with any defectors. But he could not get an answer to his question. And the intelligence officer on board the *Grayback* who was overseeing the mission still wasn't going to tell any of the SEALs that the primary language they could expect to run into was English.

The platoon members going on the operation were told that the defectors would signal with a red or yellow cloth or red light. No other details were forthcoming as to just who the defectors might be, or which country they would be coming from. This lack of information did not sit well with the SEALs, but there was nothing they could do about it.

All the officers said was that they would think about the mission plan and the men had their permission to return to their compartment.

A few hours later, the submarine suddenly moved away from the area. It had been sitting on the bottom in sixty-five feet of water about four thousand yards off the mouth of the Red River. None of the SEALs knew at the time why the submarine moved away so quickly. What was learned later was that was the time when Dry, Martin, Edwards, and Lutz were dropped in from the helicopter. They had no way of knowing the Dry had been killed on impact and that the first SDV group had found itself swimming with the passengers and crew of the second abandoned SDV.

The *Grayback* had signaled in plain back to the Long Beach—"Do not drop package. Hammerhead coming out of the Hourglass."

It was suspected that a North Vietnamese PT boat had left the nearby base and was moving in the direction of the *Grayback*'s resting place. The submarine had to move for its own protection and they had no way of knowing that the "package" had already been dropped, or that the second SDV had been abandoned.

Then the submarine stopped and bottomed again. It was about three or four hours after that when a new danger made itself known.

A sound inside the steel hull of the submarine concerned everyone on board—it was the noise made by steel chains being dragged across the bow planes of the boat while she rested on the bottom. It was an old method of detecting submarines in shallow water, dragging chains and grappling hooks behind surface boats. And it was very much the kind of technology that might be employed by the North Vietnamese.

The SEALs were all up in their compartment when the scraping sound was suddenly heard. The sound was distinctive and unmistakable, as each individual link of a chain seemed to clank as it was dragged across the bow planes. Then there was a soft, double-click sound. While the rest of the platoon wondered what might have been going on, one of the men spoke in a very sarcastic manner, "Oh great, a limpet mine."

There was a sound-powered phone that connected the compartment to the rest of ship and Hetzell wanted someone to be called up from the crew who knew how to open the outside hatch on the wet side of the hangar. There was a way to manually open the hatch by working a hydraulic pump by hand, but none of the SEALs in the compartment knew how to do it.

When the crewman came up into the compartment, he wanted to know what it was the SEALs intended to do. There was no real plan, it was just that the men did not intend to die in a steel pipe if they had any other choice. For men to whom the sea is a second home, they had another choice: They would suit up and fight it out on the surface with whoever was attacking the submarine.

The SEALs broke out their weapons and put on their bathing trunks, what they called their "blue-and-golds" for the blue cloth and gold trident. Over their trunks went their web gear and inflatable UDT vests. The weapons were locked and loaded and the men stood by. If the submarine was actively attacked, the SEALs would exit the boat and swim up to the surface. There, they would rain serious fire down on any small boats that might be in the area. The men didn't want to just drown down on the bottom with the sub; they would rather go out fighting on the surface. They knew it couldn't be a large craft that was dragging the chains; they would have heard the engines, but a PT boat or even a sampan would find they had hooked a fighting fish on the end of their chains.

Then the submarine suddenly took off again. It lifted up from the bottom and hauled out of the area at its best speed. None of the SEALs knew what had happened, but it seemed that the danger had passed. They would not be fighting it out on the surface. The gear came off and the weapons were unloaded. Stoner light machine guns, M60 machine guns, M16s, and forty-millimeter grenade launchers all went back into their respective storage containers. If it had come to a battle on the surface, the SEALs would have given a good accounting of themselves. But the chains might have been nothing more deadly than a local shrimper running his nets across the bottom. Discovery of the submarine by even a simple fisherman could mean disaster, so they had left the area.

It was hours later that suddenly the men from both of the SDVs came into the compartment. Moki Martin, Bob Conger, Lutz, McConnell, and the rest were back. It was then that the rest of the platoon learned about the loss of Mr. Dry, and just what had happened to the SDVs.

On the *Long Beach* with Edwards receiving the medical attention he required and Dry secured for his last trip back to the States, the rest of the SEALs and UDT operators wanted nothing more than to return to the *Grayback*. The submarine reported that it would send a rubber boat over to the *Long Beach* to pick up the men after dark. Hours passed by as the men waited. Finally, a Z-bird came up from the darkness to the tall steel sides of the *Long Beach*. It was the missing boat from the *Grayback*. The delay had been due to an outboard motor that had failed. The intelligence officer on board the *Grayback* had insisted that the fifteen-horsepower silenced motor be used on the rubber boat without informing the rest of the SEALs on board as to just what was going on. And the motor had remained just as dependable as it had proven to be at Subic.

The men from the submarine turned down offers to get the outboard repaired by the facilities on the *Long Beach*. They climbed into the craft, picked up paddles, and began stroking out into the darkness, rendezvousing with the sub as she lay in the darkness.

The involvement of the *Grayback* with Operation Thunderhead was over. The helicopters continued their search patterns over the planned time of the mission, but there wouldn't be any signal spotted from escaped POWs. There was a false alarm raised by the spotting of a yellow flag, but it turned out to be nothing more than a local boat.

One more incident during the mission of the *Grayback* took place to help keep the mission memorable. It was 6:15 A.M. on Friday, June 9, when the orders rang out across the deck of the *Harold E. Holt*. The ship had spotted what had to be an enemy submarine operating among the ships of the Seventh Fleet. The radar of the *Holt* had picked up the snorkel of the sub as it ran on its diesel engines. The transmission from the *Holt* rang out across the radio net. "Stone Face" (*Holt*) had a submarine spotted at three-five-zero-five and they were taking it under fire. With that announcement, the five-inch gun of the *Holt* launched its first round, right at the USS *Grayback*. Several rounds were fired at the submarine before a desperate order to cease fire was issued from the *Long Beach*.

On board the *Grayback*, Captain Chamberlain had finally turned in after a very long thirty-six hours on watch. At about 6:00 A.M., he turned the con over to his executive officer and went to his cabin in near exhaustion. It wasn't more than a few minutes after he had laid his head down on his bunk that the first shell screamed overhead and smashed down into the ocean. Though the heavy projectile had missed the submarine, the blast of high explosives reverberated throughout the hull of boat. With his feet hitting the deck even before he was fully awake, Captain Chamberlain rushed to the control room. Rapidly issuing orders, Chamberlain had communications established with the *Long Beach* even as more rounds came down from the *Holt*'s gun. If it came down to it, Chamberlain was not ready to give up his ship. He had one of the submarine's torpedo tubes made ready for firing. But he never had to fire that shot. The incoming fire from the *Holt* ceased as the *Long Beach* issued orders. The *Grayback* was once more able to continue on its way out of the area.

It wasn't until that evening that a message came in from the *Grayback* at the scheduled time. There was a great deal of relief from everyone involved with Operation Thunderhead when they learned that the unique submarine was completely unscathed. Chamberlain mentioned the poor marksmanship of the *Holt* and added that if the incident repeated itself, he would be obliged to fire back!

It seemed that even the trip back to Subic Bay wasn't going to be without incident once the *Grayback* left the Gulf of Tonkin waters. Due to the characteristics of a diesel-electric boat, the submarine could make much better speed on the surface that she could while submerged. It was while traveling on the surface that the *Grayback* ran into a force that she couldn't battle, only endure—Typhoon Ora.

In spite of the waves forcing the sub to roll on the surface, she continued under diesel power to charge up her batteries and make best speed toward Subic. Down in their compartment, the SEALs remained in their bunks and continued their journey as passengers. To help pass the time, the SEALs had taken their turn at mess duty, washing dishes and doing cleanup as so many sailors had done before them. The food on the cruise out had been everything the Submarine Force was known for. The fresh food having run out some time back, the meals on the return trip were not quite up to the same level as the earlier ones, but the SEALs had other things on their minds than eating. And when they passed through the typhoon, some of the SEALs wanted to do anything else but eat.

There was a complete investigation on the operation and the loss of a fine and promising SEAL officer. It was later determined that Lieutenant Melvin Spence Dry had died on impact during the cast from the helicopter. The situation of altitude and speed may have added to his impact, but what had killed the officer was a broken neck from hitting something floating in the water. It had just been one of the things that can happen to a SEAL conducting the kind of dangerous operations that they do. Spence Dry was the last SEAL killed in action during the Vietnam War. But due to the highly classified nature of

Operation Thunderhead, he would not receive official recognition of that fact. Even his family, his father a retired Navy captain, would be told that Dry had been killed in an operational accident while working from the *Grayback*. They would not learn the truth for years following the incident.

Though they never operate with the intention of receiving rewards or decorations, there was some disappointment in the lack of recognition of the SEALs' involvement in Operation Thunderhead. The bravery and dedication to service and commitment shown by the men of the SEALs and the UDT operators during the difficult mission speak for themselves. It took nearly thirty-six years for the mission to finally be publicly and officially recognized by the Navy. On February 25, 2008, Memorial Hall of the United States Naval Academy, Annapolis, Maryland, hosted an awards ceremony for Lieutenant Melvin S. Dry. The award citation reads:

> *OPERATION THUNDERHEAD, **North Vietnam, June** 1972:*
> *A highly classified mission to rescue U.S. POWs after they escaped from a Hanoi prison and the first combat-use of a mini wet-submersible SEAL Delivery Vehicle (SDV). Launching from USS* Grayback, *a submarine converted to support clandestine operations, the SDV met with a stronger current than expected, draining the SDV batteries and forcing the four-man element to the surface in enemy territory well short of its destination. In a valiant effort to avoid detection and preserve operational security, the officer-in-charge, Lt. Melvin S. Dry, swam out to sea with his team and scuttled the inoperable SDV. Dry and his team swam for eight hours until daylight, when they were picked up and extracted to the USS* Long Beach. *Determined to complete his mission and rescue the escaped servicemen, the following night, Dry and his team attempted a rendezvous with the* Grayback *by jumping out of a helicopter into the water in complete darkness. However, the reported conditions*

for the jump were fatally inaccurate. Dry was killed and two others were injured, one severely.

For his leadership, valorous actions, and determination to complete the mission, Lt. Dry is awarded the Bronze Star Medal with valor.

With the award, Lieutenant Dry's name was added to the honor roll of Academy graduates who lost their lives in combat for their country. Among the dignitaries, family, and friends who attended the ceremony—including Admiral Michael G. Mullen, Chief of Naval Operations and Chairman of the Joints Chiefs of Staff, as well as a member of the Class of 1968; Rear Admiral Joseph D. Kernan, Commander, Naval Special Warfare Command; Richard Hetzell, Robert Hooke, and Frank Sayle of Alfa platoon, SEAL Team One; and most of the surviving Naval Academy Class of 1968—was Colonel John A. Dramesi, USAF (Ret.).

CHAPTER 30

FINAL RETURN

There was a failure of the leadership of the prison camp that neither the SEALs nor anyone in higher command had any knowledge of. In spite of Dramesi and the other members of the escape committee having met all of the requirements put to them, permission to conduct the escape was denied. The SRO of room #7 had noted the activity and excitement of Dramesi and the men around him. That greatly concerned the man and he investigated the situation. In part, that was how he learned of the planned escape.

The SRO of room #7 immediately got in contact with the senior ranking officer of the prison camp. He pointed out what was going on and the repercussions that could come down on the other prisoners in room #7, and even those in the rest of the camp, if an escape took place. He reminded the senior of just what had happened only a few short years earlier when Dramesi and Atterberry had escaped, how the consequences of that action had made life a literal hell for most of the American prisoners in North Vietnam. The possibility of retribution by the North Vietnamese and the return of torture as a punishment was a very real threat. The prisoners had all suffered enough.

In spite of the escape attempt having been approved by outside authority, by the manner of the message of the highest authority, the SRO of the camp reversed his earlier decision. He ordered the escape committee to stand down. There would be no escape from Camp Unity or any other section of the Hanoi Hilton. Operation Diamond was over before it had really begun, and there was no means to inform the outside world of the situation quickly enough to prevent Operation Thunderhead from going forward.

On February 12, 1973, only eight months after the events of Operation Thunderhead, a new operation took place. Operation Freedom was the return of the POWs held by the North Vietnamese. Out of the 725 individuals known to be captured or interned by the Communist forces of Vietnam, 660 were eventually returned to U.S. custody. Sixty-five individuals died while prisoners, some from the injuries received while ejecting or being taken prisoner, others from the abuse and neglect of the North Vietnamese and their allies. Many more individuals were lost and listed as missing in action. Some had been simply obliterated by the violence of war. Others disappeared, and concern for them continues to this day.

On board the freedom bird flying back from North Vietnam, the cameras showed a shouting, happy bunch of POWs. One smiling man lifted up a small cloth to face the camera. That man was John Dramesi, and the object he was holding was the American flag he had so carefully made and defended.

Colonel Leo K. Thorsness, USAF (Ret.), was a prisoner of war in North Vietnam for six years. He received the Medal of Honor while a

POW for the actions he took in order to save others on the day he was shot down. The award was made in secret by President Richard Nixon so that the information couldn't be used against Thorsness by his North Vietnamese captors while still under their control.

In a conversation made during the research for this book, Thorsness remarked on a dream that many of the POWs had while they were being held. The dream was about the day that their cell door was kicked open by an armed green-clad American soldier. He would reach his hand out and say: "I'm here to take you home."

One of the SEAL operators who remained on the *Grayback* during the SDV insertion also made a remark that would have been well received by Colonel Thorsness. The man said simply: "If I had known about the prisoners, I would have swum up the Red River to go get them."

And Lieutenant Dry would have led them there to kick open the doors.

[APPENDIX]

Alfa Platoon Roster, SEAL Team One, 1972

Lt. Melvin Spencer "Spence" Dry
Lt. (j.g.) Robert. W. Conger
EO1 S. E. Birky
MMC Phillip L. Martin
PH3 Tim R. Reeves
RM3 Richard C. Hetzell
YN3 E. A. Knudson
RM3 M. J. Shortell
RM3 D. R. Hankins
RM3 B. S. Steele
ETR3 J. M. Davis
ADJAN Robert M. Hooke
RMSN Frank H. Sayle
HM2 W. B. Wheeler

Underwater Demolition Team Eleven SDV Detachment (*Grayback*)

Lt. (j.g.) John Lutz
Lt. (j.g.) Bob McGrath
Tom Edwards
Steve McConnell
Jim Couzins
Tony Drake
Scott Shaw

[INDEX]

traveling irons, 192, 198
truck park bombing mission near Package One (Ba Don), 8
20/20 rule for helicopter casting technique, 259–260, 261–262
Two-Lane Blacktop (film), 252
Typhoon Ora, 273

U2, 223
UDT Eleven, 246, 248, 280
Underwater Demolition Teams (UDTs), 200, 206, 207, 246, 248, 280. *See also* Navy SEALs; Operation Thunderhead
U.S. Air Force and Army, 1, 2
U.S. Marine Corps, 20–21
U.S. Seventh Fleet, 73, 79, 140, 167, 199, 234, 242, 251, 253, 272
USS *Buchanan*, 246–247
USS *Grayback* (LPSS 574), 236, 237–239, 241, 242, 243–244, 246, 247, 248, 249, 250, 251, 252, 253, 255, 257, 258, 259, 260, 261, 264, 268, 269, 271, 272, 273
USS *Growler*, 237
USS *Harold E. Holt*, 240, 272, 273
USS *Long Beach* (CGN-9), 240, 253, 254, 255, 256, 257, 258, 259, 263, 264, 265, 269, 271, 272
USS *Midway*, 241
USS *Oklahoma City*, 234
USS *Sutherland*, 205

Vanishing Point (film), 252
"venting the boat," 252–253
Viet Cong (VC) and Navy SEALs, 201, 203–204, 205, 206, 207, 251
Vietnam War. *See also* Blackbirds (SR-71); Camp Unity; Code of Conduct; Dirty Bird (Yen Phu Prison); Dramesi, John; Hanoi Hilton (Hoa Lo Prison); Navy SEALs; North Vietnamese; Operation Thunderhead; prisoners of war (POWs); Zoo Annex Prison; Zoo (Cu Loc Prison)
air support and infantry, integrating, 1–2
antiwar movement in U.S., 68, 153
Caucasian moving unnoticed through Asian population, 78, 80, 85, 145, 160–161, 167–168, 179, 180, 181, 220
CIA operations in Laos, 6
civilians, avoided by U.S., 54, 130
"danger close" distances, 1

halt to bombing of North Vietnamese targets called by Johnson, 153
Ho Chi Minh, death of, 198, 208
last Navy SEAL killed in action during Vietnam War, 273–274
missing in action, 277
savageness of land, 161
U.S. Air Force and Army and, 1, 2
war against North Vietnam, not declared by U.S., 130
Virginia Aviation Museum (Richmond), 233

war crimes, 12, 17, 19
War to End All Wars (World War I), 14–15
water, need for
Dramesi's first experiences, 77, 78
Hanoi Hilton (Hoa Lo Prison), 209
Zoo (Cu Loc Prison), 133
WESTPAC (Naval Special Warfare Western Pacific Detachment), 207, 245
Wheeler, W. B. (Navy SEAL) and, 279
White Beach (Okinawa), 207, 245
Wild Weasel (F-105F), 37–38
Wilson, Glenn "Red" (POW), 171–172
windblast and punching out, 35, 36, 38, 39
wing commander's name revealed to North Vietnamese, 65, 67, 70
wintergreen saved by Dramesi, 60, 71, 77
Wirz, Henry (Captain), 12
World War I (Great War, War to End All Wars), 14–15
World War II
Dramesi's youth and, 26–27
POWs, 15–17, 22, 215
punching out (ejection), 35, 36
wounded, fear of being, 10–11
wounds of Dramesi, 43, 44, 46, 49, 60, 78, 104, 109, 111, 123
wrist shackles torture, 98, 100, 102
writing demands by North Vietnamese, 101, 111–112, 113, 115, 117, 127, 128–129, 193, 210, 212

Yankee Station, 141, 199
Yen Phu Prison. *See* Dirty Bird
Yokosuka Naval Shipyard (Japan), 234

Z-birds (inflatable rubber boats), 247, 266, 267, 271
zeppelins (balloons) as military aircraft, 13

Kevin Dockery has been the armorer in the President's Guard under presidents Nixon and Ford, as well as a radio broadcaster, gunsmith, and historian. He spent time in Iraq and Kuwait during Desert Storm as what he refers to as a "corporate mercenary." As a noted military historian, he has written a number of books detailing the history of the Navy SEALs and the lives of the men who lived that history, including *The Weapons of the Navy SEALs*. He has also written a number of firearms reference books. Currently living in southeastern Michigan, Mr. Dockery follows his hobbies of raising Rottweilers, blacksmithing, and knife- and sword-making.